EARLY CHILDHOOD EDUCATION SERIES

Leslie R. Williams, Editor
Millie Almy, Senior Advisor

(Continued)

Ways of Assessing Children and Curriculum

Stories of Early Childhood Practice

Celia Genishi, Editor

Foreword by Millie Almy

Teachers College, Columbia University
New York and London

To all
learner-centered teachers,
especially Ed

Published by Teachers College Press, 1234 Amsterdam Avenue
New York, NY 10027

Library of Congress Cataloging-in-Publication Data

   Ways of assessing children and curriculum: stories of early childhood
practice/Celia Genishi, editor; foreword by Millie Almy.
    p. cm.—(Early childhood education series)
  Includes bibliographical references and index.
  ISBN 0-8077-3186-2.—ISBN 0-8077-3185-4 (pbk.)
   1. Child development. 2. Observation (Educational method).
3. Curriculum-based assessment. 4. Early childhood education—Case
studies. I. Genishi, Celia, 1944-   . II. Series.
LB1115.W439 1992
372.12'7—dc20   92-13805

ISBN 0-8077-3186-2
ISBN 0-8077-3185-4 (pbk.)

Printed on acid-free paper
Manufactured in the United States of America
99 98 97 96 95 94 93 92   8 7 6 5 4 3 2 1

Contents

Foreword

Many education books reflect their times. Only a few attempt to take their readers beyond the present. I am pleased and honored to have this opportunity to reflect on Celia Genishi's *Ways of Assessing Children and Curriculum: Stories of Early Childhood Practice*. It is a book that is well rooted in the present, but also holds promise for the future. *Ways of Assessing Children and Curriculum* emerges at what may well be called "the worst of times." Never, it seems, has agreement about a crisis in education been more widespread. Schools beset by drastic budget cuts at all levels struggle to cope with increasing parental poverty, greater diversity in children's abilities and backgrounds, and, perhaps most difficult of all, pervasive public apathy and resentment.

Early childhood education and care, to which Genishi's book is directed, face their share of these and other problems, not the least of which is inadequate compensation for staff and the related high staff turnover. Nevertheless, perhaps because of the greater diversity of their funding sources, programs for young children seem to have had more flexibility and innovation and attendant parental and public approval than their elementary and secondary counterparts. In any event, it may be, as Genishi's last chapter suggests, that the present time will turn out in the long run, and in certain respects, to be "the best of times."

I find it interesting to compare *Ways of Assessing Children and Curriculum* to two earlier Teachers College Press publications, *Ways of Studying Children: A Manual for Teachers* (1959) and *Ways of Studying Children: An Observation Manual for Early Childhood Teachers* (1979). The first, which I put together from materials collected by Dr. Ruth Cunningham and her colleagues, came out at a time when schools were still reeling from the symbolic impact the Soviet satellite, Sputnik, had had on American education. Failure to beat the Soviets into space gave focus to widespread criticism of mathematics and science education. Efforts at desegregation had begun to underscore inadequacies in inner-city schools. Experimental programs to capitalize on the learning potential of preschoolers were just getting underway. Some American educators were beginning to visit British Infant Schools, with their emphases on the development of the "whole child," an integrated curriculum, and informal assessment. Educators saw there a possible new direction for kindergarten and primary education.

The second *Ways of Studying Children*, for which Celia Genishi was co-author, followed the format of the earlier volume, but limited its scope to early childhood education. In contrast to the first edition, it included a chapter, "Study the Ways Children Think," reflecting increased emphasis on cognition in developmental psychology.

And the times? They still manifested a bit of the ebullience of the 1960's, but also the sobering experiences of the 1970's. Early childhood education had taken on new importance. A surprising variety of experimental programs had been launched and had struggled to demonstrate their effects on the improvement of later school achievement, as well as on the amelioration of some of the customary outcomes of poverty. The steadily increasing employment of women outside their homes had also increased the need for the expansion of child care programs. But President Nixon's veto of the Comprehensive Child Development Act of 1971 had brought early education advocates into confrontation with stern political realities.

It was the continuing social and political ferment in the field of early childhood education that led me to focus the 1979 revision of *Ways of Studying Children* on that field. Nevertheless, the central themes of the first edition remained. Observation was the basic method of assessment. The teacher studied children in order to promote their individual development and their learning more effectively. In studying children, teachers became learners and, in a sense, researchers, as they raised questions about the children and the curriculum, and sought evidence to suggest solutions to problems.

These themes continue in Genishi's *Ways of Assessing Children and Curriculum*. But *Ways of Assessing* differs in several respects from its predecessors. The subtitle, *Stories of Early Childhood Practice*, conveys one important difference. Not only do the children and the teachers speak out, their voices are not disembodied. In telling stories of themselves and of their life together in their classrooms, they add a reality, a completeness, that cannot be matched in the more traditional quarterly or end-of-term report usually addressed to parents. Teachers do not conceal their concerns about the children or the parents in the verbiage of objectivity. Rather, as part of the *dramatis personae*, it behooves them to acknowledge their feelings openly.

Both versions of *Ways of Studying* had emphasized that teachers, being human, are prone to experience bias—and need, as far as possible, to identify it. *Ways of Assessing* takes a more dynamic and more creative approach to the problem. As the teachers take note of their encounters with the children and their parents, they are also participating in a story-writing process in which the views of one person are substantiated or challenged by the others. Thus assessment through story-telling carries with it certain built-in correctives to the problem of bias. This is not, however, to say that the issues of reliability and validity, long of concern to those who wish to evaluate the effectiveness of early childhood education, have become less relevant. Rather, it seems, they have become more public, more subject to scrutiny. The reader will find it interesting and profitable to consider how the different stories this book tells reveal and deal with such issues.

From one point of view, in offering stories to assess children and curriculum, Genishi and her collaborators provide no new departure, for teachers have always told stories. As Genishi indicates, Susan Isaacs, writing some 60 years ago, offered an early example of such assessment. Others, many more recent, can also be cited. It seems to me, however, that this book is significant in other ways and that it probably could not, or would not, have been written at an earlier time.

In the first place, this book represents great diversity in children, their ages and their cultures; in the settings in which the curricula are enacted; and also in the backgrounds of the teachers who are involved. Despite their differences, the teachers, as Genishi points out, share certain agreements about their curricula. They all aim to provide a safe environment, to give children a variety of appropriate developmental choices, and to integrate experience across subject matter. They all try to see all children and themselves as learners. As I see it, these underlying agreements lead to a consistency between assessment and curriculum. *The Ways of Studying* authors regarded such consistency as desirable but recognized that many teachers valiantly tried to study children in settings that often placed inappropriate demands on the children.

A second distinguishing feature of *Ways of Assessing* is the nature of the collaboration among the teachers. Teachers involved in *Ways of Studying* often collaborated with one another, and some were also involved with teacher education and the faculty from universities or colleges, or with other specialists. None, as far as I know, were committed to publishing the story of their mutual efforts.

The latter commitment, it seems to me, gives new meaning, new authority and respectability to the teacher-as-researcher role. While the research aspect of early childhood education was fairly well specified in the founding days of nursery education in the United States, it seems to have slipped into near oblivion as the years went by. Recently, however, the importance of the teacher's research at all levels of education has received increasing recognition.

Genishi takes this fact plus her own deep knowledge of developmental theories, on the one hand, and of storytelling, on the other, to suggest how the much needed "theory of practice" (or perhaps theories of practice) for early childhood education may emerge. It is an exciting and challenging point of view—a view that deserves much further explication, a view that must be thoroughly understood if it is to help to release the bonds that currently constrict the effective assessment of children and curriculum. I predict that this point of view will greatly influence the field of early childhood education in years to come.

Millie Almy
Berkeley, California

Acknowledgments

My warmest, deepest thanks to:

My collaborators, who generously agreed to assemble and share stories from six early childhood settings. Working with them was pure pleasure. They, together with the children and family members of their classroom communities, gave this book its heart.

Sarah Biondello and Carol Collins at Teachers College Press for support, editorial shepherding, and timely assistance.

Sal Vascellaro, a doctoral student in early childhood education at Teachers College, for invaluable bibliographic assistance and a thoughtfully critical eye as he read early drafts of chapters 1, 2, and 7.

Millie Almy, my adviser at the University of California, Berkeley, and mentor (before I understood the word), for two decades of wisdom, humor, and friendship. Words fail to express my admiration for her strength of spirit and depth of perspective—on the field of early childhood education and on life. In the most fundamental ways she is the source of this book.

1

Framing the Ways

CELIA GENISHI

This introduction to the collection emphasizes the importance of story for conveying aspects of everyday experience in early childhood classrooms and presents the broad historical and educational contexts framing our stories.

Thinking and Communicating Through Stories

This is a book of stories, and the storytellers are teachers who are at home in early childhood classrooms. Their voices present ways of assessing children and curriculum that are embedded in everyday classroom life. Here assessment often occurs through ordinary conversations that lead to the sharing of stories, as the following exchange illustrates:

ELLEN: So tell me about today. What happened in terms of emotional development?

JOAN: Well, Tracy stands out for me—the power of his emotions and the effects it has on the whole group. I feel that I am a person who responds to the whole group too, so everybody feels the impact. OK, I remember Kata and Trish. I think they both don't have the skills yet to be friends and want to be friends and pretty much beat on each other physically and emotionally. And Mia R. going into her poor mode, needing to be held. Let me think what else. I remember Austin, really trying to tell me his dragon story in the midst of all this stuff, you know, and we were finally getting it through—I guess that's the main dramas.

(Delaney, in progress)

Joan's story is made up of the ongoing dramas of her Head Start classroom. It tells us how classroom life is lived—with characters,

1

individual and collective motives, scenes, and plots that are often unpredictable. Stories reflect the way we share feelings and experiences with others and the way we preserve experiences in memory. So for creating this book we thought storytelling made the most sense. For example, to begin Chapter 2, Jan, Joanne, Stephanie, Mary, and I began by telling stories to one another. Like Joan, we talked mostly about individual children, with an underlying awareness of the presence and identity of the group. We then wrote down some of those stories, and for us the chapter came to life.

We co-authors agree with psychologist Margaret Donaldson (1987) when she points out the difference between two kinds of thinking, one that grows out of our own life experiences and concerns and the other that grows out of problems that someone else sets for us. She says that the first kind of thinking is "embedded in the life of the mind—in a setting of memories, hopes and purposes— if not in the life of the senses and the muscles" (1987, p. 104). It is mainly that kind of thinking, full of easily recalled hopes and purposes and the sensory life of classrooms, that our stories capture. The second kind of thinking Donaldson (1978) calls *disembedded*. This is steered by logical or formal argument, by using the goals of science to describe and explain phenomena in "universal" terms that stand apart from individual experience (see also Bruner, 1986). This kind of thinking validates many of the traditional testing practices that are currently so controversial. In psychology and education those practices are most often represented as statistical data about groups and expressed numerically.

In this book we follow a different—uncharted—course because we present an argument not in formal, disembedded, or statistical ways but through stories. We hope our stories demonstrate that traditional assessment tests, which are problems that outsiders set for us, fail to measure significant aspects of children's growth and learning. We hope the stories persuade you that *teachers* can look at their own children, in the context of their own curricula, to devise alternative ways of responding to the need for assessment. The rest of this chapter provides the context for our stories and is organized around these topics: (1) definitions of the terms *assessment, young children,* and *curriculum*; (2) the politics of testing, or the recent escalation of curriculum and testing; and (3) responses to the pressure to test—from those recommending alternative testing instruments, from early childhood educators who object to most testing, and from those who support the human being/teacher as "instrument."

Defining the Focus of Our Stories

Assessment here does not refer chiefly to standardized tests or commercially available diagnostic instruments, but to *teachers' informal ways of observing and documenting development and learning*. This is also called *alternative* assessment, since it contrasts with standardized measures developed to evaluate groups or to compare one group or child to another statistically. These ways of assessing are ongoing and philosophically in tune with the primary curriculum-makers, the teachers and children; that is, they are "grass-roots" ways that grow from the ground up or from the participants out. In the chapters that follow, more elaborate and personalized definitions of *assessment* are presented, along with specific ways to do it. These include the staples of child study, observation and note-taking, as well as portfolios of child-done materials and selected work and videotapes of classroom activity.

The term *young children* is used to refer to children from birth to about age 8, although the classrooms we focus on are for children from about 2½ to 8 years of age. The term *curriculum* is much less straightforward than this. There are tidy definitions that place a curriculum within the pages of a published course of study, textbook, or teacher's guide. These textbook definitions have been part of classroom life and teacher preparation programs for a long time.

To illustrate, we present the following situations in which decisions about curriculum are preset and detailed by experts outside the classroom. A preservice teacher (Pratt, 1948) describes the content of her "methods" courses, first for the kindergarten:

> You taught children to dance like butterflies, when you knew they would much rather roar like lions, because lions are hard to discipline and butterflies aren't. All of it was designed to prepare the children for the long years of discipline ahead. Kindergarten got them ready to be bamboozled by the first grade. (p. 15)

and then in manual training:

> In the shop I had been learning to use one tool after another (someone had decided which were easier and which harder, and the tools were given us in that order), and to perform one kind of operation after another (someone had also decided the order of difficulty for these). I sawed to a line; I planed; I chiseled; I made joints, one after another, until I reached the crowning achieve-

ment, the blind dovetail. But I never made a single object! This was
the way I was to teach Manual Training to children when I was a
graduate teacher. (p. 15)

These are the words of Caroline Pratt, a contemporary of John
Dewey, in describing part of the training for prospective teachers at
Teachers College, Columbia, in 1892. Manual training is no longer
part of most teacher education programs, and Teachers College has
since changed its orientation to curriculum; but we can easily detect
the assumptions underlying these traditional activities in current
practices. We still see an appreciation for classrooms as quiet as
butterflies and separate activities that make you "ready" for the next
grade or a more difficult task. We can make our own contemporary
substitutions in the paragraph about manual training:

> (someone had decided on the sequence of skills I needed to be
> ready to read). I learned initial consonants, final consonants,
> short vowels, long vowels, all the letters of the alphabet, I com-
> pleted hundreds of worksheets. But I never read a single book!

In this book, our views of what children can do in classrooms are
neither this predetermined nor this remote from the events of everyday life. Although parts of a curriculum are certainly planned in
advance, the curriculum's most significant aspect for us is how it is
enacted, or how teachers and children carry it out in the classroom
in lifelike ways. Thus curriculum is made up of such elements as
spontaneous conversations in which children inform teachers;
children's actions and interactions with clay, blocks, water, and so
on; opportunities to create and dramatize children's own stories and
to hear or read whole books; and discussions that grow out of
disagreements or conflicts about the physical or social world. Our
definition is compatible with longstanding and still current views of
curriculum as learner-centered and organic (Ashton-Warner, 1963/
1986), experiential (Connelly & Clandinin, 1988; Dewey, 1938/1963;
Snyder, Bolin, & Zumwalt, 1992), and dialogic and negotiated
(Barnes, 1975; Freire, 1970; Lester & Onore, 1990).

When the curriculum is all these things—or striving to be—
there is an assumption that the classroom is a community in which
children and teachers all have rights and responsibilities. There is
an assumption that individuals differ from one another and, as
importantly, that they have the *right* to differ from one another. To
honor those differences, teachers ensure that children have oppor-

tunities to choose some of the experiences they will have. There is the assumption that teachers can be trusted to make decisions about which experiences are educative and purposeful and that these decisions are based on knowledge of children's own prior experiences, what they know and what their social histories are. There is the assumption that for the child the curriculum is enacted largely through action and interaction with materials and people (Dewey, 1938/1963; Piaget & Inhelder, 1969; Vygotsky, 1978). And there is the assumption that for the teacher it is enacted largely through observation and communication, both nonverbal and verbal (Barnes, 1975).

The classrooms we describe here offer choices so that children do not have to be as quiet as butterflies; their teachers' actions may range from sheltering children who act like roaring lions to occasionally teaching academic skills. Because there are a number of stories about classrooms from preschool through second grade, there is no label that we can attach to all of them. There are teachers who support a child-centered, nonacademic, play-based curriculum, as well as those who identify themselves with "whole language" principles and bilingual education. We believe the classrooms are all "developmentally appropriate" (Bredekamp, 1987), although each is a unique community that cannot be glibly categorized. Each provides a context for a constantly developing curriculum that suits those who enact it. Further, since their developing curricula are found more often in teachers' and children's ideas and interactions, not the pages of published guides, teachers create their own informal, grass-roots assessments of children's learning. So in the six school settings that you will come to know through people who live in them, teacher- and child-based assessment go hand-in-glove with teacher- and child-based curriculum. One informs and enhances the other, and both steer the cycles of classroom life.

The Politics of Testing: Why We Need Alternatives

Life in many classrooms is steered by forces outside of the teacher and children. The origins of these forces—pressures—are multiple: There is pressure from agencies that fund early childhood programs, from national mandates for accountability through standardized testing, from parents who want the best educations for their children, from other teachers and professionals whose needs are served by certain kinds of teaching and testing. In the next section we present two short stories that show how different teachers and schools respond to pressures for assessment and how the pressures affect children.

Responding to Pressure: Two Stories

Story 1. In a public school kindergarten where the children are termed "at-risk," the children are taking a widely used achievement test in reading so that they and their school can qualify for special funding. The teacher has tried to keep the classroom atmosphere as low-key as possible, and the children do not appear to be anxious or upset. They, of course, have their own ways of interpreting the test questions, something the teacher knows because she is not forcing them to be silent. For example, one item requires children to choose the picture of something that starts with the same sound as *doll.* There is a picture of a dog, and a few children say, "woof, woof" or "arf, arf," apparently thinking that this is the sound a dog makes. Nothing in the children's manner suggests that they are making a good joke. Another example: when the children are to choose groups of letters that look just like the group of letters in the test question, some children ignore the order in which the letters appear. They might match BOT with TOB or OTB. The children's responses are reasonable from their perspective but, of course, are not correct from the testmaker's (Andrea McCarrier, personal communication, 1991).

Story 2. Billy is a 4-year-old whom I have chatted with a number of times. He is an outgoing, alert, and verbally advanced child, so advanced that I think anyone familiar with young children would call him extremely bright. Billy and his family live in a large city where many children attend private schools. An increasing number of the schools give a test to children as an entrance exam, for example, the Wechsler Preschool and Primary Scale of Intelligence (WPPSI). Billy took one of these tests in a situation that was, at the very least, not supportive of a young child who was unfamiliar with testing. His mother described the building as forbidding and the tester as businesslike. She remembers the unhappiness on Billy's face when the tester took him into the testing room—"like I had just sold him into slavery," she said. The testing took an hour, the length of time required for the administration of the test. This meant that the tester took no additional time to get to know Billy or give him any breaks from the test items. Billy's score on the test was slightly below the mean, so that he could not enter the school's kindergarten in the fall. But the most serious consequence of the testing was that Billy was "traumatized for three weeks after taking the test," according to his mother. He was not acting like himself and refused to do anything new or different. He did pass the entrance requirements for another private kindergarten, so his story is not altogether a sad one (personal communication, 1991).

These stories selectively reflect the kind of standardized assessments that young children might experience and the uses to which tests are put, whether or not they match the intentions of the testmaker. The first story illustrates what happens when children's schools must qualify to receive special funding, in this case federal funds for Chapter I reading assistance; that is, most children must fail the test if their school is to qualify for assistance, despite the fact that the test was designed as an achievement measure, not as a screening instrument. Since many kindergartners are unfamiliar with such tests and the concepts of reading they include, failure is quite likely. The second story is an example of the misuse of an intelligence test that, if administered sensitively, can yield useful information about individual children. Instead it has been used to select children with the highest scores and exclude others from entering a particular institution. Thus it is transformed into another screening instrument, separating children into groups of "high" and "low" scorers.

These stories are just two reminders that children from all social groups may be subjected to inappropriate, sometimes harmful, testing situations because of policies that achieve practical adult goals. Policy makers are responding to pressures from groups who press for accountability, for "objective" ways to determine need or merit. More importantly, the two stories are poignant reminders that we deceive ourselves if we think that standardized testing is generally beneficial to young children themselves.

Despite many adults' reservations about testing, policy makers still rely on it. The next section is a discussion of the power of *standardized testing*, which strongly influences not only classroom assessment practices but also curriculum.

Responding to Pressure: Escalation of Curriculum and Testing

Our position in support of alternatives to standardized testing runs against a historical tradition in which tests have become an integral part of public education in the United States. According to Perrone (1991), the Thorndike Handwriting Scale, published in 1909, was the first widely used standardized achievement test. In the decades following, dependence on tests increased as they were used to monitor the quality of schools with minimally qualified teachers and minimal resources. In the present, changed context, many say the publication of *A Nation at Risk* (National Commission on Excellence in Education, 1983) prompted the most recent fervor for standardized testing. That report, assembled by the National Commission on Excellence in Education for the U.S. Department of Education, briefly summarized why this nation is at risk: lower student performance on standardized tests, such as the Scholastic Aptitude Tests (SAT), as well as on high school achievement tests; higher rates of adult illiteracy; the inability of 17-year-olds to make inferences or write an essay; and so on. Since our economy has changed, there is less need for unskilled workers and a growing need for service-oriented and highly skilled workers who are comfortable with technology. In addition, there is a sense that the United States is losing an international economic "war" with countries such as Germany and Japan. The Commission made a number of recommendations about what changes were needed in our schools at all levels to make our students more "competitive." These included: students' increased proficiency in English, science, math, computer science, and foreign languages (beginning in elementary school); the upgrading of textbooks' content so as to present challenging material; and a major recommendation about testing:

> Standardized tests of achievement (not to be confused with aptitude tests) should be administered at major transition points from one level of schooling to another and particularly from high school to college or work. The purposes of these tests would be to: (a) certify the student's credentials; (b) identify the need for remedial intervention; and (c) identify the opportunity for advanced or accelerated work. The tests should be administered as part of a nationwide (but not Federal) system of State and local standardized tests. This system should include other diagnostic procedures that assist teachers and students to evaluate student progress. (National Commission on Excellence in Education, 1983, p. 28)

This explicit pressure for "accountability" via standardized tests led to most states' widening the scope of their testing programs as well as continuing or strengthening traditional (textbook-driven) aspects of the curriculum. As of 1990, 47 states required public school districts to test students at some point between grades 1 and 12 (Coley & Goertz, 1990). (At that time, the exceptions were Hawaii, Vermont, and Wyoming.) In most states testing was not required before the third grade, and a common pattern was to test at the end of the third, sixth, eighth or ninth, and eleventh or twelfth grades. It is not surprising, then, that the testing industry is selling 100 million tests each year (Medina & Neill, 1990) and that students who graduated from high school in 1989 had taken 18 to 21 standardized tests during their school careers (Perrone, 1991).

Moreover, to improve American education in the next decades, the federal government recently announced the development of an "America 2000 strategy," which seems to follow up on the content of *A Nation at Risk.* One of its aspects is a proposed system for national testing, to include new measures such as "an 'anchor test' to which other tests could be calibrated" (Miller, 1991, p. 26). Writing samples and portfolios might also be considered. By September of 1993, the first examinations for fourth-graders are to be available; but because reservations have already been expressed about national tests leading to a "national curriculum," it is likely that any evaluation system will be long debated.

In response to this continuing emphasis on testing, teachers feel greater pressure to teach specific content. In general there has been an escalation of academic content even in preschools and kindergartens (Durkin, 1990; Freeman & Hatch, 1989; Gallagher & Sigel, 1987; Shepard & Smith, 1989); skills-oriented activities in reading and math fill the curriculum of many classrooms. Although most states do not require testing at the early childhood level, many school districts do in order to evaluate whether teachers have taught and children have learned the content of the escalated curriculum. A tight link then forms between curriculum content and testing. "Teaching to the test" is not new (Darling-Hammond & Wise, 1985), but its appearance at the early childhood level is recent. The publication of a parents' guide for preparing their children for preschool and primary grade entrance (Robinson, 1988, cited in Bredekamp & Shepard, 1989) is one example that would seem comical except that entrance tests have such serious consequences for children and their families.

Thus in this cycle, from curricular change to changes in testing, children take a greater number of tests that evaluate both readiness and achievement. Because such tests are designed to sort children into those who do well, are "on level," and do badly, there is an increase in the number of children who do badly (who may not have been so identified before the tests were given). These children probably have difficulty completing worksheets, sitting still, quietly attending to academic tasks, and taking paper-and-pencil tests. Although they are simply acting like young children, some are inevitably judged as not "ready" for school or the next grade. And so another problem presents itself: a greater number of "retainees" who do not fit into the narrowly defined academic curriculum. Where do they fit in this cycle? Well-intended adults have made places for children who are not ready for first grade—or, in blunter terms, have flunked kindergarten—in increasingly common "transitional kindergartens," or pre-first grades. There is no evidence from research that this practice improves children's achievement (Shepard & Smith, 1989); it may even result in lower achievement among some children in specially created transitional classes (Sternberg, 1991). So the cycle of change is complete: Adults respond to pressure for higher achievement in schools by changing the curriculum; children participate in an often overly academic curriculum; adults test the children to see whether they have learned its content; both children and teachers are evaluated on the basis of test scores; and further changes are made in the curriculum to accommodate children who are not "ready."

Responding to Pressure: Voices of Early Childhood Professionals

Many in early childhood education and development believe that the pressure-filled cycle just described is not of their making. They see "outside" groups as the main characters in the story of academic escalation or the "downward push" of elementary curriculum onto the early childhood years. These include legislators, testmakers, textbook publishers, and educators and administrators who have worked with older children and so fail to appreciate the developmental characteristics of young children. Yet early childhood professionals also have major roles to play in the story, and a number have done so by taking clear stands, either opposing narrow academic curricula and describing alternatives to them (Bredekamp, 1987; Katz & Chard, 1989; Schickedanz et al., 1990; Seefeldt, 1987) or opposing standardized tests for young children (Kamii, 1990; Perrone, 1991).

Although the majority of voices from the profession are against both narrow academic curricula and standardized testing for young children, there is a range of opinions, reflecting the controversy inherent in the story of testing and young children. One of the best-known readiness tests—and main sources of controversy—is the Gesell School Readiness Screening Test (GSRST), widely used to determine children's readiness for kindergarten. Its underlying rationale is maturationist; that is, it is based on Gesell's theory that behavior is primarily a result of maturation or aging. Thus the passage of time is more critical to development than the nature of a child's environment or experience. Many in early childhood education (including us co-authors) hold to an interactionist or *constructivist* view; we see children's development as a complex interplay among maturation, environmental and genetic factors, and the child's own thinking (Piaget & Inhelder, 1969; Vygotsky, 1978). Compared to constructivism, Gesell's theory is simplistic. Moreover, the Gesell test itself has doubtful reliability and validity (Meisels, 1987). Even some who do not oppose the test seem lukewarm in their support:

> One might conclude that although the GSRST does not demonstrate sufficient reliability and validity to justify using it as a primary determinant of grade placement, it appears to be a valuable source of information about school readiness—whatever that may be. (Lichtenstein, 1990, p. 377)

Most writers and researchers in early childhood education are equally uncomfortable with the idea of "school readiness" and strongly oppose the use of tests. The only exception is developmental screening and assessment measures when they help professionals make decisions about the need for special services (Bredekamp & Shepard, 1989; Meisels, 1987; National Association for the Education of Young Children [NAEYC] & National Association of Early Childhood Specialists in State Departments of Education, 1991). Those services should *benefit* children with particular conditions, disabilities, or gifts that require special classroom facilities or individualized curricula and help to move children forward in their development and learning. Tests that result in some children's being *excluded* from educational settings (for example, public school kindergarten) deny services that are part of all children's right to a free education (Meisels, 1987). The worst feature of such tests is that their use conveys the message that all children must fit into classrooms with narrowly defined curricula. We co-authors resist this message and take the position that classrooms and centers should not be test-driven, but rather "child-ready"; they should be flexible enough to accommodate the heterogeneity that typifies any group of learners.

The Current Situation: Encouraging Changes

As just noted, individuals and professional organizations have responded to the pressure for escalation by opposing most forms of testing for young children. They have also responded by joining others who support alternative means of assessment across all age and grade levels. In the next section alternative points of view are presented, based on the belief that better tests or instruments can be developed that are more appropriate for assessing what learners know and can do.

Responding to Pressure: Alternative Instruments

Some experts in assessment and testing respond to current pressures to improve teaching and learning within a traditional framework; that is, they believe that tests are an essential and potentially beneficial part of schooling. In a recent special issue on assessment of the journal *Educational Researcher*, educational psychologist Richard Snow (1989) suggests the need for assessment procedures that follow students' progress from the beginning of instruction through a whole course or series of courses. These procedures might include tutoring by computer, which allows the computer to adjust instruction to the learner's level of knowledge. The assessment "document" would be the computer record. Although such a document would be detailed and precise, Snow points out that no one has figured out how it can be translated into a statement of what the learner can do in the classroom in a way that is useful to teachers. Snow further describes ways to assess learners' thinking on a daily, weekly, and monthly basis. For example, on a weekly basis students might engage in a "teach-back" procedure (Gray, 1982, cited in Snow, 1989) during which they teach someone with no prior knowledge about something they have learned. The student-teacher's ways of organizing and articulating information for the listener are then assessed.

Conative aspects of learning, those having to do with motivation and desire to learn, are also part of Snow's proposal. Thus a test of students' ability to concentrate, for example, might be given. The overall aim is to assess what students should ultimately achieve:

conceptual structures, procedural skills, learning strategies, self-regulatory functions, and motivational orientations (Snow, 1989, p. 9). This range of knowledge and attitudes should include aspects of learning not usually tested (nonverbal and artistic, for example) and may be tapped by means such as portfolios, behavioral observations, and quantitative scores.

In the same journal issue, John Frederiksen and Allan Collins (1989) propose a systems approach to testing. Unlike the strongest proponents of standardized testing, the authors identify tests as a negative factor in the improvement of teaching and learning. They give examples of teachers who "teach to the test" and change their instruction in significant ways so that students will score well on specific tests (a practice that many teachers at the early childhood level admit to), even if teachers' own goals are undermined. Frederiksen and Collins argue that different kinds of tests must be developed that are "systemically valid," that encourage in students the kinds of "cognitive traits" that the tests are designed to measure. So, for example, if schools want to develop higher-order thinking, they need tests that measure such thinking, not multiple-choice tests that measure it only indirectly.

Frederiksen and Collins state that the features of such tests are based on a set of real-world tasks, such as writing, and explicit ways of assessing performance on those tasks. What makes the authors' proposal distinctive is their emphasis on accessibility of the test and its guide for scoring (which they call "exemplars") to three different groups: administrators, coaches who help the test-takers perform better, and the test-takers themselves. Practice and *self-assessment*, then, become part of the testing system. Thus the articles by both Frederiksen and Collins and Snow offer alternatives to the usual procedures of standardized testing, which often encourage a narrowing of curricular content rather than working toward a match between desirable goals (higher-order thinking, curiosity, reading a variety of books) and test content.

Further, in a special issue of *Educational Leadership*, M. E. Martinez and J. I. Lipson (1989) describe the Mastery Assessment Project at the Educational Testing Service. The word *mastery* is used to suggest learners' progress from being a novice to becoming an expert; the authors see the tests as ways of making instruction and assessment complementary. According to the authors, mastery systems provide immediate feedback, unlike most standardized tests, which either give feedback months after a test is taken or give none at all. These systems, currently being developed, would not just tell the learner whether something is correct or not; they would also indicate why. Moreover, assessment for mastery would pose real-world tasks, such as troubleshooting and planning, and students' learning would be followed via "maps" of knowledge and skills. The maps can depict progress over a period of weeks or years.

Reading Recovery, an intervention program developed by Marie Clay, uniquely embeds a focus on individual learners and teachers within a system, implemented nationwide in New Zealand, for improving reading instruction (Clay, 1985; DeFord, Lyons, & Pinnell, 1991). Notable features of assessment are that teachers, who themselves are carefully observed during a yearlong training period, learn how to take cues from first-graders having difficulty with beginning reading. In a tutorial situation, teachers assess what children know about print and guide them to acquire strategies for reading and writing that successful readers use to make sense of print. Although the program relies on teachers' ability to observe and teach, using daily "running records" of what children can read, it also incorporates standardized tests to compare Reading Recovery children with others; these are more useful as an index of achievement than of readiness. Thus Clay and her collaborators demonstrate the possibility of combining informal with formal assessment, taking advantage of teachers' abilities to see "where children are" from moment to moment and of standardized tests' function of comparing groups of learners with one another (Clay, 1990).

Finally, there is at least one major research effort to change the direction of assessment at the early childhood level. Project Spectrum (Wexler-Sherman, Gardner, & Feldman, 1988), based on Howard Gardner's theory of "multiple intelligences" (Gardner, 1983), expands the concept of assessment to include not only verbal and mathematical abilities but also musical, artistic, kinesthetic, scientific, and social talents. Instead of the traditional preschool standardized test, given by an adult to one child in a testing room, this alternative approach incorporates assessment measures into the classroom curriculum. These are administered over time in the naturally occurring settings of the preschool and are often based on observations (sometimes tape-recorded, sometimes done by researchers) of children's specific abilities (how do they tell stories, how do they sing "Happy Birthday," what does their portfolio of artwork look like?) and styles of playing and working (how confident are they, is their tempo quick or slow, how do they respond to frustration?). What results from this breadth of attention to each child is a profile, not a single test score. A by-product of this kind of assessment is that the curriculum also changes when teachers agree that the whole spectrum of activity is necessary to allow for both fully ranging development and innovative assessment.

The alternatives to assessment just summarized exemplify the growing belief that traditional means of testing and assessing are flawed. The ways that we are about to describe in the next five chapters, then, are part of a broad, still growing movement toward reform in testing at all levels of schooling. Within this movement we are all in agreement that assessment measures must change, that they must be responsive to what is taught in the classroom, and that what is taught should be guided by worthwhile goals, not by the content of standardized tests. There is also agreement that learning goals should not be superficial; they should promote such things as critical thinking, expressed orally and in print, which develops over time. Still, there are important differences between our "ways" and the proposals of the authors discussed above. Like most features of formal testing, these authors' ideas originated *outside the classroom.* So although all authors state that teachers are necessary participants in any meaningful reform of testing, their proposals, with the exception of Reading Recovery, leave control in the hands of researchers, testmakers, or administrators. Further, except for the work of Wexler-Sherman and colleagues (1988), the proposals are aimed at students who are at the upper end of or well beyond the early childhood years. In the next section, a contrasting framework for our alternative approach is presented.

Responding to Children: Human Beings as Instruments

At this point we shift from a discussion of *systems* of assessment and *instruments* that can be widely adopted to a focus on individual children and teachers in their own classrooms. We begin to see the *teacher* as the primary instrument for developing the curriculum and assessing the children who contribute to its development. A third short story illustrates the kind of assessment that teachers initiate and control:

Story 3. Eddie was not making progress in his class of 4-year-olds. We teachers tried everything we could to make this year work out for him. Finally, we moved him to a class of 3- and 4-year-olds, thinking that being with younger children would help. He's been in my class for two weeks, and it is too soon to tell if he is being helped. I feel his main problem is that he cannot keep up socially with his

peers and so he becomes anxious and acts out. He is very bright but
very impulsive. He is the only child who is not making progress in
his socialization this year, and this is holding back his development
in other areas. His mother wants to send him to a structured preschool next year, and I think something different should be tried.
Anyway, I have until the end of May, and I'm determined to get him
feeling better about himself at school (Jan Waters, personal communication, 1991).

This story illustrates one kind of child- and teacher-based assessment featured in this book. Focused on an individual child as he
tries to adjust to the group experiences of schooling, it is an informal
assessment, a teacher's anecdote expressing concern that a child is
not adjusting socially in preschool. A few of the complexities of early
childhood education are implied—the broad purposes of schooling,
the need to attend to multiple aspects of development, the need to
take parents' wishes into account. Although the teacher's and her
co-teachers' observations lead to judgments about Eddie's development, she never refers to a test or a stark number that tells us
definitively how to judge this child. Since her assessment is ongoing
and closely linked to the curriculum that child and teacher experience, it is a sample of the variety of ways of assessing contained in
the following chapters. It is clearly not what most school districts
and policy makers rely on. We make no claim that this approach is
new. Instead we see ourselves in a historical context that has always
valued the human being—in psychology, as an observer of behavior
and development, and in education, as the main determinant of
curriculum and assessment, as we defined those terms earlier. Documenting child behavior has been an activity of students of development for about a century. In the United States, the first investiga-
tions by child study specialists at the end of the nineteenth century
were descriptions of individual children (Baldwin, 1960). Carefully
following development has been associated with a range of research
activities, from longitudinal growth studies conducted by developmental psychologists (Bayley, 1933, 1955) to the psychoanalytically
based early education movement in England (Isaacs, 1933/1972).

At Malting House, a school for young gifted children, Susan
Isaacs kept careful records, which she said were intended for both
psychologists and educators. For example:

Frank invented a new game, in which all the others joined, following his instructions happily. They all had to sit on a rug, with their

hands behind them, and one child went round unclasping their hands; then they all had to chase and catch him, the one who caught him being the next to go round behind. Later on, the children asked Mrs. I. and Miss B. to "make a bridge," while they ran round and under the bridge as a "train." (Isaacs, 1933/1972, p. 95)

Numerous observations such as these formed the basis for Isaacs's analysis of the children's social and psychosexual development.

Interestingly, Isaacs presented her data and interpretations for psychologists separately from those for educators; she wanted to be able "to face the facts dispassionately" and not prejudge their meaning (Isaacs, 1933/1972, p. 3). This view of the observer as dispassionate and objective has been characteristic of traditional—also called *positivistic*—research and assessment (Guba & Lincoln, 1989). Objective observation is based on the assumption that "distance" between the observer and the person or event observed is necessary. But there is a different view of observing that is more often associated with researchers in anthropology and education than in psychology, which does not require distance and places the observer in the same setting—the same research "space"—as the person or event observed (Eisner, 1991; Genishi & Dyson, 1989; Guba & Lincoln, 1989; Johnston, 1989).

In this kind of research, the observer may already be a part of the setting, as teachers who study their own classrooms are. As active participants, they may want to initiate a change in the setting. For example, those doing action research (Wann & Foshay, 1954) seek to answer questions about their own classrooms. The goal here is to affect teaching and learning in a direct way so that although teachers may have the abilities of a scientist who can observe dispassionately and systematically, their objectivity is not the primary concern. Educational improvement that is sensitive to children's development and learning is. Classroom child study done by teachers shares this goal (Almy & Genishi, 1979; Boehm & Weinberg, 1987; Genishi & Dyson, 1984), as does the growing teacher-researcher movement (Bissex & Bullock, 1987; Burton, 1988; Cochran-Smith & Lytle, 1990; Strickland, Dillon, Funkhouser, Glick, & Rogers, 1989).

Since the 1970s, educators (Carini, 1975; Perrone, 1975) have written about the impossibility of separating the observer, often the teacher, from what he or she observes, often children and their behavior. Citing philosophers such as Husserl and psychologists such as Jung, Carini (1975) illustrates a method of observation and record-keeping called "documentation" that depends on the observer's dwelling in a particular setting over time. In its emphasis on setting, the method is similar to that of participant observation, used often by anthropologists and ethnographers as they study a culture or settings within a culture (Erickson, 1986). Participant observers, like classroom participants, cannot stand apart from the phenomena around them; instead they try to see patterns in what occurs around them. Eventually, they interpret what they see, and their interpretations are drawn from immersion or participation in the setting. If the setting is a classroom and the teacher is the participant observer, interpretation grows out of interacting with children over time and is often presented in the form of case studies (Genishi, 1991).

There are now growing numbers of practitioners—teacher-researchers—and researchers who create portraits and stories of classroom interaction through participant observation. Like the teachers contributing to this book, practitioners study the learning of children in their own classrooms as they develop the forms of assessment that suit their curricula. Researchers who are not classroom teachers tend to study developmental processes, such as those involved in becoming literate (Bussis, Chittenden, Amarel, & Klausner, 1985; Dyson, 1989). Thus they are part of the encouraging changes supporting child-oriented practice.

Those associated with the whole language movement (Edelsky, Altwerger, & Flores, 1991) have been particularly influential in disseminating ideas about both alternative curricula and assessment. Whole language is defined as a philosophy of education that is grounded in theories about child development (a constructivist view) and language acquisition, a process that all children experience from birth and upon which classroom learning can build. The philosophy is compatible with developmentally appropriate practice in that it is learner-centered, interactive, and respectful of teachers' abilities and knowledge. Like others, whole language proponents point out that learner-centered, alternative curricula are not adequately assessed by traditional tests. So teachers have formulated their own ways of evaluating the development of children's spoken language, literacy, and knowledge and ability in science, social studies, and so on, sometimes as part of teams of whole language teachers and sometimes on their own (Cambourne & Turbill, 1990; Goodman, Goodman, & Hood, 1989; Harp, 1991). As a result, teachers' voices have gained strength as they tell stories from their own classrooms.

Learners' spoken and written language is the primary basis for other approaches to assessment as well. Everyday assessments are found in the dialogue that often occurs as children learn to read and teachers discover what children know and do not know, not just in terms of what words they know but also of what they understand about the workings of print (Genishi, McCarrier, & Ryan, 1988). Chittenden (1990), providing another approach, has collaborated with teachers who use focused discussions as one way of assessing primary grade children's learning in science. He is also currently working with groups of teachers using the *Primary Language Record* (Centre for Primary Language Education, 1988) to assess a broad range of young children's language-based abilities. It is designed to accompany children from grade to grade and incorporates the unusual feature of parental assessment.

Portfolios, originally used with older children, are an increasingly popular means of documenting progress over time (Wolf, 1989). They may contain samples of artwork, writing from journals, or any other documents that teacher and/or child select. In fact, they are so popular that advertisements for commercially published portfolio "kits" now offer "everything you need for a portfolio approach to assessment." Everything, of course, but the heart of the portfolio, the child's own work.

When publishers make "informal" ways of assessing available, it is obvious that the world of education in general has heard the call for reform in testing. Further, changes are appearing in statewide policies. The California Assembly recently mandated "developmental profiles" (Herrell, 1991) for each child in certain child-care programs. Early childhood educators are exploring instruments like those in the *Primary Language Record* and Marie Clay's techniques for assessing children's knowledge about print (Clay, 1991) to help caregivers develop such profiles. Other states, such as New York, while holding to their requirements for achievement testing, have begun to explore alternatives to it. They seem to take the position that standardized tests have a purpose, that of comparing one group of children to another, and that alternatives to testing may provide information the tests do not. Vermont, in contrast, recently instituted a statewide program of portfolio development in reading and math to replace achievement tests.

Regardless of what state agencies mandate, our view is that the heart of what children learn is best captured by the careful ear and eye of teachers. In the coming pages, then, we offer stories in our own voices from six early childhood settings: two private preschools, one in Columbus, Ohio, and the other in New York City; public kindergarten, first-grade, and bilingual second-grade classrooms, respectively, in the urban settings of New York City, Berkeley, and Phoenix; and a public second-grade Foxfire classroom in rural Tennessee. The collaborations among authors, based on classroom teachers' coursework at schools and colleges of education and recommendations from friends, resulted in five varied chapters that describe young children of differing backgrounds and abilities. Their classroom communities cover a broad span both programmatically and geographically, although the range is not exhaustive and does not represent all early childhood sites. None of us, for example, have written about alternative assessment in the significant setting of day care (see Leavitt & Krause Eheart, 1991). Still, we hope that the issues, principles, and ways of assessing embedded in these chapters touch teachers in the audience, whatever their setting, so that they are able to see themselves and their children in our stories.

References

Almy, M., & Genishi, C. (1979). *Ways of studying children* (rev. ed.). New York: Teachers College Press.

Ashton-Warner, S. (1986). *Teacher.* New York: Simon & Schuster. (Original work published 1963)

Baldwin, A. (1960). The study of child behavior and development. In P. H. Mussen (Ed.), *Handbook of research methods in child development* (pp. 3–35). New York: Wiley.

Barnes, D. (1975). *From communication to curriculum.* Harmondsworth, England: Penguin.

Bayley, N. (1933). Mental growth during the first three years: A developmental study of 61 children by repeated tests. *Genetic Psychology Monographs, 14,* 1–92.

Bayley, N. (1955). On the growth of intelligence. *American Psychologist, 10,* 805–818.

Bissex, G. L., & Bullock, R. H. (1987). *Seeing for ourselves: Case-study research by teachers of writing.* Portsmouth, NH: Heinemann.

Boehm, A. E., & Weinberg, R. A. (1987). *The classroom observer: Developing observation skills in early childhood settings* (2nd ed.). New York: Teachers College Press.

Bredekamp, S. (Ed.). (1987). *Developmentally appropriate practice in early childhood programs serving children from birth through age 8* (expanded ed.). Washington, DC: National Association for the Education of Young Children.

Bredekamp, S., & Shepard, L. (1989). How best to protect children from inappropriate school expectations, practices, and policies. *Young Children, 44*(3), 14–24.

Bruner, J. S. (1986). *Actual minds, possible worlds.* Cambridge, MA: Harvard University Press.

Burton, F. (1988). Reflections on Strickland's "Toward the Extended Professional." *Language Arts, 65,* 765–768.

Bussis, A., Chittenden, E., Amarel, M., & Klausner, E. (1985). *Inquiry into meaning: An investigation of learning to read.* Hillsdale, NJ: Erlbaum.

Cambourne, B., & Turbill, J. (1990). Assessment in whole language classrooms: Theory into practice. *Elementary School Journal, 90,* 337–349.

Carini, P. F. (1975). *Observation and description: An alternative methodology for the investigation of human phenomena.* Grand Forks, ND: University of North Dakota Press.

Centre for Primary Language Education/Inner London Education Authority. (1988). *Primary language record.* Portsmouth, NH: Heinemann.

Chittenden, E. (1990). Young children's discussions of science topics. In G. Hein (Ed.), *The assessment of hands-on elementary science programs* (pp. 220–247), Monograph of the North Dakota Study Group on Evaluation. Grand Forks, ND: University of North Dakota Press.

Clay, M. M. (1985). *The early detection of reading difficulties.* Portsmouth, NH: Heinemann.

Clay, M. M. (1990). Research currents: What is and what might be in evaluation. *Language Arts, 67,* 288–298.

Clay, M. M. (1991). *Becoming literate: The construction of inner control.* Portsmouth, NH: Heinemann.

Cochran-Smith, M., & Lytle, S. L. (1990). Research on teaching and teacher research: The issues that divide. *Educational Researcher, 19*(2), 2–11.

Coley, R. J., & Goertz, M. E. (1990). *Educational standards in the 50 states: 1990.* Princeton, NJ: Educational Testing Service.

Connelly, F. M., & Clandinin, D. J. (1988). *Teachers as curriculum planners: Narratives of experience.* New York: Teachers College Press.

Darling-Hammond, L., & Wise, A. E. (1985). Beyond standardization: State standards and school improvement. *Elementary School Journal, 85,* 315–336.

DeFord, D. E., Lyons, C., & Pinnell, G. S. (1991). *Bridges to literacy: Learning from Reading Recovery.* Portsmouth, NH: Heinemann.

Delaney, E. (in progress). *Early childhood teachers' implicit theories of emotion: A study in teacher thinking.* Unpublished doctoral dissertation, Teachers College, Columbia University, New York.

Dewey, J. (1963). *Experience and education.* New York: Collier. (Original work published 1938)

Donaldson, M. (1978). *Children's minds.* New York: Norton.

Donaldson, M. (1987). The origins of inference. In J. Bruner & H. Haste

(Eds.), *Making sense: The child's construction of the world* (pp. 97–107). New York: Methuen.

Durkin, D. (1990). Reading instruction in kindergarten: A look at some issues through the lens of new basal reader materials. *Early Childhood Research Quarterly, 5,* 299–316.

Dyson, A. H. (1989). *Multiple worlds of child writers: Friends learning to write.* New York: Teachers College Press.

Edelsky, C., Altwerger, B., & Flores, B. (1991). *Whole language: What's the difference?* Portsmouth, NH: Heinemann.

Eisner, E. (1991). *The enlightened eye: Qualitative inquiry and the enhancement of educational practice.* New York: Macmillan.

Erickson, F. (1986). Qualitative methods in research on teaching. In M. Wittrock (Ed.), *Handbook of research on teaching* (3rd ed.) (pp. 119–161). New York: Macmillan.

Frederiksen, J. R., & Collins, A. (1989). A systems approach to educational testing. *Educational Researcher, 18*(9), 27–32.

Freeman, E. B., & Hatch, J. A. (1989). What schools expect young children to know and do: An analysis of kindergarten report cards. *Elementary School Journal, 89,* 595–606.

Freire, P. (1970). *Pedagogy of the oppressed.* New York: Continuum.

Gallagher, J. M., & Sigel, I. E. (Eds.) (1987). Special issue: Hothousing of young children. *Early Childhood Research Quarterly 2*(3).

Gardner, H. (1983). *Frames of mind: The theory of multiple intelligences.* New York: Basic Books.

Genishi, C. (1991). The research perspective: Looking at play through case studies. In B. Scales, M. Almy, A. Nicolopoulou, & S. Ervin-Tripp (Eds.), *Play and the social context of development in early care and education* (pp. 75–83). New York: Teachers College Press.

Genishi, C., & Dyson, A. H. (1984). *Language assessment in the early years.* Norwood, NJ: Ablex.

Genishi, C, & Dyson, A. H. (1989, April). *Making assessment functional: Fighting what comes naturally.* Paper presented at the annual meeting of the American Educational Research Association, San Francisco.

Genishi, C., McCarrier, A., & Ryan, N. N. (1988). Research Currents: Dialogue as a context for teaching and learning. *Language Arts, 65,* 182–191.

Goodman, K. S., Goodman, Y. M., & Hood, W. J. (1989). *The whole language evaluation book.* Portsmouth, NH: Heinemann.

Gray, L. E. (1982). *Aptitude constructs, learning processes, and achievement.* Unpublished report, Stanford University, Stanford, CA.

Guba, E. G., & Lincoln, Y. S. (1989). *Fourth generation evaluation.* Newbury Park, CA: Sage.

Harp, B. (Ed.). (1991). *Assessment and evaluation in whole language programs.* Norwood, MA: Christopher-Gordon.

Herrell, A. L. (1991). *Assessment in early childhood programs.* Sacramento, CA: California State Department of Education.

Isaacs, S. (1972). *Social development in young children.* New York: Schocken. (Original work published 1933.)

Johnston, P. (1989). Constructive evaluation and the improvement of teaching and learning. *Teachers College Record, 90,* 509–528.

Kamii, C. (Ed.). (1990). *Achievement testing in the early grades: The games grown-ups play.* Washington, DC: National Association for the Education of Young Children.

Katz, L. G., & Chard, S. C. (1989). *Engaging children's minds: The project approach.* Norwood, NJ: Ablex.

Leavitt, R. L., & Krause Eheart, B. (1991). Assessment in early childhood programs. *Young Children, 46*(5), 4–9.

Lester, N. B., & Onore, C. S. (1990). *Learning change: One school district meets language across the curriculum.* Portsmouth, NH: Boynton/Cook.

Lichtenstein, R. (1990). Psychometric characteristics and appropriate use of the Gesell School Readiness Screening Test. *Early Childhood Research Quarterly, 5,* 359–378.

Martinez, M. E., & Lipson, J. I. (1989). Assessment for learning. *Educational Leadership, 46*(7), 73–75.

Medina, N., & Neill, D. M. (1990). *Fallout from the testing explosion: How 100 million standardized tests undermine equity and excellence in America's public schools.* Cambridge, MA: National Center for Fair and Open Testing (FairTest).

Meisels, S. J. (1987). Uses and abuses of developmental screening and school readiness testing. *Young Children, 42*(2), 4–6, 68–73.

Meisels, S. J. (1989). High-stakes testing in kindergarten. *Educational Leadership, 46*(7), 16–22.

Miller, J. A. (1991). Bush strategy launches "crusade" for education. *Education Week, 10*(31), 1, 24–26.

National Association for the Education of Young Children & National Association of Early Childhood Specialists in State Departments of Education. (1991). Guidelines for appropriate curriculum content and assessment in programs serving children ages 3 through 8. *Young Children, 46*(3), 21–38.

National Commission on Excellence in Education. (1983). *A nation at risk.* Washington, DC: U.S. Department of Education.

Perrone, V. (Ed.) (1975). *Testing and evaluation: New views.* Washington, DC: Association for Childhood Education International.

Perrone, V. (1991). On standardized testing. *Childhood Education, 67,* 131–142.

Piaget, J., & Inhelder, B. (1969). *The psychology of the child.* New York: Basic.

Pratt, C. (1948). *I learn from children: An adventure in progressive education.* New York: Simon & Schuster.

Robinson, J. (1988). *The baby board: A parents' guide to preschool and primary school entrance tests.* New York: Acro.

Schickedanz, J. A., Chay, S., Gopin, P., Sheng, L. L., Song, S.-M., & Wild, N. (1990). Preschoolers and academics: Some thoughts. *Young Children, 46* (1), 4–13.

Seefeldt, C. (Ed.) (1987). *The early childhood curriculum: Review of current research.* New York: Teachers College Press.

Shepard, L., & Smith, M. L. (1989). *Flunking grades: Research and policies on retention.* Lewes, England: Falmer.

Snow, R. E. (1989). Toward assessment of cognitive and conative structures in learning. *Educational Researcher, 18*(9), 8–14.

Snyder, J., Bolin, F., & Zumwalt, K. K. (1992). Curriculum implementation. In P. W. Jackson (Ed.), *Handbook of research on curriculum* (pp. 402–435). New York: Macmillan.

Sternberg, D. (1991). *The efficacy of an early primary transitional program as an alternative strategy within a pupil-placement policy.* Unpublished doctoral dissertation, Teachers College, Columbia University, New York.

Strickland, D. S., Dillon, R. M., Funkhouser, L., Glick, M., & Rogers, C. (1989). Research currents: Classroom dialogue during literature response groups. *Language Arts, 66,* 192–200.

Vygotsky, L. S. (1978). *Mind in society.* Cambridge, MA: Harvard University Press.

Wann, K., & Foshay, A. (1954). *Children's social values: An action research report.* New York: Teachers College Press.

Wexler-Sherman, C., Gardner, H., & Feldman, D. H. (1988). A pluralistic view of early assessment: The Project Spectrum approach. *Theory into Practice, 27*(1), 783.

Wolf, D. P. (1989). Portfolio assessment: Sampling student work. *Educational Leadership, 46*(7), 35–39.

2

Learning to See the Learning of Preschool Children

JAN WATERS
JOANNE FLYNN FRANTZ
STEPHANIE ROTTMAYER
MARY TRICKETT
CELIA GENISHI

This chapter focuses on a private preschool in Columbus, Ohio. Its main themes are emotional safety, a curriculum that emerges in response to individual children, and the importance of communication among children, teachers, and parents. The sections marked "Celia's Voice" are a weaving together of all collaborators' voices, oral and written.

Lizzie's Story: *Mary's Voice*

It is very early in the school year at SYC (School for Young Children). On this morning Lizzie's mom is going to leave Lizzie for the first time at the school. The teacher can see this is hard for Lizzie. Her eyes are big; she grips her mom's purse. Her mom says: "Lizzie, now don't you cry. I already feel bad enough. I'll be back." She leaves. Lizzie stands wooden, looking down, biting her lip. The teacher comes close to Lizzie, gets down next to her and says, "At this school, Lizzie, it's OK to cry," which is what Lizzie immediately proceeds to do. The teacher says, "It's so hard to have your mom leave." Lizzie cries harder, and her body relaxes. The teacher comes closer to put a comforting arm around Lizzie. Lizzie stiffens again and pulls away.

The teacher moves back and says: "Lizzie, you feel so bad. Would you like to write a letter to your mom and tell her how you feel?" Yes, she would. The teacher gets a marker and paper. She asks Lizzie if

she calls her mother "mom" or "mommy." "Mommy," says Lizzie.
Writing what she is told, the teacher repeats to Lizzie,

Dear Mommy:
I miss you. I want you here now. I want you to come back. I
hate this school. I love you.

"Would you like to keep this letter?" Lizzie says, "No." The teacher
tells Lizzie, "I am a person who really likes kids, and I'll take care of
you while you are here until your mom comes back."

She has stopped crying and looks around. The teacher says:
"You know, Lizzie, I know there is a place in this room where kids
can just watch what's going on. Would you like to see where it is?"
Yes, she would. The teacher takes her to the book corner, where she
can see everything in the room but is somewhat secluded herself.
Within five minutes Lizzie, on her own, leaves the book corner.
Within a few minutes more, she is giggling with another little girl
and engaging in active play.

Lizzie is 3 years old, and she knows to be sad when her mom
leaves, to cry about it when she knows that it is safe to do so. She
knows she doesn't want this big person, whom she doesn't know, to
hold her. She knows she needs time to check this place out and then,
on her own and in her own time, venture out. She knows a lot.

Her feelings have been accepted, listened to, and respected. She
has been freed up to find her own way to work through this hard
process on this morning of coming into a new environment without
the comfort and protection of her mom.

This is a true story, and I am the new teacher trying out for the
first time on my own the skills that I have seen modeled at this
school. It feels great for me and for Lizzie, and on top of that, it works.
I call what I see as SYC's most unique quality "emotional safety"—or
the ability to provide this safety on a consistent basis. It is so easy to
shame a child with a word, a glance, a gesture. That shaming doesn't
happen here. For me as a teacher, as I give to a child the assurance
that all her feelings are acceptable in a very concrete way, I give that
assurance to myself as well. And that feels good.

SYC has a low turnover rate for preschool teachers. The average
number of years of teaching here is five to seven years. This makes
for a very experienced staff with much time to learn about and work
with children. There is a real consistency of philosophy at this
school with a wide range in childrens' ages—from 2 to 5 years old—
and in personality of teachers. I believe this happens because we

allow teachers to be individual and unique in the process of learning to be teachers. We give them the same support, space, respect, and boundaries that we afford the children.

I remember that as a new teacher I was aware of my reluctance to involve myself in angry conflicts between children. No one confronted me about this apparent weakness that I felt in myself. I found myself washing dishes or cleaning up when there was an angry confrontation taking place. I imagined resentment and unspoken criticism from the other teachers. Finally, I asked Jan, the director, if she had noticed my actions. Her response was that she thought I was probably not comfortable with these situations and that as I gained confidence, when I was ready, I would move into them. Being accepted as I was provided me with the "emotional safety" to move into exploring my world as a teacher, to try my ideas, to trust my judgment—I felt motivated and encouraged.

An "Assessment Spiral": *Celia's Voice*

In her brief story Mary introduces you to SYC as she incorporates the major themes of this chapter: the importance of *accepting* children's and teachers' own styles and giving them a sense of "emotional safety"; of *seeing* what children feel and do; of *providing a curriculum* or environment that is responsive to children's needs and styles; of *contextualizing* needs and styles within their family and out-of-school experience; and of *communicating* what children feel and do to others. All of these themes make up our view of assessment, which is also reflected here:

> The tremendous learning that goes on daily at our school is not readily visible to many people. The purpose of this handbook is to help parents learn to "see" the learning that occurs at SYC. Our interest in young children's learning is grounded in the knowledge that children feel good about themselves as a consequence of their own achievements. By becoming more aware of the learning that happens at SYC, I feel parents can also come to appreciate the learning that happens at home. (Waters, 1990, p. 1)

This is part of the introduction to Jan's handbook about SYC, entitled *Learning to See the Learning: A Parent's Guide* (Waters, 1990). Like Mary's story, Jan's paragraph also addresses key themes of this chapter: particularly seeing children's learning and communicating with parents about it. Everything that happens at, and sometimes beyond, SYC seems to be intimately tied to the processes of *seeing what and how individual children learn*, a more meaningful phrase for us than the word *assessment*. Thus we use it as a framework for defining and describing our ways of assessing.

That phrase suggests a number of questions: Who is doing the *seeing*? Is the *what* our curriculum? How do we as teachers construct the curriculum? What are the ways of seeing *how* children learn? And can we understand the *how* without knowing about out-of-school contexts? To give order to the answers to these questions, we have used an "assessment spiral" (see Figure 2.1), which specifies the important people and contexts that contribute to our seeing. At the center of the spiral, daily life at school makes up the *curriculum that develops in the community of the classroom*, a context that children, parents, and teachers all participate in and influence. The arrows indicate interaction and communication between and among these groups. The teachers are also influenced by and contribute to the community of Columbus and, beyond that, to their professional field, that of early childhood education. In turn, what they bring from the field into the classroom influences children and their parents. Finally, adults' visions of how children fit into the outermost loop, the larger society, influence expectations of what and how children should learn.

The rest of the chapter deals primarily with the heart of the spiral and is arranged in the following way: (1) history and description of SYC, (2) the parents' role early in the school year, (3) children's stories, the center of the classroom community, (4) themes shaping the curriculum, (5) our ways of assessing, (6) the outer loops—the pressure for kindergarten readiness, (7) teachers collaborating and teachers learning, and (8) an epilogue.

The Community of the Classroom: History and Background

The developmental story of SYC provides a frame for viewing processes of learning, teaching, and assessing. The beliefs of the current staff are grounded in a child-centered philosophy, presented next.

Some History

Lee Row and Janet Stocker, the founders of SYC, based the school's curriculum on their dream, a place where young children's

FIGURE 2.1 Assessment spiral

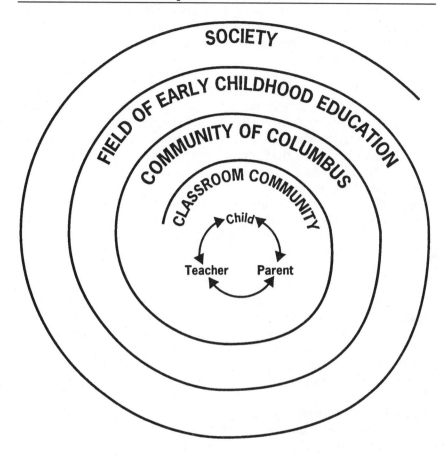

creative thinking and problem solving could develop largely through free play and art activities. The founders and their teachers planned their curriculum by imagining that they were children. They attempted to enter the child's world and build a program that allowed children to interact with one another in places filled with child-focused materials. That interaction would be the fertile soil upon which young children could grow and develop into autonomous playing children.

Lee and Janet were especially concerned with the protection of children's rights. Their rules for SYC classrooms reflect the respect that adults there have for children and include the following: Children have the right to feel safe; children have a right to uninterrupted play; no one will be allowed to abuse someone emotionally or physically; and everyone is responsible for his or her own actions and the effect they have on other people. Rules such as these still underlie the SYC curriculum.

In 1969 the First Unitarian Universalist Church in Columbus decided to sponsor SYC as a social outreach program for the community. The school is still housed there, although the SYC staff independently develops its curriculum. The church's Sunday School classrooms provide an ideal setting: They are spacious, with ceiling-to-floor glass windows that reveal large grassy areas used as playgrounds. Surrounding the classroom building are a wooded area and field, which extend the "classroom space" considerably. Although the physical site has not changed, SYC has grown since 1969 from two classes with 40 students to nine classes with 150 students. It now has 15 part-time teachers, an office administrator, and the director, Jan, who also teaches a class. We teachers work in teams of three, and each team has a head teacher who is ultimately responsible for the class.

The children range in age from 2½ to 5 years old; most, according to the occupations of their parents, are middle-class. Although in the past few mothers worked, now about 50% of them do and so make arrangements for day care while their children are not at SYC. A small number (3%) of children are on "scholarship," and almost every class includes a special-needs child. In 1990 tuition for eight months ranged from $145 for children attending one day per week to $1,170 for children attending five days per week. Almost all the children are Caucasian, as are the teachers, who are all women. Children who are members of ethnic minorities usually make up about 3% of the group and have recently been African-American, East Indian, and Japanese. In short, SYC serves a largely Caucasian middle-class community in which most parents share the social and educational values of teachers and staff.

An Overview of the Curriculum

Parents often enroll their children in the School for Young Children after an initial visit because they like the "feel" of what they see during the visit. They usually know they do not want a highly structured program and prefer a "play" program. They want their children to have a positive introduction to school, and they want their children to be treated kindly by the teachers. . . .

> We want to assist our young learners in building knowledge
> and skills that will enable them to become eager learners, creative
> thinkers, confident problem solvers, and sensitive, compassionate
> human beings. (Waters, 1990, p. 1)

These paragraphs also come from Jan's handbook for parents. They
are a capsule description of the curriculum and of teachers' goals for
SYC learners. More elaborate goals include the following:

1. To help children and families make the transition from home to
   school.
2. To respect the dignity and character of each child.
3. To preserve and nurture the inborn creativity of each child.
4. To allow each child to question, explore, and develop at her or his
   own rate and to be active partners in the learning process.
5. To help each child move toward his or her optimal potential for
   social, intellectual, emotional, moral, and physical growth.
6. To encourage and facilitate the child's striving toward independence.
7. To develop trusting relationships with both children and parents.
8. To help children begin to learn the process of schooling.
9. To respond to parenting needs.
10. To foster communication among the children, teachers, and
    parents.

We work toward these goals within a curriculum that is emer-
gent: In part we teachers systematically plan and construct it based
on what we know and what we have done before; in part the children
determine it by their responses to what we plan. Our abilities to
observe and "read" those responses help us modify plans and create
new ones. The daily schedule reflects this dynamic view of curriculum. It allows for much child choice, some adult structuring, and
much communication. On a typical morning at SYC, children arrive
between 8:30 and 9:30 A.M., and at 9:30 the school day officially
begins. Until 11:10 children play freely in any area of the classrooms.
Paints and markers are available at all times, and each day the
teacher plans a special art activity. At 11:05 teachers announce that
pick-up time, a transition period, will begin in five minutes. Everyone is responsible for putting away whatever she or he had played
with that day. When a certain area is very busy, a teacher will write
brief notes about who plays with what and with whom. These notes

make up a portion of the daily notes that teachers write every day after class.

After pick-up time comes the more structured rugtime, directed by a teacher. The 2-year-olds have a short (5- to 10-minute) rugtime, whereas the 3-year-olds meet for 15 to 20 minutes or as long as the group of 18 children maintain interest. Activities include finger plays, songs, puppet shows, or a parent sharing a talent. Here children begin to learn rules for social participation in a group.

The 4-year-olds have "minirug." Each of the three teachers chooses a topic and draws a picture of what the topic will be. Children then make tickets and sign up for the topic of their choice. There are eight slots for signing up, so each teacher gets about one-third of the class for minirug. Lunch follows rugtime and minirug and is a social time with teachers and children sharing conversations and sometimes lunch. At 11:45 the class divides into three groups for story-reading and talk about the story. School ends at noon. (A similar schedule, except for lunchtime, is followed in the afternoon as well.)

Parents: Getting to Know the Classroom Community

What happens in any classroom grows out of a community history, and at SYC parents are the first to contribute to that history when they fill in an application for their child. So the first step for all teachers is simply reading the applications for children in their respective age groups. This tells us about the family, including number and ages of siblings and parents' occupations. Parents list particular concerns or information they think will be of interest to teachers, including the child's previous experience in groups or characteristics such as shyness or aggressiveness. Lengthy notes often indicate parents who will want a lot of support from the school.

The second step is a meeting of the three teachers for each age group or classroom. This is a chance for teachers to get to know one another better if they have not worked together before and to collectively review applications. Jan sees that each team of teachers is balanced in terms of the group's strengths. Some are good at art, others at puppet shows; some outgoing, others quiet. At the meeting we ask who has siblings, who is new to the school, how many boys and girls there are at each age level. Differences in class composition are most evident at the 4-year-old level. One group of 4-year-olds tend to be less mature and may need to focus on separating from parents and adjusting to one another, the teachers, and school routines. The second group usually have had more experience at SYC and with peers. With them we focus on facilitating peer communication from the start. Thus, broad plans for curriculum stem from the characteristics of the children in each group.

The Sunday evening before school starts, an orientation for all parents is held. This is a requirement because we feel that the year should begin with communication between parents and teachers. We distribute school policies, calendars, daily schedules, and class rosters. We also present a series of, we hope, entertaining skits called "A Day at SYC" in order to portray important elements of our philosophy and curriculum. Although these vary a bit from year to year, the basic topics remain the same: how we deal with separation of child from parent; the importance of playing and its connection to learning; setting limits; respecting creativity; and learning how to participate in groups.

During the year we encourage parents to continue their communication with us informally when they bring or pick up their children. We also have two other scheduled contacts with them, the home visit and parent coffees. We visit the homes of every 2- and 3-year-old in the fall. In addition, we visit the homes of any 4- and 5-year-olds who are new to the school. During the visit the child's teacher spends about half an hour with the child doing whatever the child chooses to do while the rest of the family is elsewhere in the house. We hope that this visit gives us more information about the child and also strengthens the bonds between home and school, teacher and child.

Parent coffees are scheduled by the head teacher of each group, who decides on the appropriate format. She may choose specific topics to discuss or just let parents talk. Teachers might impart information about child development so that both parents and teachers can discuss individual children within a common framework. Often the information builds up parents' confidence about their ability to be parents at the same time that teachers gain new insights into the children. These coffees can also initiate informal parent support groups.

Children: The Center of the Classroom Community

This section represents the center of the chapter, as well as the center of the classroom community. We first let the stories about three children "speak for themselves" and later discuss common themes and our ways of remembering children and events. The children contrast in informative ways: Jimmy, at first a "withdrawn" 3-year-old; Adrienne, a "handicapped" 3-year-old; and Morgan, a "difficult" child, whose SYC career spanned his life from 2 to 5 years of age.

Jimmy's Story: *Stephanie's Voice*

Jimmy's 3-year-old year at our school was a quiet one. He did not exhibit concern about being separated from his mother, yet he seemed subdued and unwilling to participate in many activities. He chose instead to stay in a small area in the lunchroom playing alone with the marble game or quietly looking at books. He looked content in this small area that he could control. The teachers tried to establish a good relationship with him by having many conversations with him and allowing him his space. He always responded when spoken to but rarely initiated any talking. Many 3-year-olds prefer at first to play alone or next to other children, rather than with them, so his teachers hoped that as he matured he would branch out and become interested in other children.

In September of his 4-year-old year Jimmy seemed to maintain the same level of comfort he had shown the previous spring. In fact, he was quite self-assured and chatted comfortably with his new teachers; he even reminded one to put out the snacks. He still seemed reluctant to interact with other children, reacting instead of initiating. For example, he stood up for himself when another child tried to take the marble game from him. Then he began to claim the small area around the game for himself, as he had done the year before. We saw him look longingly at our playground and the other rooms of the school, but we weren't able to get him to try them out. We tried many strategies to get him to venture out and finally succeeded. Outside at last, Jimmy took up a position on our climber and tried to control who came on with him by demanding cheese curls in "payment." Since the school rule is that the climber is for all the kids, no one followed Jimmy's new rule, so he retreated back to his small, safe area.

As the weeks passed, Jimmy adopted a "teacher's-helper" role for himself and watched but would not join in activities. We knew that he was very bright and verbal and began to devise intellectual activities that might appeal to him, attract other children to him, and lure him into other areas. On his mother's advice, we found an old typewriter and told him that he could take it apart and "be the boss of it." He started to do this on a table near his area; but since his work involved tools, we asked him to do it in the room with a workbench. He enjoyed trying to take it apart, and other kids were fascinated with the effort. He enjoyed their attention and as days passed finally let them join in. Everyday he asked for the typewriter and let Nate and Michael, who consistently wanted to play with it, have more and more input. The typewriter was nearly demolished, so we put up a sign in the office asking that parents donate other broken machines. At about this point the two other boys were getting bored and wanting Jimmy to do other things with them. We were thrilled as we watched him try different types of play, and when the weather turned nice, the play turned to running and chasing games on the playground. Jimmy was running and chasing with the best of them. He never asked us for the "take aparts" again.

As we teachers tried to analyze this transformation, we realized that we had all assessed Jimmy's "true nature" to be a quiet, intellectual one. His parents and even Jimmy himself seemed to have this view, as he appeared to enjoy only solitary and mechanical activities. All of our observing and conferring for the last year and a half had led us to that conclusion. Yet once Jimmy felt more confident and safe, he consistently chose the more physical and social types of play. Maybe he was always yearning to run and chase but got "stuck" in familiar routines. As he stayed with those routines, though, he had the time to develop relationships with peers—and time to get his emotional, social, cognitive, and physical sides together. He left SYC looking so confident and happy, and we were thrilled that he had discovered the physical part of himself before beginning kindergarten.

Adrienne's Story: *Jan's Voice*

Adrienne started the school year in early November about six weeks after the beginning of the school year. She had turned 3 on October 15, whereas the rest of the class had turned 3 by September 30, so she was underage for the class. Underage children are considered on a trial basis if there are openings in the class.

We usually request that parents stay in the parent room, not in the classroom, when their children do not want them to leave. This helps us assess whether the child or the parent has a problem with separation. Because of her age and because Adrienne is visibly, physically different from other children, I agreed when her mother asked to stay in the classroom to help her daughter acclimate to the school.

Adrienne's difference is that she has only one hand. Her left arm ends below her elbow. I felt watching child and mother together would help us teachers understand their relationship and deal with children's talk about Adrienne's lack of a left hand. So we began to watch Adrienne's behavior with her mother and her classmates. Her mother asked us for help in explaining to the other children that Adrienne was born with only one hand. Mother and teachers decided to see if Adrienne wanted to answer the children's questions herself. If she did not, her mother would answer them.

I remember in the housekeeping corner John Paul asked Adrienne what happened to her hand. Adrienne remained silent. After a few minutes her mother said, "She was born that way." John Paul looked at both of his hands, wiggled them around and said, "I'm glad I have two hands." Adrienne's mother said, "Oh are you?" John Paul and Adrienne continued playing in the kitchen, "making dinner."

During those first days, Adrienne stayed close to her mother, often crying if her mother was out of sight. Anytime there was a problem with another child, Adrienne fled to her mother. During lunchtime Adrienne seemed to need a lot of help from her mother managing her lunch box and food. At first Adrienne's contact with other children happened mainly when others questioned Adrienne about her missing hand or when she would play with her friend Josh, who was a friend outside of school.

I made a home visit to Adrienne's house about a month after she began school. During this visit, Adrienne decided we should play with her zoo set, and she directed the play entirely. At home she did not exhibit an overdependence on her parents but appeared very self-sufficient. I remember playing with Adrienne for 45 minutes or so with her parents watching from the other room in an unintrusive way. During the home visit Adrienne and I made physical contact with pats and hugs, something that had not happened at school.

As the school year progressed, the class became interested in a house that was being moved into the neighborhood from another location. We would take walks across the field to look at the house and discuss what was happening to it. By this time Adrienne was letting her mother leave during classtime. Adrienne always asked to hold a teacher's hand on these walks, and we began to notice she seemed thrown off-balance on these walks through the rough field. So we began to assess her physical development because we saw her in a context other than the classroom.

As more time went by, we noticed that Adrienne seemed to be interested in watching an active group of boys play at superheroes. She watched at great length and sometimes acted fearful of their play. However, one day we noticed her wearing a Batman cape and swinging a sword. She became very assertive as Batgirl and would tell the boys to "stop that" when they got too scary. She also became fascinated with tiger suits and liked to play tiger houses.

In February I had a conference with Adrienne's mother, who seemed pleased with the way the school year was going. She expressed some concern over Adrienne's dominating of her friend Josh, and we discussed her problems in getting along with peers outside of school. Adrienne's mother said that Adrienne had a prosthesis, but she never wore it. We talked about the progress Adrienne had made in taking care of her own needs and her growing ability to take care of herself at school. By this time Adrienne had been totally accepted by the other children, and she was well liked.

Toward the end of the school year, we noticed a return of Adrienne's fearfulness. She asked teachers to hold her during these times and then would go off and play again. One teacher theorized that we were outside more and that outdoor play was more taxing for Adrienne. Another teacher wondered if there might be a change in her parents' work schedules that might be affecting her.

The next fall, about to turn 4, Adrienne entered school in a class with many new classmates. Children soon started questioning her about her handless arm. Her reaction was either to walk away or say in a loud voice, "I don't want to talk about my arm!" Teachers explained to her that some children were curious about her missing hand and that a teacher would answer questions if Adrienne did not want to.

During the first few weeks, Adrienne would curl up on a teacher's lap and talk about missing her mom. We were concerned because she seemed angry around the other children, and they were avoiding her in their play. We stayed in close touch with her mother to plan strategies—such as writing notes or making phone calls home and bringing security objects from home—that might help Adrienne cope with anger or feelings about separation.

She began to play alone with swords and guns and told teachers she was a policewoman, riding a big wheel and dressed as a policewoman. We were about to invite her mother in to talk to the class about Adrienne's being one-handed when Adrienne seemed to change dramatically. After a day when both her mother and father brought her to school, she seemed happy all day. From that point on, she spent most of her days active and involved. She became friends with a rather aggressive boy named Andrew, and the two engaged at length in sociodramatic play with rubber animals. I have noticed that she has also progressed in her climbing and jumping. Her shorter arm seemed to present a balancing problem when she used large-muscle equipment last year. She seems to have figured out how to balance herself and to enjoy large-muscle activities.

I had a conference with Adrienne's mother a few days ago, and she is pleased with her progress in school. She is worried, though, because at home Adrienne has taken to hitting and shouting at her mother. Since we have seen none of this kind of behavior at school, I suggested that her mother encourage Adrienne to talk about why she is feeling angry and not let her hit or shout. Her parents are considering a private school kindergarten next year because she is showing an interest in reading. I suggested that whatever school they choose, a lot of time be spent helping Adrienne cope with the inevitable questions about her seeming handicap.

Over time we have been able to watch Adrienne change—not in a "straight-line" way—from a frightened, dependent little girl to a sword-swinging, climbing and jumping, competent member of her class. Her assessment picture became more complicated but in most ways clearer as teachers talked with her mother, observed her in different situations, and interacted with her and her peers.

Morgan's Story: *Joanne's Voice*

The 2-year-old year. Morgan Jones began at SYC in the 2-year-old program when he was 2 years and 9 months old. He entered school as a larger-than-average, stocky, blond-haired and blue-eyed boy, the diapered, verbal, and much-loved son of two older parents (his mother was about 40 and his father, over 60). Morgan's mom, Karen, stayed with him in the classroom those first few weeks, as all 2-year-olds' parents are requested to do. Morgan seemed eager to explore the environment and the nine other children in the class as long as Karen was close by.

These first few weeks are a get-acquainted period for parents, teachers, and children. We hope that parents will slowly come to trust that SYC is a safe place for the child, that the child will have fun, and that the teachers are willing listeners and advisers if advice is requested. Morgan's teachers that year were Ann and Janet. Ann routinely talks individually with parents during the first two weeks of school, asking such things as: Are they working on potty training?

What are the child's fears? Does the child have a favorite security item? Ann learned that Karen had been hospitalized for meningitis earlier that year and that separation from his parents and potty training might be problems for Morgan.

In their afterschool notes, which we teachers regularly took, Ann and Janet recorded early on that accepting rules such as picking up things you played with were a challenge for Morgan, since there were no firm limits set at home at this point. At pick-up time Morgan would get mad, stomp his feet, and start to cry. We often physically help a child's hands pick up toys. Since Morgan did not like physical contact with the teachers, he wanted no part of that. He would go further into hysterics. Morgan's next response was to try to hide at pick-up time. Clearly that was a game Ann and Janet could not encourage!

After many note-writing sessions, Ann and Janet decided to give Morgan several minutes warning before pick-up time. They would tell him what he needed to do so that he would not be overwhelmed and could focus on one segment at a time. Ann remembers cajoling Morgan with comments like, "Which do you want to pick up first, the red or the blue blocks?" This plan seemed to work.

Ann and Janet also felt that Morgan would accept school rules more easily if he knew the teachers better. In early October Janet arranged to do a home visit, which is done for each child new to the school. Janet remembers roughhousing with Morgan and having a fun time. She felt that Morgan trusted her more after this.

After the first three weeks of school, Karen began leaving SYC while Morgan was there. Since emotional issues and separation were difficult for him, Janet set up a routine. Janet would hold Morgan, and they would both watch Karen leave and shout, "See you later, alligator!" Although Morgan was very talkative, he did not acknowledge or express his emotions. Janet remembers working on this, modeling expression of feelings, and helping him dictate letters to Karen:

Dear Mommy,
    I miss you. I want you to be at school with me.
                                    Love,
                                    Morgan

When Karen was hospitalized with a relapse of meningitis later in October, Morgan was fine at school while she was in the hospital. After she returned home, though, Morgan again had a hard time, one day crying for more than 15 minutes. The teachers knew Morgan needed more emotional support, more hugs and holding, as separation from Karen again became the most important and difficult issue for him.

Socially Morgan was a leader. A gang of children had begun to form in the class, a very interactive group of 2-year-olds. Morgan and Danny were attracted to each other from the first weeks and laughed together, making silly noises at rugtime. They were joined by Elizabeth, Graham, Willy, and sometimes Evan, while they made pretend airplanes and gas stations with chairs. Together they engaged in a range of activities, except for small-motor activity, which Morgan avoided. His imagination and verbal ability served him well in social situations.

By late January Ann and Janet noticed changes in Morgan, which they recorded in their daily notes. Danny and Graham rejected him, and he cried hard when this happened. Apparently Morgan liked to be the boss—in control. They speculated that this need for control might have been linked to his mother's rehospitalization, since "losing" one's mother is a young child's ultimate loss of control. At about this time Morgan also began testing the school rules in a different way. One day while the class was outside riding bikes in the fenced-in play area, with no teacher in sight, Morgan opened the gate and led children on bikes out to the parking lot. When Ann caught up with Morgan and established firmly the rule that only teachers open gates, Morgan became very upset. It was clear that Morgan did not like to make mistakes. Ann and Janet decided to follow up with a puppet show the next day in which Little Bear, the 2-year-old puppet, did the same thing that Morgan had done. The teachers wanted to demonstrate and model that it is OK to make mistakes at school, but you need to follow the rules even if you don't like them. Morgan watched in rapt attention.

Janet remembers spending the majority of time at the annual parent conference with Karen talking about Morgan's emotional development and his difficulty in verbalizing feelings. Janet came away from the conference feeling that Karen really did trust the school.

As Morgan ended the academic year with the other 2-year-olds, he was still testing school rules, still wearing diapers, still not liking small-motor activities, but also being highly social and verbal. The summer following that year, Morgan attended playcamp, an SYC activity. Jan remembers that Morgan began pooping in his diapers quite often. She spent a lot of time in the bathroom with him helping him change. Her main concern was that this behavior was interfering with his social life, since other children wanted to avoid the way he smelled. One day Jan and Morgan sat on the bathroom floor together as Morgan wept. He told Jan that he pooped in his diaper because he wanted to be a baby. She then told him he could pretend to be a baby, but he had to change whenever he pooped. She later recounted what Morgan had said to his mom, who, Jan thinks, applied the same rule at home. Maybe Morgan would stop pooping in his diapers when he got tired of changing and cleaning up. He eventually did.

The 3-year-old year. My first reaction to Morgan that fall was utter fascination. He seemed to have an 8-year-old's vocabulary and manner, trapped in a 3½-year-old's body. His mother brought him on the first days, and they were usually among the first to arrive. His mother said he did not like the confusion when other parents and children arrived. (Young 3's are often overwhelmed by the larger class size and greater space in the rooms.) Until his friend Danny arrived, Morgan would look anxious and want his mom to stay in the room with him. He always had a plan of what Danny and he would play and what props would facilitate the plan: swords to play pirates, outfits for Batman and Robin. Morgan still liked to be boss!

Since the 3-year-old group was larger than the 2-year-old group, it was difficult to give Morgan the special attention that Janet had given him the year before. Morgan's parents tried giving him good-bye hugs and letting him wave until they were out of sight, but he kept wanting to run after them. After they left, he would look tense but would say: "I'm fine. Leave me alone."

We read children's body language and often find it a more accurate indication of adjustment than a child's words. One day, as Morgan's parents left and I watched him fighting back tears, I scooped him up in my arms to reassure him as he was saying that he was not sad. Morgan pulled back and yelled, "You let go of me!" He was crying, turning red, retreating under the cubbies, and continuing to yell, pointing at my face the whole time. I felt utterly frustrated and helpless. Here was a child who needed reassurance but would not accept it. He was a little boy trying hard to be an adult, a little boy trying to deny his vulnerability and feelings of sadness and loneliness. I discussed the problem with my co-teachers, Mary and Lela, and we decided to describe this scene at a schoolwide meeting.

At one of our bimonthly teachers' meetings, our topic was Morgan—as he had been a number of times before. We role-played the scene I just described; I played Morgan. I remember identifying with Morgan and feeling alone and scared as I yelled at the teachers. As a result of the brainstorming and suggestions that followed, we decided on a more indirect approach with Morgan. We felt it was important to continue to model expression of feelings and have puppets verbalize being sad and missing a parent. Despite our natural inclination to comfort Morgan physically, we decided this threatened him. We agreed to make occasional physical contact by touching him on the arm or patting him on the back when he was in a good frame of mind.

Then, there was the day Morgan's lunch box fell on his head, an incident Lela clearly remembers. Morgan went to get a toy out of his cubby, and his lunch box fell out and hit him—hard—on the head. Lela, who was the teacher in the room, moved toward him to make sure he was physically OK and to reassure him. He began yelling at her: "You get away from me. Don't touch me. The lunch box did not hit me." Lela was intimidated and so kept her distance as she tried to reassure Morgan verbally. Here again was a scared little boy who did not want to admit he had made a mistake. We acted this scene out, too, at a teachers' meeting, with Lela playing Morgan this time. Lela again felt the scared little boy in Morgan, but we also sensed Morgan had too much power. As a result of the other teachers' suggestions, we decided to continue encouraging Morgan's expression of feelings, but we also had to start limiting his yelling. We began to give direct feedback, such as: "Morgan, I don't like it when you yell at me. It hurts my ears." We expected progress to be slow, but Morgan was normally so charming and delightful that we really wanted to help him overcome these frustrating times.

Socially Morgan continued to be very interested in other children. Control and yelling were factors in his social life as well. As a 3-year-old Morgan could play with Danny or Graham individually, but it was difficult for the three of them to play together. Graham and Danny would begin to hit each other; Morgan would not hit but would start yelling: "I'm not playing with you now. Go away." His yelling further escalated the conflict.

We spent a lot of time, as we do with many of the 3's, problem-solving with Morgan, Danny, and Graham. When a problem arose in play, a teacher would ask, "Is there a problem here?" Then each boy would tell his version of the story. We find direct confrontation is the most effective way of changing inappropriate social behavior. Being able to tell someone "It makes me mad when you won't let me play" or "Don't yell! We don't want to play with you when you yell" is an important life skill. Over time Morgan's yelling at peers began to decrease.

I was responsible for Morgan's parent conference during the 3-year-old year. We spent a lot of time discussing Morgan over the Christmas break on conference-planning day. We agreed that his emotional development still needed to be the focus of the conference. We pooled our daily notes and compiled a picture of him socially, physically, and cognitively. At the conference his mother, Karen, shared her feelings of frustration about Morgan's yelling at home and not talking about underlying feelings. She gave us an insight when she said that it was important in any conflict for Morgan to save face. She also said she was concerned about Morgan's role in the Morgan-Danny-Graham triangle, and I said I would watch this closely. Karen was not concerned about Morgan's lack of small-motor activity in school, since both she and her husband were artists and Morgan painted often at home. She thought SYC was a great social setting for her son, since he was an only child. I thought the conference was helpful for parent and teachers.

The 4-year-old year.　　Morgan began the 4-year-old year looking more relaxed than the year before. He had gone to playcamp during the summer, and separation was not a problem. He let his other teachers and me hold him when he was upset or frustrated. Janet, who had been his teacher when he was 2, had a particular knack for being silly with him when he was in a situation in which he needed to save face. In November he was upset for a few days when a new routine began, called minirug, when a child picks from among three activities for 15 minutes of the day. The distress with the new routine was short-lived; in a few days he was enjoying it.

Morgan's social world was expanding. He began to play doctor with Natalia and Spike, and Bryce was now often a playmate. And he was no longer yelling at other children! Morgan, Graham, and Danny were usually able to talk through problems themselves. We viewed this in disbelief and amazement. We watched Morgan continue to blossom as he turned 5 in the fall. Looking so much more self-assured, he liked a variety of activities at minirug—games, acting out stories, science, animals—his enthusiasm was contagious. By December Morgan was beginning to choose craft (small-motor) activities and trying to write his name.

One day in January when Morgan went to the bathroom, the heavy bathroom door that was usually propped open was closed. After trying in vain to open it, he came running around the corner, desperately saying that he needed help. By that time, he had wet his pants. But this did not upset him. His parents had left a set of dry clothes for him, and he calmly allowed he would change himself. What progress! He could admit he had had an accident, verbalize it, and problem-solve. Furthermore, he was very proud he had done it all by himself.

Morgan also became the great problem solver of the class, which he often demonstrated in social situations. By January a large group would often play together: Morgan, Danny, Bryce, Max, Elizabeth, Caitlin, sometimes Evan and Joshua. If a conflict arose, Morgan often solved the problem. With exuberance, he'd announce, "I know, I've got an idea!" This was a big step beyond the 3-year-old year when he had shouted orders to the whole class.

In the spring the large-group play continued, with Morgan usually the hub of the activity. Ninja Turtle play was very popular, and "sewers" were constructed inside and out. On nice days large groups would play with water and sand and construct lakes and rivers. On several days Morgan worked side by side with petite Melonia (who had been afraid of Morgan's yells the year before). Morgan listened to Melonia's ideas about how the rivers and lakes should be connected in the sand and helped her build them.

On the last day of school it was difficult for Morgan to say good-bye. He knew he would be returning for playcamp, although the teachers would be different. For the teachers it was very difficult to say good-bye to Morgan. He had gone from being one of the biggest challenges in the school at ages 2 and 3 to one of the most delightful and engaging children by his 4-year-old year. Again, we marvel at the process of development in a supportive environment.

A postscript: *Jan's voice.* One day at summer playcamp, I noticed Morgan and Danny over by the tire swing. Morgan appeared to be crying, and I slowly started moving toward the boys to figure out why. I stooped down by the swing and said I could see that Morgan was sad and was concerned about him. Morgan said, "You tell her, Danny." Danny told me that Morgan was sad because Danny's kitten had been killed by a car the night before. I said when a pet dies it is a sad time. Morgan then proceeded to tell me about how his tadpole had died after living only one day and how a goldfish of his had died "because the bigger fish had eaten all the food." Morgan seemed sad at the injustice of the tadpole's and goldfish's deaths. Tears streamed down his face, and I empathized with him. I asked Morgan and Danny if there was anything they wanted to do.

Morgan said to have a funeral. What would they do at the funeral? Morgan said play music. What kind? Morgan said Teenage Mutant Ninja Turtle music. At story time we read *The Tenth Good Thing About Barney* (Viorst, 1971), a story about a cat that dies. I asked Danny if he wanted to mention any good things about his kitten, and he said no.

Morgan had changed tremendously since I had seen him as a 3-year-old. He expressed his feelings very well. Instead of being over-whelmed by his feelings and striking out tyranically, he was able to verbalize how he felt. This dissipated his anger. He played well with his friends, used problem solving in an exceptionally mature way, and had found his place in a group of classmates.

Story Themes Shaping the Curriculum: *Celia's Voice*

The themes of our first assessment story, Lizzie's, reappear in the others. Accepting others so that they feel "emotionally safe" is dominant; a child's emotional self receives attention first. Woven throughout the stories are words such as *angry, crying, feelings, upset*—all part of a vocabulary of emotion. We know that both adults and children need to feel as safe in school as they do at home; they need to overcome fears about failure or separation. In order to help children feel safe, we *accept* the child as she or he is. Thus children hear no verbal suggestion that they act like "big" boys and girls, and there are no specific objectives or expectations for all children. Instead we have a general expectation that they will all grow and develop.

At the same time, we observe what children do and feel and *problem-solve* with parents' help; we develop plans for dealing with children's emotions within the contexts of school and home. Hugs and holding are available when the children are ready for them. In many cases we help children verbally *express* what they are feeling, through short letters to a parent or through statements such as, "I don't like it when you yell at me." Plans are flexible, and we change them if children do not respond well to them.

Problem solving and the talk it generates are mainstays that weave through plans to help children develop physically, socially, and cognitively as well as emotionally. As a social being, the child is learning about the needs and desires of others while finding her or his own place in the classroom community. Problem solving almost always grows out of a specific situation, observed or participated in by one of us teachers. It can be long term, as in Morgan's diaper problem. We had to deal with the problem every time it occurred, but we also talked about ways to solve it with one another, his parents, and Morgan himself. As Joanne said, Morgan did it "all by himself"—he had, with some skillful help along the way from caring adults.

Talk about problems can also lead to shifts in curricular activities. When Stephanie and her colleagues were puzzling over Jimmy's solitary behavior, they observed that he liked to tinker, so they found a broken typewriter that became an "activity" for him and eventually for others. At other times children's interests created class projects, as when children were curious about the neighborhood house that was being moved. In addition, children developed curriculum and solved problems independently of us teachers; building sewers in the sand was one example.

In this child-centered school, then, we work with children "where they are." Often their emotional lives are primary; and understanding those lives is a matter of seeing things from the child's point of view, not from the point of view of a textbook or test. Separating plans for children's emotional development from the social, physical, and cognitive is not possible, since these realms overlap and progress in one realm affects the others. Morgan's sadness over the death of Danny's kitten, for example, involved the children's emotions, their relationship with each other, and possible learning from a book. So our participation and careful observation help us follow the child's lead to shape the curriculum. Children move toward new understandings and behaviors that help them deal independently with their experiences and with the consequences of what they do. Together, we and children move toward creating niches for each child within the classroom community and toward each child's sense of uniqueness and autonomy.

Our Ways of Assessing

Observing and Taking Notes: Conferring with One Another

People who have heard or read our stories have been impressed by the detail included about children's behavior and teachers' discussions. Our main "way" of remembering the details is taking daily notes so that we can review what we saw, thought, and discussed.

What we write is selective, and as our stories show, we each have our own style of remembering and telling. We are not trying to document everything that occurred; instead, we want to note in anecdotes or a few phrases *salient behaviors, patterns* that emerge from recurring ones, and *changes* in a child's behaving, thinking, or feeling, including *developmental milestones* (for example, participating at rugtime for the first time) and *problems*.

Our note-taking begins on the first day of school when each class is split in half, each half attending for one hour. Parents are asked to stay in the classroom so that parents, children, and teachers can begin to establish trusting relationships from the very beginning. We observe how parent and child interact: Who is doing most of the talking? Who is making choices about the child's activity? How does the child interact with the classroom environment? Is she or he physically active or cautious? Are child and parents happy or anxious? (See Figure 2.2 for sample notes.)

On the second day, children stay for the full two and a half hours. Parents are encouraged to stay in the parent room, adjacent to each of the classrooms, and children may see them whenever they like and tell the teacher they are doing so. So the beginning of the year is a period of gentle adjustment, and the end of each day, like all days throughout the year, is a time for us to share, confer about, and record observations about every child. We save the notes and occasionally pass some on to teachers the following year.

Playing Roles

Our daily observations, brief conferences, and note-taking often help us articulate unformed ideas about children and their development. When we get "stuck"—for example, when trying to help Morgan express his feelings—we also use role-playing to take us a step further in understanding a problem. The school founders, Lee and Janet, used the tool often, and we continue to do so. At teachers' meetings we reenact a specific situation for a few minutes, then stop and discuss what the players might have been feeling. The discussion usually gives a different perspective on what both the child and we teachers are experiencing. This leads us to articulating thoughts and insecurities and formulating possible solutions. Even though some new teachers feel self-conscious about the dramatizations at first, participation has been magnificent because of the insights it offers.

FIGURE 2.2 Examples of Joanne's and Stephanie's notes

Darren Arndt	Jewell Browne	Vernon Kane	Jessie Loudon
Tina says he doesn't went to come to school. Good group member. Very creative. Dressed up in tutu. 10/18	Played w/ Michael. Ninjas making popcorn. Became Moira's daddy, Jessie's mommy, older sister.	Face paints. Played w/ magnets.	Watched Laura play baby. Pushed Jake M. Visit on Thurs. Face paints.

11/12/90

Lila – Brought birthday cookies. Didn't want me to sing Happy Birthday. Mom stayed all day, and she loved it. Played safety corner game. Flitted a lot w/ Ken.

Michael – Remembered which group he washed hands with. Does he hate John ditching him after pre-care?

Liked all the crafts very much.

Carolee – Very ill with coughing. Dad came to get.

Conferring with Parents

Observing, note-taking, and role-playing are ways to learn about children and, thus, shape the curriculum. They are also the basis for annual parent conferences, since parents, too, want to learn about their children's learning. After the three-week winter break in December and January, we prepare for the conferences by pooling notes and talking with one another at a special meeting, which we are paid to attend. We capitalize on our different perspectives: One of us might know a child's physical development, whereas another might know about the child-parent relationship.

Much of what we discuss with parents has already been presented in different ways, through our statement of goals and through our stories. Figure 2.3 shows our child assessment guide for each conference; it acts as an organizer and summarizes how our curricular goals are linked to assessment. We feel free to select the questions that are most relevant to each child and skip the ones that are not.

These guiding questions reflect the chief curricular goals for children and ourselves: feeling emotionally safe, adjusting to the classroom community, and communicating verbally about needs, feelings, and interests. *Communication* always plays a role in our learning, teaching, and assessing. For us *talk* is as important a "way" of assessing as careful observation: through talk children and we learn more about each other and the world; children, parents, and we identify, follow, and often solve problems that accompany development; and through talk all of us then celebrate signs of growth.

The Outer Loops: Responding to Pressure for Kindergarten Readiness

We wish our curriculum and ways of assessing children could be independent of pressures outside the classroom and the children's homes. As noted in Chapter 1, this is no longer possible. The local media highlight and publicize test scores, and parents seem to think of nothing else. They naturally expect us to help their children be "ready" for the world of kindergarten, whether this is in a public or private school. So from the beginning of the 4-year-old year, we encourage parents to visit their local school and get to know its expectations for kindergartners. Joanne, the head teacher of the 4-year-olds, does this with her colleagues when they hold a parent

FIGURE 2.3   Assessment guidelines for parent conferences

A. Adjustment to the world of school
   1. How did the child enter school? Leave at the end of the day?
   2. How does the child feel about coming to school?
   3. What does the child enjoy doing at school?
   4. Does the child initiate activities by her- or himself?
   5. How is the child's rugtime behavior?
   6. Does the child seem interested in rugtime?
   7. Can the child express her or his ideas in small group?
   8. Does the child take care of own belongings (lunch, cup, toys)?
   9. Does the child usually follow school rules?
   10. Does the child try new activities, take risks?
   11. Does the child communicate needs to teacher? How?
   12. Does the child demand and require a lot of teacher attention (to deal with separation, follow rules, interact with peers)?
   13. Is the child able to wait for turns to play, talk, or use equipment?

B. Social relationships
   1. Does the child trust teachers and seek them out? Accept comfort?
   2. Does the child know teachers' and some kids' names?
   3. What type of play does the child engage in (solitary, parallel, dramatic)? Is this age-appropriate?
   4. Who are the child's playmates? What do they do together?
   5. Can the child set limits on playmates and assert her or his own wishes and rights?
   6. Is the child a leader or follower or both?
   7. Does the child verbalize likes, dislikes, ideas to peers?
   8. In a play situation can the child listen to others' ideas, compromise?
   9. How does the child enter play?

C. Emotional development
   1. How is the child's self-esteem?
   2. How did/does the child handle separation?
   3. How does the child handle frustration?
   4. Does the child express feelings at school? Negative and positive? Or does child deny feelings?
   5. What does the child do when she or he is angry?
   6. Is the child able to empathize with peers?
   7. Does the child attempt to take care of own needs? Know when to ask for help?

D. Physical development
   1. How are the child's large-motor skills? What type of large-motor activities does the child like?

FIGURE 2.3   (continued)

 2. How are the child's small-motor skills? What type of small-motor
    activities does the child like? Does the child participate in art/craft
    activities?
 3. How are child's body movements: fast, slow, clumsy?
 4. Do child's hearing and vision seem normal?

E. Cognitive development
   1. Is the child's attention span age-appropriate?
   2. Does the child demonstrate problem-solving skills?
   3. Does the child respond appropriately at rugtime?
   4. Does the child know colors and shapes?
   5. Does the child show awareness of numbers?
   6. Is the child interested in books?
   7. Does the child show interest in and knowledge of writing: letters of
      alphabet, own name, making signs, writing letters, labeling things?

F. Goals
   1. What areas does the teacher see the child "working on"?
   2. What are the parents' concerns and goals for the year?

coffee specifically to deal with kindergarten. They present current research about "summer birthdays," or the youngest children in the class, and answer questions about choosing the appropriate kindergarten. Within the five or so school districts our children usually attend, there is a wide variety of expectations, some highly academic and some that would match our own views of what is appropriate for 5- and 6-year-olds.

According to Joanne, a major source of information as she and her colleagues imagine their 4-year-olds as kindergartners is their observation of the children's participation in minirug, a period of about 15 minutes when children choose one of three activities in one of our three rooms. This allows the teachers to observe each child in our most structured situation, a small group (about eight children) focused on a single activity. Teachers ask themselves questions related to the cognitive portion of the child assessment guide shown in Figure 2.3 such as: Does the child try the chosen activity? Does she or he contribute to discussion? Can she or he sit for a period of time (about 10 minutes by the end of the year)? Teachers can see a lot during this short time, and this kind of assessment helps us to demonstrate to parents that we understand real-world pressures—that we know what kindergartens require. We urge parents to take this kind of information into account, along with what they know about their children's emotional and social lives at SYC, their own perceptions of their children, and the expectations of the kindergarten they are considering.

Occasionally we think a child may *not* be ready for the typical kindergarten, for example, if she or he behaves in ways that would cause problems in the classroom. In this case we talk with parents about what we have seen in situations such as minirug and suggest choices: staying at SYC for another year; attending a different, more structured preschool; or choosing an appropriate kindergarten that is "child-ready" and not narrowly academic. We do not think of this as a kind of "retention," but as a way of continuing to respond to the child's own developmental needs.

Conclusion: Teachers Collaborating, Teachers Learning

We end this chapter in a way that reflects the nature of our collaboration, which was cooperative and harmonious, and that gives a sense of the relationships that developed. This story is the root of the chapter; it shows that the collaboration was a highly personal endeavor with professional purposes. We begin with a word on "where our ideas came from." As you saw, most of them came from the teaching and administrative experiences and stories of Jan, Joanne, Stephanie, and Mary. How the stories came to be chosen and organized in this form grew out of conversations that we had. At first these seemed rambling, but later they showed us that we all had ideas—some we did not even know we had—about assessment and about early childhood development and practice. Articulating the ideas with one another made them "real" and helped us give shape to this chapter. In fact, just as *talk* was a major "way" of assessing children and curriculum, it was our most important way of deciding what to write. Eventually Celia took responsibility for organizing and editing what was written, but everyone judged whether the stories were true to the teller's spirit and purposes.

There was another more subtle collaboration that we hardly ever discussed and that is apparent only with hindsight: collaboration with other early childhood educators, theorists, and researchers that we took for granted as we talked. Like most teachers, we incorporated and adapted other teachers' ideas and principles. The vision of the school's founders, Lee Row and Janet Stocker, for example, is still the foundation of the curriculum. The voices of psychologists and theorists such as Maslow (1970), who developed a hierarchy of needs, can be heard as background for our emphasis on emotional safety. Erikson (1963), who wrote persuasively about the development of trust and autonomy in early childhood, and Vygotsky (1978), who viewed learning as first social, then internalized, also influence this chapter's content. In addition, the research of Balaban (1985) on separation and Cochran-Smith (1984) on the development of literacy in preschool settings has influenced what we think and do. This "hidden collaboration" makes us part of an ongoing dialogue among ourselves, authors, and colleagues in professional organizations, which in turn influences the more down-to-earth, public collaboration and dialogue we have with our children and their parents.

Now to the collaboration among the five of us authors. Our work together began in 1989 when Celia asked Andrea McCarrier, then a doctoral student at Ohio State, if she knew a teacher or teachers who regularly did informal assessments of their children. With no hesitation, Andrea suggested Jan, a former classmate at Ohio State. Jan and Celia's first extended talk was over hamburgers at a luncheonette called Teddy's Frosted Mug. As Jan tells it, she was not sure she and her staff could collaborate with Celia, since they did not assess the children. (And she was not sure she could talk to her, since she was an "author.") On the other hand, Celia seemed tuned into children: She had accepted and eaten 4-year-old Tanya's pre-licked Doritos at lunchtime. As Celia remembers that first talk, Jan and her colleagues did do the kinds of teacher-based assessment she sought as the core of this chapter. And Jan seemed impressively "with-it" regarding early childhood practice; she had even coordinated the lengthy process of becoming accredited by the National Association for the Education of Young Children. More impressive, her driving interest seemed to be the children. In fact, after that lunch Celia felt much more sure of a developing relationship than Jan, though both felt comfortable with the other. And this feeling of comfort soon extended to the five of us.

As you have seen, the staff at SYC certainly were involved in informal assessment; their work spanned the "assessment spiral" of school, community, profession, and society at large in complex ways. Yet at first we as collaborators had to negotiate the meaning of *assessment* because, like many people, Jan, Joanne, Stephanie, and

Mary thought of *assessment* as standardized measures or formal tests that fail to take into account how their children feel, behave, and think in the varied contexts of SYC. As we said earlier, we felt more comfortable with the phrase *seeing what and how individual children learn* than with the word *assessment.* Here are some of our comments:

> STEPHANIE: At first I thought, "We don't assess children at our school!" One attempt at a schoolwide standardized hearing and speech evaluation reinforced our mistrust of this type of assessment. After 3-year-old William spent his five minutes with the therapist, she indicated to his parents that there were major problems with his speech. We were flabbergasted, because William loved talking to us and had a very advanced vocabulary.
>
> JAN: I think before we started this [chapter], assessment was a dirty word, or I felt we should be doing it in a more formal way. But who can stand to do that around here? I remember how much stress the parents felt that time we tried giving the Gesell [a widely used test of school readiness].

After the school year had ended, Celia asked the teachers to have a discussion, without her there to influence them, about assessment to show how their views differed or had changed over the last few months. Later, when Celia listened to the audiotape of the discussion, she realized that her collaborators were sounding a bit stilted and bored by the topic, as if they had already voiced their thoughts on assessment. Without realizing it, Celia had given a "test" on assessment—and it was appropriately resisted. Still, we offer these comments because they reflect much of what we said and thought during our collaboration:

> JAN: Well, I would say that we know our kids well, and I think that's assessment, knowing the kids. Other people might think assessment means kids are here, here, and here (*gestures to show three different levels or heights*). I don't think of it that way. It means I know different parts of the child; I know what that child is socially; I know the emotional tone of the child; I know what their physical abilities are. And intellectually, that "goes across" the whole program of the school. Not how many letters or numbers do they

know, but how well do they communicate? What are they interested in?

MARY: How I feel about *assessment* is that I feel very comfortable with it since we've been working on this chapter. Because it doesn't intimidate me, because assessment is what we've been saying; it doesn't have to have that formalized meaning.

After completing this chapter, it feels as if "assessment is what we've been saying." It is also what Jan, Joanne, Stephanie, Mary, and their colleagues have been *doing* for years: seeing as fully as possible what and how individual children learn. And just as importantly, it involves communicating what you see and know to others: parents, other teachers, administrators, and national organizations.

Epilogue

Every story of collaboration should have a sequel, and this one happily does. Our collaboration was disrupted when Celia moved from Columbus to New York. We would not recommend long-distance co-authoring, but by phone, mail, and visits, we have remained collaborators and friends who will keep in touch informally and professionally.

Although Celia viewed SYC as a "model" preschool for its community of children and families, the teachers do not believe that SYC is a perfect place. As teachers, we would like to see learning more clearly in some of our children, although every child is making progress in at least one realm. Our collaboration has made us more confident of our expertise, and we enjoy re-seeing aspects of assessment that we wrote about here. For example, when we see Mary soothe and comfort a crying child on the first day of school, we say to ourselves, "Another Lizzie story!" And we expect to have new stories to tell as we continue to develop ways of assessing our children and curriculum. We are realistic enough to know that no matter how good our communication is with families, our knowledge and understanding of a child is always "in progress."

We have already experienced an enlightening cycle of learning and assessing since we wrote this chapter. As Jan tells it, we participated in a workshop early last fall given by Rebecca Kantor, a teacher in child development at Ohio State. The topic was the value of small groups in preschools. Many of the social skills that children need to operate successfully in school have to do with getting along in a group, and it is easier for children to learn this by first experiencing small groups.

To follow up on the workshop, in place of rugtime and minirug, we divided our 3's and 4's into small groups for a 15 to 25 minute period each day when we do things like puppet shows, science experiments, or drawing to music. Each teacher of 3-year-olds has six children in her group, and each teacher of 4-year-olds has seven or eight. We grouped the children according to personality traits about the second or third week of school, considering the personality of both child and teacher. Our purpose was to facilitate the process of learning group behavior, so while these groups have a teacher-planned activity, the focus is less on the activity than on developing a group identity.

A fringe benefit of this grouping, we notice, is that we are seeing each child in a more complete way earlier in the year. Since the small-group activity can be loosely structured, children participate at will; thus when they do participate, we see engaged and motivated children set apart from the whole group. What we see adds to the picture we are accumulating of each individual. Adjusting to the change in format has not been easy, and we have had many meetings to discuss the groups. We sometimes wonder if they are too structured, if we are giving in to pressure to be more "like kindergarten." It is a developmental process to learn how small groups work for us.

This short story strikes us as the right ending to the longer story of our collaboration. No single idea or activity—or test—makes up our portrait of a child. Only many experiences over time, seen and heard with interested and caring eyes and ears, can do that. Thus collaborative learning and assessment are continuous. To echo the themes of Mary's opening story about Lizzie, we still begin by accepting children's and adults' own styles and offering a sense of emotional safety within the classroom community; we still work to provide a curriculum that responds to individuals' needs and styles; we still try to understand children within the contexts of both school and home; and we still communicate what we see—and now assess—to parents and others. This chapter extends our communication and assessment spiral to an audience of readers. We invite you to join us in "learning to see the learning."

Authors' note. We would like to dedicate this chapter to the memory of Lee Row, one of the founders of SYC.

References

Balaban, N. (1985). *Starting school: From separation to independence.* New York: Teachers College Press.

Cochran-Smith, M. (1984). *The making of a reader.* Norwood, NJ: Ablex.

Erikson, E. H. (1963). *Childhood and society.* New York: Norton.

Maslow, A. H. (1970). *Motivation and personality,* 2nd ed. New York: Harper & Row.

Viorst, J. (1971). *The tenth good thing about Barney.* New York: Macmillan.

Vygotsky, L. S. (1978). *Mind in society.* Cambridge, MA: Harvard University Press.

Waters, J. (1990). *Learning to see the learning: A handbook for parents.* Unpublished master's project, Ohio State University, Columbus.

Linking Curriculum and Assessment in Preschool and Kindergarten

MARTHA FOOTE
PATSY STAFFORD
HARRIET K. CUFFARO

The authors describe their work in a New York City private school, whose history is rooted in the civil rights movement, and a public school kindergarten, also in New York. Although the teachers have somewhat different assessment needs, they illustrate the insepa-rability of curriculum and assessment in settings that reflect the social and ethnic diversity of New York.

Introduction: *Harriet's Voice*

While this chapter consists of three distinct voices—those of Martha, Patsy, and myself—in actuality the chapter grew out of our conversations. In the give-and-take of our talking, as we questioned, commented, expanded, confirmed, and questioned again, this chapter took its present form.

Our work together began when I proposed to Martha and Patsy that they join in writing about how each used her curriculum—the activities, content, and interactions of the classroom—as a means for assessing children. I was the "connecting link" between them because Martha and Patsy did not know each other prior to the writing of this chapter, although both had been graduate students at Bank Street College of Education. As Director of the Intern and Assistant Teacher program, I had interviewed both when they applied to the program. My connection to each increased while they were completing their degrees. I became Martha's supervisor during her yearlong fieldwork, and Patsy was a student in my Foundations course. With time they both became cooperating teachers for the

Intern Program, and during the writing of this chapter I supervised the interns working in their respective classrooms.

In the months in which we worked together, many things were said and learned about assessment, about curriculum, and about children and teaching. For each of us, the meetings after school, the conversations over food, the questions raised, the laughter and thinking, and the off-the-topic talk all were richer and more complex than what we had outlined initially at our first meeting. As we talked about the progress of their writing at our meetings, about the connections between curriculum and assessment, we wondered if I should also contribute to the writing of this chapter. We decided that my task would be to describe the themes and questions that surfaced during our conversations, to be the participant observer. That description appears at the end, following Patsy's and Martha's writing about their respective classrooms, their philosophy, and the connections they make between curriculum and assessment.

Philosophy of Teaching: *Martha's Voice*

When I was growing up in a small town in central New York, I never once considered becoming a teacher. I was going to be a chemist, a veterinarian, or a pediatrician. I loved playing with young children, but I had had such an uninspired educational experience as a child that I could not imagine joining the same profession as those colorless adults of my past. When I went off to Swarthmore College, a small, liberal arts college outside Philadelphia, I was pleasantly surprised to discover that many of my newfound friends had enjoyed as children a creative and challenging school experience. The anomalous brilliant teachers who provided a few stimulating spots in my schooling were often the norm elsewhere. My attitude toward the profession began to change, and because I enjoyed children so much, I decided to look into teaching as a possible career.

After college I went to work with preschoolers at a day-care center in Brookline, Massachusetts. I had many definite ideas as to what kind of educational experience was appropriate for young children, but I had no theoretical background to support my beliefs. I felt that young children should be allowed to play and to experiment without the fear of being wrong or right. I felt that they should learn to respect their classmates and to treat them with consideration. I also wanted my students to feel free to express their feelings honestly and openly. After a year at the day-care center, I knew that if I were to become the kind of teacher I envisioned myself being, I needed to go to graduate school. That's when I headed to New York City and enrolled at the Bank Street College of Education.

My philosophy of teaching has been further refined as a result of my studies at Bank Street. As a student there I was influenced by the work of the child psychologists Piaget (Piaget & Inhelder, 1969) and Erikson (1963). I grew to believe that it was imperative for teachers to have a firm knowledge of child development so that they would know how their students were viewing the world around them. From that base, teachers could develop a curriculum best suited to their students' age group; that is, the curriculum would be at the children's level.

As a student I also learned how to set up my classroom to be a child-centered environment. I do not believe children should be spoonfed information by a pedagogue; instead, they should be allowed to explore and experiment freely with a variety of open-ended materials in a safe and secure learning environment. I see my role, then, as guiding my students in their explorations, providing them with materials, and asking questions of them to encourage further growth and understanding. The learning that ensues is a result of each child's own experiences. Also, it is a kind of learning that is understandable to a child because it takes into account his or her developmental abilities.

Goals of Teaching

My teaching goals center around four major areas of developmental growth for a child: social, emotional, cognitive, and physical. In fact, I design and structure my classroom so that these four areas can be constantly evaluated by observing the children interacting with the different elements of the classroom. My goals for social growth center around my belief that young children have the ability to learn to respect the rights and feelings of others. Thus I emphasize the importance of sharing both materials and ideas. My goals for emotional growth are based on helping children to express emotions honestly and in consideration of others. Cognitively, I look for a child's developing ability to think logically, to use words and ideas clearly, and to apply knowledge. My goals for physical growth include the development of small- and large-motor coordination. All in all, I want my students to enjoy learning and to feel happy and comfortable in their school setting.

In many ways I can also see that these goals are a reflection of the schooling I believe I was denied. I know firsthand the negative effects of uninvolved, callous teachers. As a result I try to make my own classroom the antithesis of my past experiences. If my students like school, I know I am on the right track.

Description of School

Upon completion of my graduate studies in 1987, I took a position as a head teacher at the Manhattan Country School in New York City. The school was founded in the mid-1960s in response to the civil rights movement, and its underlying philosophy is one of equality for all regardless of racial or cultural differences. Today it is the most integrated, nonsectarian independent school in the United States, with a student population of approximately 50% white, 30% African-American, 15% Latino, and 5% Asian-American. The school staff is also a racially and culturally diverse group. In an effort to uphold the school's commitment to pluralism, the school has devised an innovative tuition system that operates on a combined basis of sliding-scale fees and voluntary contributions. Thus the school is comprised of children from varying socioeconomic as well as racial and cultural backgrounds.

The school is located in an old five-story townhouse in Manhattan near the border separating the affluent East Side from the inner-city neighborhood of Harlem, which is about three blocks away. The school's founder and director, Augustus Trowbridge, believes that the building was destined to house the school because of its proximity to various neighborhoods in New York City. In fact, more of the student body lives in Harlem than on the East Side, although the school also attracts students from Manhattan's more middle-class Upper West Side as well as working-class neighborhoods in the city's other boroughs of the Bronx, Brooklyn, Queens, and Staten Island. Children use various modes of transportation to come to school: city-operated schoolbuses, subway trains, city buses, the family car, and walking. The city block on which the school is located is made up primarily of large, prewar apartment buildings. Madison Avenue with its green groceries, pizza parlors, newsstands, and small retail stores is half a block to the east. Central Park is half a block to the west, and the entire student body uses the grassy playing fields and playground facilities there for recreation and outdoor time.

The school also owns a small, diversified, working farm, located about 150 miles away in the village of Roxbury, New York, in the

Catskill Mountains. The farm program was established to give Manhattan Country School students a broader range of experiences with the natural processes of the world around them, be they on the farm itself or in the surrounding woodland.

The school is made up of ten classrooms, one for each of the age groupings, which range from a mixture of 4- and 5-year-olds to the eighth grade. There are approximately 18 children in each group. Our director, Augustus Trowbridge, is the original founder and director of the school, and he continues to guide the school in its original mission as a school for all children. There is also a lower school director, Lois Gelernt, and an upper school director, Kallyn Krash, who serve to advise the teachers.

Overall Curriculum of School

Because the school is multicultural, the teachers at the Manhattan Country School are provided with a unique, ready-made source for their social studies curriculum; that is, the diversity of their student body. In fact, the school has designed its curriculum so that each classroom provides a study that sequentially fits into an overall scheme of multicultural learning and understanding. The younger children learn about one another, their own families as well as their classmates', and their various neighborhoods. The third- and fourth-graders study Native Americans, immigration, and slavery. The fifth- and sixth-graders study ancient civilizations and Asian, African, and European history. Finally, the seventh- and eighth-graders study United States history from precolonial times to the present. Because each classroom is comprised of a culturally diverse student population, the teachers, especially of the younger children and middle grades, are able to use their students' backgrounds as the backbone of their studies. While the students are learning about various cultures and peoples, a respect and understanding for those individuals different from themselves is fostered. The racial harmony that is promoted at this school is of the purest kind, a result of actual, day-to-day living and understanding.

Description of Classroom

This is my fourth year teaching the youngest children in the school, the 4- and 5-year-olds. An intern teacher who is working on her graduate studies at Bank Street College works as an assistant. The class is comprised of 18 children, 8 girls and 10 boys. Racially, there are 8 African-American children, one Asian-American, and 9 white children. Although the classroom is physically small, there are many areas of activity. The block area takes up about one-third of the floor space and is a vital part of the curriculum. Three tables across from the block area are used for seated activities such as working with clay, doing jigsaw puzzles, drawing, and making collages. Near a corner of the room there is a water table that becomes a sand table in the winter and is then replaced by a woodworking bench in the spring. In the open dramatic play area the children use hollow blocks to make tables, trains, or airplanes for their play. The other areas in the room consist of a book shelf and corner, counters for both science materials (shells, rocks, leaves, seeds) and math manipulatives (pattern blocks, Cuisenaire rods, Unifix cubes, stringing beads), and a painting area. We also cook in the classroom once a week.

The children are free to play at all these various areas, and the room becomes very active with the children engaged in their chosen areas. Blocks clatter on the tile floor as builders construct apartment buildings and hospitals. Voices in the dramatic play area can be heard calling "The train is leaving in three minutes!" as the participants scramble to find their seats, clutching briefcases and train tickets. Across the room painters quietly experiment with brush-strokes and color mixing. Water splashes in the water table (and on the floor) as children play with funnels and pumps. I feel there is a joyful and creative atmosphere in the classroom as the children enthusiastically participate in the various activities. Although angry outbursts sometimes arise as two children both want to play the big sister or one child refuses to share a block car, we talk together to reach satisfactory resolutions to these inevitable early childhood conflicts.

A typical daily schedule looks like this:

8:30– 9:00	Arrival
9:00–10:00	Morning meeting followed by worktime, then clean-up
10:00–10:30	Special (music, movement, or library)
10:30–11:00	Circle time and snack
11:00–12:00	Outdoor playtime
12:00–12:15	Story
12:15– 1:00	Lunch
1:00– 1:45	Rest
1:45– 2:45	Outdoor playtime
2:45– 3:00	Dismissal

Classroom Curriculum

When I speak of my curriculum, I am referring to every part of my classroom: all the materials we use, all the themes we explore, all the ways we structure and schedule our 6½-hour days. Although it becomes necessary for me to dissect my curriculum in order to discuss and explain it, the integration of all these pieces into a coherent whole is the ultimate goal of my teaching.

In an attempt to organize this section, I will discuss my curriculum under these different headings: social studies, mathematics, language arts, science, and Spanish. Within each topic, I hope the reader will see how the curriculum is ultimately integrated.

Social studies.   Because this is the first year that these children have met and come together as a group, I choose to concentrate my social studies curriculum on having the 4- and 5-year-olds learn about one another. The children make graphs showing what their favorite foods are. They write and tell stories about their lives outside of school. They make body tracings and paintings. In the spring our study culminates in a series of home visits in which I take five children with me to visit a classmate's home (while the intern teacher remains at school with the other children). Every child has a trip to his or her home, and the other children and I become "sociologists," discovering what pets the child has, what his or her favorite toy is, what view of the city can be seen from the windows of the apartment or house, and so on. The information that we glean from these trips is disseminated in the classroom in a variety of ways. The children partake in group discussions, make charts and graphs, construct block buildings of their homes, and cook foods that are family favorites. With the school's multicultural perspective, I find the home visits particularly beneficial in helping my students learn that although their classmates may look different or engage in unfamiliar customs, there are also universal similarities among children and families. As we investigate the unfamiliar, we discover that differences are not to be feared or mocked, but appreciated and enjoyed. Thus, even though a classmate has brown skin and her mother has white skin, that mother is just as special as our own. And she just might take out her guitar and sing songs with us on the home visit, just as our father did on our home visit.

Mathematics.   The children in my classroom work with a variety of manipulative math materials, such as Cuisenaire rods, Unifix cubes, number lines, attribute blocks, and pattern blocks. They also work with such found materials as rocks, acorns, shells, and buttons. With these materials they count, classify, compare, order, match, and make patterns. These growing mathematical skills and abilities are carried over into other classroom activities as well. When the children cook, they count the number of apples that are being used. During block clean-up, the children make stacks of "like" blocks—for example, all the triangles, all the squares—before putting them on the appropriate shelves. The snack helpers are asked each day to think mathematically as they set the table, count place settings, and then divide their amount of crackers into equal portions.

Language arts. My students have the opportunity to develop their language arts skills throughout the school day. The value of voicing one's opinions and ideas clearly and coherently is stressed, as well as the importance of listening to others. For example, children listen and respond to one another at group discussions, when resolving conflicts, and during their games of dramatic play. They see their ideas written down on paper when they dictate stories to their teachers or write signs to hang on their block buildings. They begin to recognize meaningful words written in the classroom: their classmates' names on the cubbies and job chart, as well as words on the daily schedule and morning message. The children are also read books and poems on which they comment and from which they infer meanings.

Science. The theme of the science curriculum is change and growth. Because we spend so much time in Central Park, the children have the opportunity to observe the natural changes of the seasons. A deciduous tree is "adopted" by the children in the autumn and closely observed through the winter and spring. Materials such as leaves, seeds, and nuts are collected to sort, study, and classify. Within the classroom the children plant orange seeds in September and watch the plants grow through the school year. We prepare and cook foods from seeds—granola, peanut butter, toasted pumpkin seeds. We also observe butterfly eggs hatch into caterpillars, which grow large enough to form chrysalids, from which butterflies emerge. The butterflies are then released in the park; however, we still have our drawings and stories by which to remember them. As the children observe all the natural changes that are occurring around them, they in turn document the growth and changes that have happened to them in their lives. They bring in photographs of themselves as infants and toddlers, which they use to write stories about their "younger years." Parents bring in babies to the classroom; the children observe and play with them as they learn more about the infant and toddler years. By discovering the stages that a child goes through in his or her development, the 4- and 5-year-olds have a better understanding of the changes they underwent to become the children they are now. Thus this piece of our science curriculum becomes integrated with the social studies investigation of ourselves and one another.

Spanish. As a multicultural school in a city where Spanish is widely spoken, the Manhattan Country School promotes both the learning of the Spanish language as well as an understanding of Latin American culture. With the 4- and 5-year-olds, Spanish is introduced through the use of songs, finger games, and simple books. We then begin to use Spanish to identify foods at snack and lunch, to count, to identify colors, and to play games at circle time. Basic greetings are also learned, which the children then use to welcome one another in the morning. The cooks in the school are Spanish speakers, and the children learn the names of various foods and how to ask for seconds at lunchtime. I work to instill in the children a feeling of ease upon hearing the language as well as some beginning words and phrases that they can use to feel a part of the classroom Spanish activities.

Assessment

When I think of assessment, I see it in terms of how my students are doing within the framework of my classroom. Because I work in an independent school, I am not bound to district guidelines or requirements. However, the lower school director, Lois Gelernt, and I have discussed in depth our views of what we think are appropriate developmental goals for this age group. These goals are the ones that I have kept in mind when setting up my classroom and designing my curriculum. Thus I adhere to these goals consistently through my education program, from planning and inception to evaluation and assessment.

The assessment that I do in my classroom is achieved through a variety of methods. First of all, I find it very helpful to keep a daily record of worktime choices. For each child I record his or her initial choice, any subsequent choices in the course of the worktime (children are free to move to other open areas of the room), and the names of classmates with whom the child was playing. I will also jot down any other relevant material, such as the type of building that the child constructed in the block area, what role the child adopted in the dramatic play area, or whether the child initiated or followed others' ideas in group play. I try to record this information during worktime itself, either during a lull or during the last few minutes before clean-up. If I am unable to grab those few minutes during the day, I will reflect and record with the intern teacher after the children are dismissed. I find these records especially beneficial because they help give me an overall picture of a child's interests in the classroom. By compiling the records over a period of time, I can see patterns of worktime and playmate choice, as well as gauge a child's ability to focus on activities and whether or not this ability has been increasing.

Another record-keeping device I use is an index card file with a section for each child. I use this file to record any behaviors or comments I have observed that help support a picture of the child that I am forming or, on the other hand, that seem so out of the ordinary that I want to keep the incident on record. I try to note these events as soon as possible after they occur. If I know I cannot soon get to a note card, I make a mental note of the incident that I will later write down.

Aside from the written records I keep, I constantly discuss the children's behaviors and daily incidents with the intern teacher in my classroom. At our weekly meetings as well as during snatched moments of worktime, we share observations, make inferences, and discuss the emerging patterns we have been forming. It can sometimes put a strain on our working relationship if we see an incident or development differently, but I think that more often than not, our different perspectives help us to see our students more richly. Instead of holding one overriding interpretation, I have another adult's observations and ideas to help me gain a deeper picture of my students. I hope the same holds true for the intern's view of the children.

Another person with whom I share observations is Lois Gelernt, the director of the lower school. Lois visits for 15 to 20 minutes in the classroom on an average of three days a week. She also spends one lunchtime a week in the classroom with the children. I consider Lois an "in-house expert" whose observations and insights I value. (She taught in New York City for about 20 years, including 8 years as the teacher of the 4- and 5-year-olds at Manhattan Country School.)

We meet formally for an hour a week, but we also schedule extra meetings if necessary. We also grab moments during the day to discuss specific issues.

During these meetings with both the intern teacher and Lois, we try to spend time discussing a number of children. Although the children who have been requiring extra teacher attention tend to be the ones who jump to mind at a meeting, I will also make a point of remembering the rest of the class. As a result, I feel that we are all staying on top of the progress of the 4- and 5-year-olds, the individual children as well as the group as a whole.

Another tool I use for assessment is the children's work itself. Because the children do not engage in any kind of worksheet activities in my classroom, the kinds of material I save are dictated stories, paintings, collages, and drawings. The ability to comb through a couple of month's worth of a child's work is invaluable to me. I can see what themes a child has been exploring in his or her artwork or what subjects are of greatest importance in a child's stories. The growing proficiency in using a paint brush, pencil, or crayon can be tracked. I can also note any increase in details of representational artwork.

The assessments that I prepare are intended for a variety of sources. First of all they are for me. In order for me to feel that I am fulfilling my responsibilities as an educator, I need to know as much as possible about my students' classroom lives. Once this knowledge has been accumulated through observations and note-taking, I can then discuss and interpret it with the intern teacher and Lois. This process is a constant one that continues through the school year. Through it I can better see which areas of my curriculum are working (or not working) for individual children and which aspects of their development are progressing or lagging. I can then change and adapt my program in the ways necessary to make it more beneficial for my students' growth.

Second, I use my assessments in preparing for conferences with and reports for the parents of my students. The school schedules three 30-minute conferences a year for teachers and parents, one each in November, February, and May. However, if necessary, I will schedule more. In order for me to feel that I am conveying an accurate picture of a child's school experience to a parent, I need to have as much material as possible to do the job. I have found the kinds of assessment I prepare helpful to me in this respect. By organizing the information under such headings as "primary worktime choices," "areas of recent growth," or "areas of social difficulty," I can then present a coherent and detailed picture to the parents. Hopefully the parents will then use my information as a springboard to enrich the conference with details of their own. Together we can then enact plans to help and encourage a child in his or her growth.

In April of every year I prepare my annual written report for parents. This report is the culmination of all the assessment I have done throughout the year. It is an overall review of the child's year that chronicles his or her growth in the cognitive, social, emotional, and physical areas. I usually feel that if my conferences have been comprehensive, then this report will come as no surprise to the parents. The conference in May then becomes an opportunity to discuss the report with parents and to emphasize the directions in which I see the child growing and the difficulties in which he or she may continue to need support.

Finally, I see my assessments eventually as a tool for the school to use as the child continues through the school. Lois serves as the adviser for the teachers of the students aged 4–5, 5–6, 6–7, 7–8, 8–9, and 9–10. Thus the information that she has garnered with me can then be used to help subsequent teachers in their work with these children. Lois will be able to recognize patterns of behavior in the future and advise the teachers as to which teaching strategies were found to be most effective in the 4- and 5-year-old and any subsequent classrooms through which the child has passed. My conference write-ups and written reports are also kept on file in the school so that a teacher can read them to gain a portrait of a child when he or she was in the 4- and 5-year-old group.

Assessment of a Child

As an illustration of the kinds of assessment I do, I have chosen to look at one of my students in more detail. Five-year-old Ellis is white, and he lives with both parents and his sister in a middle-class, ethnically mixed neighborhood within the affluent, predominantly white East Side. His mother takes Ellis and his 10-year-old sister (she is in the fifth grade) on the one-mile ride to school either on a city bus or in the family car every morning. This is Ellis's second year in the 4- and 5-year-old group, a phenomenon that occurs regularly because of the mixed-age groupings at the school. In fact, Ellis's sister also spent two years in the 4- and 5-year-old group, first as a 4-year-old and then as a 5-year-old, before I began teaching there. Of all my students I have chosen to share my assessments of Ellis because I see him as a child who has particularly benefited from Manhattan Country School. At another school with a greater emphasis on the development of discrete skills (recognition of letters, oral counting to 100, etc.), Ellis might have become withdrawn and insecure. However, a different picture of Ellis, one that incorporates aspects of his growth not easily measured in a standardized way, is about to emerge for the reader.

Last fall I saw Ellis as a very quiet, reticent child who was often found playing happily by himself. He displayed many immature speech patterns that included the incorrect substitution of various consonants, and I felt that the physical difficulty he had in speaking often prevented him from talking with classmates and teachers. At the end of the morning meeting, when the children would choose an area of the room in which to work, Ellis would ask to go to the bathroom. Upon his return to the classroom, he would quietly take a jigsaw puzzle from the puzzle rack or a piece of paper and crayons from the art shelf. He would then silently involve himself with his activity, remaining focused until clean-up time.

In the winter of his first year in the 4- and 5-year-old group, Ellis began seeking out the friendship of another child in the room, Kunio, a Japanese boy who had come to the United States at the beginning of the school year and was experiencing his own difficulties with language. As of February, the two of them were choosing to play together, drawn together by their mutually gentle and respectful manner of play, as well as by their shared interest in Teenage Mutant Ninja Turtles. Laughing constantly, but speaking minimally, together they began to try classroom materials and activities that they had previously ignored—block building, sand table, and painting. Outside they were deeply involved in acting out such fantasy games as Teenage Mutant Ninja Turtles and Batman. These fantasy games provided a premade script for their play, thus precluding much need to communicate verbally. Although still predominantly reserved at circle times, Ellis cautiously began to participate a bit, contributing to discussions or making inferences about a story being read.

I was very pleased by Ellis's progress as the school year ended. He remained very close to Kunio; however, he also developed relationships with other classmates and no longer played exclusively with his one friend. His use of materials expanded and deepened: By the springtime he was regularly building houses in the block area and engaging in interactive dramatic play with the other block builders. For example, his block people would go to sleep at night, tucked into the beds Ellis had made; then they would drive in cars over to another block builder's swimming pool and dive in. He was also concentrating more on the art materials in the room. His collages, paintings, and drawings became more detailed and intricate, often revealing an interest in and understanding of symmetry and balance in composition. However, he remained inhibited in his use of materials; he used shapes only of the same size and kept them limited to one area of the background. (See Figure 3.1.) His participation in group discussions continued to increase as he began to share more of his own experiences and ideas with the group. He also seemed very happy and more comfortable at school, experiencing upset usually only on Thursdays, the day when his sitter rather than his mother picked him up. On those days Ellis would often complain of a stomachache or become teary as pick-up time approached.

The decision to keep Ellis in the 4- and 5-year-olds' room was much discussed by Lois and me. We both thought that Ellis had grown tremendously during the year; however, he remained one of the youngest in the group, both chronologically and developmentally. We thought that another year with the 4- and 5-year-olds would truly benefit him. He would be one of the two oldest children in the room; however, there would be other children just a bit younger than he to provide intellectual and social stimulation. Because Ellis would be returning to a room in which he already knew the routines and materials, he would most likely be seen as a leader by his classmates. Because the materials in the room are open-ended, however, his involvement with them would continue to grow and expand. We also thought that Ellis's self-confidence would thrive as a result of being one of the oldest in the group. Instead of looking up to his older classmates, as he had throughout the past year, his new classmates would be looking up to him. I discussed my recommendation with Ellis's mother at our conference in May, and she agreed that another year in the 4- and 5-year-old group was the most appropriate placement for her son.

It is now the fourth month of Ellis's second year with the 4- and 5-year-olds. I continue to assess his progress, and it is very exciting for me to compare where Ellis was a year ago with where he is now. Although during the first two weeks of school Ellis chose to play by himself and looked unhappy when he saw his former classmates, including Kunio, in the 5- and 6-year-olds' room, he soon got to know his new classmates and was happily forging new friendships. While he has been developing these new relationships, his use of materials has also greatly expanded. His block buildings are more detailed, and although he continues primarily to build houses, he has also constructed hospitals with sick beds, cafeterias, and doctors' offices. His dramatic play in the block area is richer as well. The block people sit down at tables for meals made by Ellis from plasticene, they climb treehouses for fun, and they take classes at a neighbor's karate school. He spends a lot of worktime with art materials, and his drawings and paintings are now representational. The interest in symmetry is still apparent in his collages; however, his compositions are even more intricate and expansive, since Ellis is now layering and spreading shapes of various sizes across the entire background. A more detailed and richer visual experience results. (See Figure 3.2.) His involvement with math materials has grown, and he now makes intricately symmetrical designs with pattern blocks and Cuisenaire rods as well. He is also more communicative, freely talking to his friends and teachers throughout the day. There are still immature speech patterns evident, and his parents are currently arranging for a specialist to test him; however, Ellis no longer seems hampered by his difficulties in speaking. He even goes off with his sitter willingly on the days his mother works late. All in all, Ellis is more actively engaged in the activities of the 4- and 5-year-olds' room this year and is a more integral member of the group. He appears to be happy and comfortable, and it is very heartening for me to see these positive changes occurring for him.

As I look ahead to the next few months, I have some goals in mind for Ellis's continuing development. For example, the home visit curriculum will begin soon, and I will assess the kinds of connections Ellis makes on these trips: whether, for example, he recognizes similar bus routes on certain trips. After a visit I will be interested as well in hearing what kinds of information about the visit Ellis shares with his classmates at the circle-time discussions, and how much detail is involved. I will also be keeping an eye on his block buildings, looking for new and different types of buildings—some perhaps seen on a home visit. As I assess these various intellectual areas of development, I will also be continuing to observe such particulars as how Ellis reacts to conflict, anxiety, and disappointment and how he works through group relationships and negotiates leading and following balances. At this point in time I see a child whose creative ideas are best expressed visually, although his verbal abilities are continuing to grow. He is emerging in the group as a leader whose kind and gentle manner is attractive to his classmates. His self-confidence can be seen in the ease with which he tackles materials as well as in his desire to try new activities. This kind of assessment is not one I could do if I limited myself to standardized

FIGURE 3.1   Collage by Ellis, April 1990

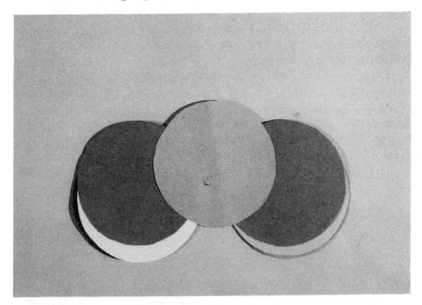

FIGURE 3.2   Collage by Ellis, October 1990

(In both Figures 3.1 and 3.2 the black and white reproduction process makes the collages appear more sophisticated and refined than the multicolored originals.)

measures. I believe that by following my method, I gather a more complete picture of Ellis, one that is more relevant to the kind of teaching I do.

The year is progressing well, but the assessment never stops. It cannot. As a responsible educator I need always to know how my students are doing and what I can do to help encourage and support their growth. Only by using that knowledge conscientiously and completely will I believe that I am upholding the responsibilities of a teacher.

Philosophy of Teaching: *Patsy's Voice*

I grew up in the southeast part of Ireland, the third oldest in a family of nine children. Although my formal education was very traditional, I had a hands-on education at home that has strongly influenced my belief system and the way I teach now as an adult. My parents were always around and provided us with a variety of opportunities for experiences. We took many day trips to castles, rivers, mountains, and old ruins. My parents read to us, told us stories, and sang songs with us. They talked to us and encouraged us to ask questions and to think for ourselves. Our summers were spent outdoors exploring nature and developing our large-motor skills as we climbed, jumped, ran, and swung from branches. We had a pretend house where we engaged in dramatic play. We built castles and houses using bales of hay and straw. We always had a ready supply of art materials for rainy days. Our house was filled with books, and reading was fostered. Life was not all fun and games; we all had responsibilities on the farm and in the house, and we were expected to take our responsibilities seriously. My father was very involved with social issues in the community, and we were encouraged to participate. Education was important to my parents, and we were expected to work hard and to achieve good results.

My philosophy of teaching has developed as a result of these experiences and has been strongly influenced by studying as a graduate student at Bank Street College of Education and by my experience as an assistant teacher with a master teacher.

My philosophy is child-centered. I believe that children are motivated to learn. I believe that children learn by doing, by experiencing. By providing the materials and the opportunities for experiences that foster the child's self-esteem and independence, the teacher can use the child's natural curiosity to explore and learn. Children should be encouraged to work independently or in small groups and to do as much as possible for themselves rather than seeking direction from adults.

The teacher's role is to stimulate and extend the children's interest and to observe and assess the children's progress in the classroom. Children should be involved in the care and upkeep of the classroom and the materials. Children should be allowed to work at their individual levels, expressing themselves through a variety of materials, both structured and unstructured. They should have many opportunities to use language to express themselves, both orally and in writing, both in group and in one-on-one situations.

Goals of Teaching

My teaching goals are influenced by my philosophy of teaching. As this is the first year of formal education for many of the children, I want all of them to have a positive experience and to feel good about coming to school; to become independent thinkers and learners; to be able to express their ideas clearly and to ask questions; to be able to apply what they have learned to new situations; to feel good about themselves and be able to express their feelings; to respect one anothers' rights and feelings and be responsible members of our group. Most of all, I want to develop a love of learning in each child.

Description of School

This is my third year teaching at Public School 11 in New York City. (I had previously worked at a private school.) The school is situated in Chelsea, on the West Side of Manhattan, a culturally mixed, predominantly white and Hispanic neighborhood. The area is also economically mixed, including both welfare recipients and two-income families.

The school is an old five-story building, built in 1924 and still heated by coal. The classrooms are large, with lots of windows. There is an alternate junior high school on the top floor of the building. The school has a swimming pool in the basement, and all children, from kindergarten up, take swimming lessons once a week. There is a large play area on the street level, with two large sandboxes and a wooden climbing apparatus. A smaller playground on the second floor, with climbing equipment and tricycles, is only used by the early childhood classes.

There are 452 children from prekindergarten to sixth grade, and some attend a gifted and talented program. The principal, Angelo Casillo, formerly a teacher at the school, encourages the teachers to work together in clusters by grade level. He both gives teachers autonomy to work within the curriculum framework and makes himself available to us. He also likes to spend time in classrooms getting to know the children. The early childhood teachers in our school, most of us relatively new to teaching, meet often to talk about budget, units of study, the children, and other early childhood issues. There is a real team spirit among us that is very supportive.

Our district provides considerable opportunities for staff development, such as workshops on hands-on math and science, whole language, conflict resolution, and integrating the curriculum. Staff developers work with teachers in their classrooms, helping them to implement new approaches. Curriculum guidelines are mandated by the city and the state. The kindergarten curriculum manual emphasizes hands-on, child-centered activities, which I found very helpful when I first started teaching in the public school system.

Description of Classroom

My kindergarten class is made up of 17 children, 9 girls and 8 boys. One child is Asian–American, four children are Hispanic, and 12 are non–Hispanic white. All but two of the children live within a 15-block radius of the school. We are part of the gifted and talented program in the school, which means that the children are accepted into the program based on their scores on a standardized test. All the children in my class have had prekindergarten experience as well, six of them in our school's prekindergarten program. My curriculum, however, is no different from that of the "regular" kindergarten teachers, so I tend not to focus on the way my children have been classified. I work with an intern from Bank Street College of Education, who is in my classroom four days a week for five months of the year.

My classroom is spacious and colorful, with six large windows. It is divided into eight clearly defined work areas for math, science, writing, reading, block building, dramatic play, woodworking, and art. The block building and reading areas are carpeted and also used for meetings. There are a piano and other musical instruments from different cultures in the classroom. Groups of tables, which are used for art activities and other seated work, are in the center of the room. The children use the carpeted area a lot and can be seen sitting or lying on the carpet while doing a puzzle, playing a game, or reading a book. The atmosphere of the room is busy and inviting. There is always a buzz of activity, sometimes accentuated by the louder sounds of blocks, woodworking, or musical instruments. We have a pet rabbit, named Twinkle, that roams freely around the room. We also have two mice, four snails, and numerous darkling beetles in terrariums.

The children arrive between 8:40 and 8:50 in the morning. They draw pictures or read books until everyone has arrived and we begin our day.

A typical daily schedule looks like this:

8:50	Meeting—children choose where they will work
9:05	Work centers—six to eight choices
10:20	Snack
10:30	Playground
11:00	Specials—computers, music, science, or swimming
11:45	Story time
12:00	Lunch and playground
12:50	Language arts worktime
1:50	Work centers
2:30	Story time
2:45	Dismissal

Kindergarten Curriculum

It is very difficult to talk about curriculum by subject, since all the subjects are interrelated. Everything that I do in the classroom is influenced by my belief system. I work with each child on her or his own level. One of the most important things for a kindergarten child, I think, is to learn how to work within a group: how to get along with one another, how to share space and materials as well as ideas and thoughts, and how to deal with the inevitable conflicts that arise in everyday life. By making the children socially aware and responsible, I am preparing them for their role in life as members of different groups, the school, the community, and the human race. That is why Conflict Resolution, a citywide school program that offers training to teachers, is such an important part of my teaching. It does not just happen when we sit down and discuss a topic; it happens all day long. Children learn to resolve their conflicts in creative ways; they learn to respect each others' rights and feelings. We role-play conflicts, such as disputes over toys or hurting one anothers' feeling, and the children try to come up with win-win solutions. We read books, such as *The Hating Book* (Zolotow, 1969), that are related to our topic. We talk about prejudices and how it feels when someone is prejudiced against you. We read books and sing songs from different cultures. These discussions help build children's self-esteem, confidence, and social consciousness. Children in the fifth and sixth grades are trained as mediators and help resolve disputes on the playground.

The ideas presented in Conflict Resolution overflow into our social studies as we learn about people's needs and how they meet these needs, first within the family, then within our school, and finally within our neighborhood. The social studies topic has to start with the child's own experiences and has to be relevant to the child. All other subject areas are integrated into the social studies topic. Children visit workers in the school and interview them; they return to the classroom and record their observations by drawing pictures and dictating stories. The block and dramatic play areas offer the children further opportunities to express their understanding of information they have gathered. Books related to our trips are read; letters of thanks are written to the workers we saw. Through our various activities the children begin to understand that teachers and custodians have other identities, such as mother, father, husband, or wife. The age of our school lends itself to social studies. For example, we watch the coal being delivered to our school and learn that it comes all the way from Pennsylvania. Exposed color-coded pipes go from the basement to our room, and we learn how the school is heated. Looking at old photographs of graduating students, the children notice that the ethnic makeup of the school was different 40 years ago. Change is also noted by looking at the outside of the school and seeing how different the school's architecture is from buildings that are built today.

The math area is supplied with a variety of math manipulatives and found materials that lend themselves to exploration through manipulation. This hands-on approach helps children understand underlying concepts of math before they are required to master skills. The children help collect the found materials—such as keys, buttons, shells, bread tags, and bottle tops—and take pride in our collection. We also have many math games, both bought and made, which involve one-to-one correspondence, number concepts, patterns, and sorting in a fun way. The games are mostly noncompetitive, which is appropriate for this age group. I follow the *Mathe-*

matics Their Way (Barrata-Lorton, 1976) and *Explorations 1* (Coombs & Harcourt, 1986) formats.

I use a whole language approach to teaching reading and writing. The children are immersed in language, both written and oral, all day long; however, we do have a language arts worktime after lunch each day. This time is specifically for language-related activities, and the children move from one activity to the next. We write a news chart at a group meeting every day. The children take turns telling their news as I write it on the chart. The children help me to sound out the words. When something new comes up, I bring it to their attention and explain its use. Frequently used words become part of the children's sight vocabulary. Through repeated demonstrations the children begin to learn punctuation, capitalization, left-to-right progression, sentence structure, and phonics. Because it is the children's own news, they have a vested interest in the chart. They love to copy their news down to take home to their parents, tracing the letters on the chart with their fingers and reading back their news. We also write lots of different charts—of experiences, letters, and favorite poems—to model correct writing and punctuation.

At writing workshop the children are encouraged to write and illustrate their own stories using invented spelling. Each child has a writing folder with an illustrated alphabet chart. The children sit in small groups and help one another sound out the words for their stories. At first a child might write down a string of letters or scribbles with no letter-sound correspondence. But over time, the child will begin to use the initial and ending sounds. Middle consonants and vowels will come, again with time. For example, in Figure 3.3, using a combination of invented and conventional spellings, Evan writes, "Today it is going to rain." The children share their stories with the class at a share time at the end of language arts time. They are also asked to use invented spelling to make signs for their block buildings and dramatic play.

We have teacher-made language games that reinforce the skills the children are learning. These games can be played individually or in pairs. We have a listening center where children read along with a tape of their favorite book. Most of the tapes are commercially made, but I have made a few as well.

We invite older children to come to our classroom to read to the kindergartners and to write down their stories. Parents come in to read their children's favorite books to the class. We read picture

FIGURE 3.3 An example of the illustrated "Daily News" by Evan. He writes, "Today it is going to rain."

books and chapter books at story time, twice or three times a day. Many of the books that we read are related to what is happening in the classroom.

Art is a major part of our classroom. Children are given opportunities to express themselves using different media. Painting, drawing, clay, collage, and woodwork are always available as a choice during worktime. Special art projects such as printing, puppetry, papier-mâché, murals, sewing, weaving, and 3-D construction are available at different times during the year. Children are invited to represent their experiences after trips, cooking, science, and other activities; and their art is put together with their own dictation to make books.

Our dramatic play area consists of hollow blocks with which the children construct the props required for their play. Vests, hats, and pieces of fabric are available for the children to use for dress-up. Other props, such as briefcases, bags, food containers, kitchen utensils, and toy money, are available should the children need them. Children act out their concerns, questions, and observations of the world around them.

Dramatic play also occurs in the block-building center, and this activity is always available for children to choose. The children are encouraged to cooperate with one another as they construct their buildings. They also have to plan ahead, solve problems, and make decisions among themselves as they work with the blocks. Following trips, the children are often asked to use what they have seen in their buildings. In their buildings, children discover relationships between the different-sized blocks as they explore balance, symmetry, classification, and patterns.

We have a wide range of musical instruments from different cultures. The children are invited to use them. We talk about the correct way to use them, what they are made of, and where they came from. We sing popular children's songs, and the children create their own songs.

We study science using the investigation-colloquium method. The children have time to investigate what we are studying and then discuss their findings with one another. They come up with questions about the topic and use these questions to go back and investigate further. We read books to find out more about the subject. The children go back with their new knowledge and continue to investigate. Topics of study include snails, plants, sinking and floating objects, and magnets.

Our study of chicks this year started with a discussion of eggs and chickens. We wondered if chicks could hatch from eggs that we bought at the store. We talked about what conditions the egg would need for a chick to grow inside, compared the yolks of a fertilized egg with an egg from our cooking supplies, and finally put 24 fertilized eggs into the incubator. We checked the temperature and humidity every day for 21 days, which seemed forever to the children. Everyday someone would ask if they were ready to hatch yet. Another child would point to the chart and show them how many more days we had to wait. We read books to make the waiting easier and to see what the chick looked like at each stage. Finally, on the morning of the twenty-first day we heard a chirp, followed by more chirps. By the end of the day we had four very wet and tired chicks and 17 very excited children who could not keep away from the incubator. By the next morning we had 15 baby chicks—some yellow, some brown, one black, and the rest every color in between. Every child in the school came through our room to see the new arrivals. Most were fascinated by the variety of colors. One child remarked, "They're all different colors, just like people." Another child was very happy to see a black chick and said, "Hey Bro', give me five!" The children shared the responsibility for taking care of the chicks. When they were two weeks old we took them to a farm and left them "safe" with other chicks.

Cooking is also an important part of our science curriculum. The children cook once a week in small groups. The intern in my room is usually responsible for this activity. The food being cooked is usually related to something else that is happening in the room; for example, when we finished the book *The Gingerbread Rabbit* (Jarrell, 1964), we made gingerbread rabbits. The children who are cooking that particular day are responsible for bringing in the ingredients needed, but everyone gets to eat the final product. Cooking also incorporates other curriculum areas, as children weigh the flour, count the eggs, read and discuss the recipe, and record and report on the process.

There are many units of study going on over the course of the school year. Because in our school the prekindergarten children study themselves and their family, I begin the kindergarten year with a study of the school, which usually runs through the end of January. The second half of the year we study the immediate neighborhood. We begin a unit on plants around the end of November, when we plant winter bulbs indoors and out. This unit continues over the year, with children bringing in seeds from food they have eaten. We plant them in our classroom first, and then some of them are planted outdoors in our small garden (a plastic children's pool filled with soil). The farm trip is our main trip of the year. Our other trips are neighborhood walking trips related to social studies—for example, to visit different merchants. All are related to classroom activities and so are purposeful within our curriculum.

As there are so many holidays throughout the year, I choose not to make them the focus of study units. Instead, the day before a holiday we discuss it and may read a book or two about it. Sometimes our cooking project is related to the holiday, or we sing some holiday songs.

Assessment in Kindergarten

Assessment, for me, is a way of seeing if the children are progressing as they should socially, emotionally, intellectually, and physically. I use many forms of informal assessment in my class-room to chart each child's development throughout the year, based on a solid understanding of child development theories and stages of development as well as a good knowledge of curriculum.

One of the most important ways that I assess children is through my discussions with the intern in my classroom. Having another adult who knows the child almost as well as I do is very helpful. We can discuss the children's behaviors, problems, and pro-gress, bringing our own observations of each child to the discussion. We talk about our goals for the child and about what areas the child needs help with and then suggest ways of working with the child to reach these goals.

I keep a journal in which I write down my informal observations, ideas, and concerns. This journal contains my personal interpreta-tion of things as I see them in the classroom. I also do more objective, formal observations of the children in different situations and write down what I hear and see without any judgments or opinions. Then I look back over these observations and look for patterns of behavior. I do not do this type of observation as often as I would like, as it is not always practical for me to do so. However, having an intern means that it is sometimes possible for one of us to take time out to do an observation without interruptions. I do this mainly for children I am trying to understand or about whom I am concerned. Even though these observations are focused on one child, I collect information about other children, too, because of their interaction with the child being studied. I also often jot down anecdotes of things children say or do, and later in the day I fill in the background information. When children are working on a project, I like to watch them at work and later talk to them about what they did. Listening to children's dis-cussions at group time provides information about their thinking and learning.

I use checklists to keep records of where each child has worked, the skills they have learned, and what they need to work on more. I have a language arts checklist and a math checklist. The children also use a simple checklist to record what areas they have worked in. (See Figure 3.4.) They keep this in their work cubbies and fill it in during the day. They know that if they have not worked in an area for a while they will be expected to work there.

I also keep a portfolio of each child's work during the year. This shows the child's progress in many areas of the classroom. I include art samples, dictations, beginning writing, and samples of their math work. At the beginning of the year I have each child do a self-

Where did you work today?

name: _____

	Blocks	Clay	Art Project	Painting	Woodwork	Science	Math	Reading	Listening	Writing	Games	Dramatic Play	Manipulates	Dollhouse
13														
12														
11														
10														
9														
8														
7														
6														
5														
4														
3														
2														
1														

portrait. I do this again every few months, and I include these in their portfolios. This is particularly useful for parent conferences, as it helps me explain how the child is doing and provides me with concrete examples to show the parents.

Meetings with parents, both formal and informal, provide useful insights into each child. I believe that parents know their child best and can often provide information that helps to understand the child's behavior. Constant communication with parents is important so that the child feels that there is a connection between home and school. Also, things that happen at home can have direct or indirect effects on things that happen in my room. I often write about my discussions with parents in my journal.

Discussions with other teachers and professionals who work with my class are also helpful in understanding a child. Hearing how a child copes in different situations helps me assess how I deal with him or her in my classroom. Things that happen to the child during the day outside of my classroom—for example, a conflict on the school bus or in the lunchroom, often have an effect on how he or she will act in my classroom. Therefore I like to keep in contact with the people who work with the children.

By observing children, whether formally or informally, I learn a lot about how children learn and also about my teaching. I assess how the set-up of the classroom is working, and I often change things around to see if that works better. I review whether children are learning what I want them to learn. What worked with one group does not always work with another, and so I have to reassess my way of doing things. I frequently read my early childhood books to assess if I am on the right track. I have a few favorites, such as *The Learning Child* (Cohen, 1972) and *The Block Book* (Hirsch, 1984), that I read over and over again. I also read the curriculum guides to make sure I am covering everything I am supposed to be covering. I never think that I am doing enough in my classroom. I always have the feeling that there is so much more I could be doing. I like to get reassurance from fellow teachers, parents, the principal, and advisers from Bank Street that I am doing OK.

There are other means of assessing children that I feel come from "outside" my classroom. Under New York State law, all children entering the public school system must be screened to identify children with special needs so that they may get an education appropriate to their needs. The screening is done in the child's primary language; assesses the child's physical, cognitive, language, and motor development; and includes a health report. Classroom teachers receive individual profiles of all children in their classes so that they can identify areas of the children's development that require further investigation. Teachers then do classroom observations and informal assessments to determine if any child needs to be referred to the school review committee. I find this screening tells me more about what children know than about potential problems. For instance, children in my class with emotional problems often score very high on this test, yet the results show no indication of behavioral problems. In this case, teachers' observations seem more accurate than the standardized test.

Assessment of a Child

Teachers often center their observations on individual children. I chose Evan as the focus of my assessment, since he is a typical 5-year-11-month-old child who intrigues me. The oldest child in the class, he is tall, blond, and usually smiling. He lives with his mother, father, and 8-year-old brother. This is Evan's first year at our school, since his family has just moved to New York. Evan talks a lot about his family and his pets. He looks up to his older brother and seems proud to have a sibling in a higher grade. Evan's health is excellent, his large- and small-motor skills are well developed, and he rarely misses school. He gives one the sense of being a child who is well cared for. Evan has had preschool experience and attends an afterschool program.

Evan comes to school each day with one of his parents or his friend's parents. He enters the classroom eagerly, hanging up his coat in his cubby and smiling at his teachers. Sometimes he comes up to me and tells me something about home or shows me something he has brought. He then quickly becomes involved in an activity with a friend. He chats animatedly with the other children who are working nearby, sometimes displaying his good sense of humor. He likes to joke and sing silly songs. Here he is singing a rhyme about diarrhea:

> DEREK: That's disgusting.
> EVAN: Yeah, and it smells too. (*He chuckles to himself.*)
> EVAN: Carlos has a polka dot tail. You know that song about a polka dot tail.

Then he continues singing to himself.

Evan is a quiet child until he becomes comfortable in a situation. Once he is comfortable, he can be very sociable, but even then he is never loud. He is well liked by his peers and is especially popular with the girls in our class. This aspect of Evan particularly intrigues me, since he does not look for their attention; yet there is often a girl holding his hand, sitting with an arm around him, or mothering him in some way. I suspect that he is popular with the girls because he is gentle and soft-spoken and he allows them to be in charge.

Evan and Andrea are playing with the doll house, setting up the furniture:

> EVAN: What will we put in this room?
> ANDREA: Nothing.
> EVAN: Nothing! Can't we have a dog?
> ANDREA: No!
> EVAN: Some people have dogs in their house, you know.
> ANDREA: I said no!
> EVAN: How about a baby kitten?
> ANDREA: Yes, a kitten is OK.
> EVAN: Good! I'll get a kitten.

They continue playing.

Evan moves from activity to activity. He rarely needs teacher intervention because he can share and compromise, but he will request it if he feels that things are unfair. When he does have a conflict, it is usually with his best friend, Carlos, and they usually resolve it verbally. However, he mostly plays in the same areas each day unless encouraged to move to something different.

He particularly enjoys block building and can build complicated structures cooperatively with other children. He can sustain interest in a project over a period of a few days. As part of the social studies unit on our school, Evan, with three other children, re-created our classroom in amazing detail using unit blocks. Evan and the other children copied the children's paintings hanging around the room and hung them in their building. They also included the piano, my desk (with me sitting at it, even though they have never seen me there), and the pets in their homes.

Evan loves books and can often be seen sitting with his favorite books, turning the pages, totally immersed in the story. He is always eager to "read" to the class, who seem convinced that he can really read. He chooses a new book that the other children have not read yet and confidently makes up his own story for the pictures. His enthusiasm for books is contagious, and he often involves a friend in his reading of a book. Evan wants desperately to be able to read and write. I think that this might stem partly from the attention given to his brother, who is just learning to read, and partly from his love of books.

When we had a book fair at school, Evan arrived very excited. He had brought his own money, which he had saved all by himself, to buy a book just like the one we had in class. He proceeded to tell us how he had gotten all the money from various sources and how he was going to buy his very own copy of *The Popcorn Dragon* (Thayer, 1989/1953). He handed me two little containers of coins, and I opened them to find mostly pennies. I did not comment but decided that anyone who loved books so much should have the one he wanted. I took him to the fair and bought him the book he wanted.

Evan loves to copy the daily chart and to take it home, especially when his news is on the chart, and he likes to read the books made by the class, especially the book of similes. His contributions to this book were original: "as crunchy as a carrot," "as hard as walking on your hands," and "as dark as sleeping in a tent at night."

At the beginning of the year, Evan's contribution at writing workshop was a picture about which he would tell a story. When I asked him if he would like to write down the story, he seemed eager and proceeded to use "grown-up" writing (scribbles) to which he pointed as he read back his story. After a while, as he became more confident of his knowledge of letters, he began using strings of letters, one letter representing each word with little or no correspondence between sounds and letters. As the months passed, Evan started writing just a word or two for each picture using beginning and ending consonants. This progressed into short sentences that included sight words from our daily chart. When Evan returned from winter vacation, he seemed much more confident about his writing. He now was ready to write a book, and so he began "The Adventures of Link." He did not need to rely on short words or sight words anymore now; he was willing to sound out any word that he needed for his story, even if the spelling was invented. He drew the pictures first and then wrote a sentence for each picture, demonstrating that he understood concepts about how print works and that he was beginning to control the skills needed for conventional writing. He likes to read his written story at share time and answer his peers' questions. When one of his classmates is sharing, Evan often asks a question about what the child has written. Evan's writing and reading reflect what is taught at our daily news time. His skills are average for the children in my class, and I suspect that he will be reading by the end of the school year. Other activities that Evan enjoys are math and art. In math he can copy or continue a given pattern or can create his own. He can sort using different variables, such as size or color, or using different senses, such as touch or smell. Evan can count using one-to-one correspondence up to 20 and by rote much higher. He rarely chooses to go to the math area to work, preferring to work in other areas; but when he does go there he becomes involved and works for a long time. With art activities, Evan is always eager to try a new project. He spends a long time working at a painting, carefully mixing the colors to achieve the desired hue. He often does more than one painting at a time, and his paintings are usually abstract. He also likes to work with clay, chatting with the other children as he shapes the clay, usually into pizza or hot dogs. As with the medium of paint, Evan seems more interested in the process of using the clay than in saving what he has made.

Evan usually participates in our class discussions. His contributions, both questions and comments, are relevant and thoughtful. He speaks in a low voice, and he sometimes blushes when he speaks. When called on to give his news for the chart, he usually says he needs more time but raises his hand a few minutes later with some news, usually about his family. This has been a real area of growth for Evan, since he rarely participated in discussions earlier in the year. I think that he feels very comfortable in the group now and feels that his contributions are valued and respected.

Evan has grown a lot since he joined the class last September, both academically and socially. He is a confident child who can be responsible when he needs to be and yet is still very much a young child. He is helpful to his fellow students and to his teachers, and once engaged in an activity he can sustain a real interest in it.

In this kindergarten Evan is a child who is neither very "advanced" nor a problem, so this focused look at him has helped me see what his strong and vulnerable areas are. In fact, I have no major concerns about him, but I would like Evan to articulate his needs more in social situations and not to always give in to what the other child wants. I sometimes wonder why Evan takes this role in dramatic play situations, since in other situations, such as block building, he is an initiator and a leader. I would like to understand this aspect of Evan better. I will also encourage him to be more varied in the activities he chooses, since I think he is inclined to stick with his favorites unless encouraged to move to a different area. I would like him to be able to do this by himself and not need teacher intervention.

The Participant-Observer Comments: *Harriet's Voice*

Each time we met we taped our discussions. In our initial meeting we talked about what each teacher usually did in terms of assessment in her classroom: Martha relied on her good memory; Patsy collected children's work in folders, which were filed in a closet cabinet. Patsy also had each child indicate on individual charts the area in which he or she would work that day. Faced with the task of writing about assessment, each decided to be more "systematic and conscientious" in her data gathering and written observations.

Later discussions revealed how their systematizing and conscientiousness became active habits and the benefits each had gained. As Patsy declared, "I've become a compulsive collector!"; she went on to say that the folder she had for each child now was placed near her desk for easy access. Statements about collecting samples of children's work sparked a lively exchange of helpful suggestions on curriculum. In this conversation Martha realized that what she collected ". . . validated my memory. Now I look more closely. I have actual concrete evidence, data, and anecdotes. I have detail for my generalizations." For Patsy, each piece placed in a folder raised questions. "Am I being selective? What place does this piece have in the folder? In my thinking? *This* piece shows another part of development or *here* this piece shows what I'm trying to say about this child, what it is that I'm thinking." Martha added to her earlier observation. "Now each piece is part of a continuum. I have previous pieces to compare them with and can see how a child is moving along. It gives it perspective for me. I see it as continuous."

The gaining and taking of perspective appeared frequently in discussions. The charts on which children checked the areas in which they chose to work served not only Patsy but also the children. "They can see what they've been doing. I don't have to point it out." Similarly, the self-conscious task of writing about assessment, reflecting on the process while engaged in it, made Patsy realize that she was also assessing herself. "It's made me think more about things, how well I do, how well the classroom works." Pieces came together and made sense, as when she observed, "I remember when I read Carini's work on assessment thinking 'how could you focus on one child and know the others?' But now I see with all the *interactions* that happen I do know more of one child *and* the others." For Martha, reflecting led to greater clarity and affirmation concerning her curriculum. "I can see more clearly how I set up my room and how it does serve me well in assessing the children. It's almost as though I've got a complete circle going. All the parts fit well together." Patsy added: "Assessment is a way to see that everything is working for the child, the classroom, your teaching. Assessment is your way of telling that everything is going as it should . . . whether things are going well or not. . . . Assessment makes you ask 'do I need to change?' . . . and to change not only big things, but also small ones."

And as both Martha and Patsy wrote in their sections above, the systematic and conscious data-gathering habits they developed also helped immeasurably in conferences with parents.

Throughout the writing, and our conversations, the theme of affirmation kept surfacing—to affirm their view of children and of learning. Sharing their thoughts, learning from each other, and exchanging "teacher talk" were a genuine source of support. In Patsy's words: "It was all in there but I needed help to bring it out, to think more deeply. Our talking stirred things up."

What also was "stirred up" in one of our meetings was their reactions to standardized testing. In a prolonged conversation between them, they spoke of the limitations of standardized testing, of how little such tests added to what they already knew about the child, of the highly specific, isolated nature of the information obtained. As Patsy observed: "The tests don't pick up what I'm looking for in kindergarten. . . . Both children were asked to reproduce shapes. They scored the same, but they are so different! There's no range in tests. And with _____, what does it tell me that she knows her address? It doesn't show the problems she's having in the classroom. What the tests show is that they can do workbooks." Martha added her observations: "When the 5-year-olds are screened, the scores don't surprise me. The scores don't reveal the child. The teacher can tell if there's a motoric problem. And I think . . . oh! stop looking at such tiny particulars that don't help me really understand. I have this big picture of the child and I think that's what's important. I can pull out the details, not just fancy words and labels."

Patsy and Martha talked of their own school experiences with standardized tests. Martha remembered the attention given to ". . . intellectual development. That is who I was. If I didn't get 100% on a test I was crushed by that. The academic was all that was prized and known about me, and that's how I saw myself, my identity. My social skills weren't developed, but I didn't get help with that. The focus was on academics." Childhood memories of schooling brought to the forefront their aims as teachers; what they considered important to know about each child; their striving to understand the complex, interrelated nature of development, its tensions and contradictions. Understanding for Patsy and Martha meant to know each child as a whole person, a person embedded in the story of family; to know each person's questions and curiosities, their joys, their fears, their struggles and satisfactions. Understanding is to know how each child views his or her world and place in it—whether it is a large or small world, a comfortable or shaky place to be, a world to encounter enthusiastically or cautiously. To know one's address or to draw a shape were isolated moments in the deeper and richer understanding they sought.

At the same time, what they sought did not quiet the doubts they experienced when others focused on test scores and academics. Their comments merged to be one voice. "You look at the kids, each one. You look at everything, not just the academics, but you wonder, 'am I holding them back?' You have doubts. But then, what makes a whole person? Isn't that the question? There are choices." What was evident was that what supported both Martha and Patsy in their times of doubt was their commitment to the philosophical framework guiding both their practice and the choices they made about curriculum and development.

Our time together made me, as the participant-observer, understand anew how important and necessary it is for teachers to have time to talk together, to tell their stories about children, to question and share doubts, to articulate their goals and the detail of their curriculum, and to have the time to record their thinking, the time to write what they know. Faced with the formal task of writing about Ellis and Evan, Martha and Patsy *experienced* the satisfaction and worth of being "more systematized and conscientious" about assessment. The opportunities to learn from experience that they offer children they gave to themselves.

In the conversations of Patsy and Martha I heard the talk of teachers who were firmly grounded in theories of development and, equally as important, who knew in detail the learning opportunities of the materials and activities they offered children. What they offer children in their classrooms is time, time to use the present fully while leading the way to future mastery and accomplishments. And it is in their observations of how children use materials, their noting of the daily interactions and struggles that occur, and the questions they ask themselves over time, that Martha and Patsy assess each child's journey and their own teaching.

References

Barrata-Lorton, M. (1976). *Mathematics their way: An activity-centered program for early childhood educators.* Menlo Park, CA: Addison-Wesley.

Carini, P. (1975). *Observation and description: An alternative methodology for the investigation of human phenomena.* Grand Forks: North Dakota Study Group on Evaluation, University of North Dakota Press.

Cohen, D. (1972). *The learning child.* New York: Pantheon.

Coombs, B., & Harcourt, L. (1986). *Explorations 1.* Don Mills, Ontario: Addison-Wesley.

Erikson, E. H. (1963). *Childhood and society.* New York: Norton.

Hirsch, E. S. (Ed.). (1984). *The block book.* Washington, DC: National Association for the Education of Young Children.

Jarrell, R. (1964). *The gingerbread rabbit.* New York: Macmillan.

Piaget, J., & Inhelder, B. (1969). *The psychology of the child.* New York: Basic Books.

Thayer, J. (1989). *The popcorn dragon.* New York: Scholastic. (Original work published 1953.)

Zolotow, C. (1969). *The hating book.* New York: Harper.

4

A Social Perspective
on Informal Assessment

Voices, Texts, Pictures, and Play
from a First Grade

SARAH MERRITT
ANNE HAAS DYSON

As the authors in Chapter 3 explored the link between curriculum and assessment, the authors of this chapter illustrate the complex interactions among the social and academic and the goals of groups and individuals, of children and their teacher. The class-room in which children's voices are often in the foreground is in Berkeley, California, another culturally diverse setting.

After the last good-bye, I [Sarah] close my classroom door and breathe in the quiet of a classroom at the end of the day. I walk around the classroom, stopping to pick up a crushed crayon, a crumpled paper, a pencil. I straighten books, retrieve paper math coins from a box of puzzles, and rearrange the dinosaur table, the wildflower table, and the ocean table, all centers of classroom study. As I go through my end-of-day rit-ual, I find the artifacts left by my first-graders: Tanya's chalk-board messages, Marie and Kayla's tens and ones columns, Christina's little-girl-crossing-the-bridge picture, and Warren, Justin, and William's sorted dinosaur figures. There are the piles of journals and pictures, reading logs, and class-made books.

Like archaeologists, we as teachers live amidst the "stuff" of human life—the child creations that are evidence of a full life. These pictures, messages, displays, and records are the tangible remains of human activity, created for some purpose and embedded in complex

94

ways into the social life of the classroom community. And also like archaeologists, we use these artifacts as materials for reflection, although, unlike them, we are allowed more direct access to human activity itself. And so to these materials, we add our own observations, captured on tape or note pad. We use these artifacts to search for patterns in how individuals participate in the learning activities of the classroom, patterns that help us understand how and what the children are learning and how we might best support that learning.

In this chapter, we focus on a first-grade classroom in a multiethnic school in the East San Francisco Bay Area, and we discuss the ways in which Sarah, as teacher, assesses—gathers artifacts and reflects on the progress of—her children. Our perspective on informal assessment is broader and, at its core, more social than many visions of assessment. Consider, for example, one of Sarah's artifacts, a letter by DJ (Daryll) to T (Tahrique) about Justin:

Dear T Man Y
wen are You
gon to ptos x in
we aBot B Justin
love DJ

As kindergarten and primary grade teachers, many of us have become expert at figuring out the unconventional but intelligent academic efforts of young students like Daryll. We collect work samples, like Daryll's letter, record anecdotal notes, and tape students' reading; and we know too how to use such artifacts to document progress in particular skills. For example, using DJ's letter, we might comment on the visual spelling strategies evident in his mixed-up letters in the word *stop* (*ptos*) or his *we* for *me*; or the phonological awareness suggested by his *x in* for *asking*; or the reasons for his use of capital letters in odd places. However, commenting on such emerging skillfulness is only part of the picture. To understand Daryll and his ways of learning, we must somehow use our artifacts to uncover the voices that lay buried within them and, thus, to come to know the individual behind the tumbled words and the classroom relationships that gave birth to those words. Clearly, Daryll's story is intertwined with the stories of his two friends, Tahrique and Justin.

In our chapter, then, we hope to emphasize the importance of considering the *social* beings whose voices are embedded within the artifacts we are collecting. Our own voices as co-authors matter, too,

in viewing the children's social life, for we are cooperatively orches-
trating the child voices readers will hear. So, we begin by discussing
how we come to be collaborating within this chapter and by elabo-
rating upon our perspective on informal classroom assessment. We
then introduce Sarah's classroom and give an overview of the key
ways we informally assess children's learning in school. Next, we use
information gathered through informal assessment to construct
stories about children's classroom lives. In these stories, we will
stress both the uniqueness of each child and the social linkages that
energize and shape children's lives as friends and classmates. We
hope providing realistic stories, filled with both insight and still
puzzling questions, will provide readers with a sense of the rich
possibilities of informal assessment. Finally, we close by reflecting
on the importance of taking a social perspective on informal assessment; that is, of acknowledging how central human relationships
are to what individual children learn in our classrooms, to the kind
of classroom communities we build, and to the kind of future we
imagine for ourselves and for the children.

A Dialogic Vision

As co-authors, we were first brought together by our concerns
for individual children's learning and for the classroom social life
that supports and hinders that learning, as we each explain below.

Sarah's Voice

One summer day in Maine, as my mother and I sat on the front
porch reading *The New York Times*, she handed me Fred Hechin-
ger's "About Education" column. It was about Anne Haas Dyson, a
researcher and professor at the University of California at Berkeley
who was interested in children's academic and social lives, as revealed through their early writing and talking. As I read, I had a real
sense of this classroom, the children, and this A. H. Dyson. I felt
heartened that Professor Dyson thought that kids' social lives and
friendships were important for their academic development. I remember reading the article and reflecting on my own first-grade
classroom right outside of Washington, D.C. I was so inspired by this
column that I immediately wrote to Professor Dyson. I told her how
much I enjoyed the article and respected her work. Naively, I asked
if she had written anything more on this early writing/talking con-

nection. She graciously and modestly wrote back to me, sending me several articles and telling me about the educational journal *Language Arts* (in which she and Celia Genishi were the Research Currents editors). I wrote to her again, inquiring about studying for a master's degree at Berkeley. And characteristically, she generously wrote back, encouraging me to apply. And so quite happily I moved from the East Coast to the West Coast to study with her.

Anne's Voice

One summer day in August, as I sat wading through mail and paperwork, a new student walked into my office. I had anticipated meeting her, as she had sent me samples of her children's work, postcards of children playing, and quotes from Sylvia Ashton-Warner throughout the year. Clearly, this Sarah Merritt was a person who took great delight in her children and who also had great respect for her work as a teacher. From her letters about her students in Washington, D.C., I had learned that our views of children and of teaching had much in common. For us both, a great deal of the joy of teaching young children comes from being allowed entry into a rich and interesting world, one peopled with beings from a place now past, that of childhood; in this place, both Sarah and I had witnessed important social dramas played out in ways less masked than in our own adult worlds: "Be my friend." "I won't be your friend." During her year at the university, we talked often about how school learning figured into children's social world and about how knowing this world helped us in our work as educators. Sarah stayed in the East Bay another year to teach first grade, but now she is going home to the East Coast. Writing this chapter has presented us with an opportunity to discuss formally the ideas that brought Sarah and me together and to celebrate the kind of dialogic learning that happens—for both teacher and student and at all levels of learning—when academic learning takes place amidst much sharing of experiences (and of laughter).

So we are cooperatively telling this story. Sarah sees with the eyes of the teacher who takes seriously her concerns that all children achieve the academic goals of her school as well as that doing so be socially meaningful. She worries about her decisions and her children's progress; she takes pride in their successes and is frustrated by those days when children seem lost, when friends seem to be leading them off onto paths whose productivity she questions. "Any redeeming qualities here?" she asked Anne one day as a group of children were playing (what, we weren't sure), "or should I start to worry?" Sarah knows that social relationships within the classroom can be messy, raucous, silly, fierce, and funny. She wonders, am I doing what is best for the children? Are they learning? What are they learning? Isn't it too loud in here? Are they on-task or off? Are the social relationships productive or destructive? How do I support those students who seem to have a difficult time interacting with others? These are the questions Sarah brings as an active listener, knower, and observer of the students in her class.

Although Anne has been a teacher, she now sees with the eyes of a researcher. She is freer to find those frustrations "interesting," those unanticipated paths "intriguing," being less directly responsible for the children's learning. And, while her questions are much like Sarah's, she is relatively more likely to wonder about the class in more distant language, to consider with Sarah the insights into teacher observation and documentation—the new perspective on assessment—that might be gleaned from discussing Sarah's own grappling with the particulars of her children's daily dramas.

So our writing has indeed been dialogic. We have pushed each other up close to Sarah's children and back again, wondering how the artifacts Sarah has gathered reveal not only her children's learning but also the ways in which teachers themselves learn about the social and academic constraints and opportunities shaping children's classroom lives.

A Multifaceted Approach to Assessment

Our approach to assessment is multifaceted. First, we are interested in how individual children are learning the knowledge and skills we judge as valuable for them. Children learn from active engagement with the world around them, as they construct and gradually transform their understandings of the world (Piaget & Inhelder, 1969). Moreover, children give shape to their understandings by making use of the symbolic tools available to them in their cultures (Vygotsky, 1962). Thus we want to understand individual children's interests, their understandings about the social and physical world, and their ways of using the tools of learning, including talk, writing, and reading.

At the same time, however, we know that individual learning takes place amidst relationships and that these important relationships include not just those between teachers and children but also among children themselves (Dyson, 1989; Vygotsky, 1978; for a practical discussion of this theoretical point of view, see Cazden, 1988). Indeed, much of the energy of a 6- or 7-year-old is spent doing "social work," that is, working to be accepted and valued by peers (Rubin, 1980). Thus our second concern centers on understanding individual children's behaviors from the perspective of their own emerging social goals. The social life of a classroom provides an important window through which to view academic development, because each child's ease or discomfort, sense of competence or failure, of alienation or acceptance, is affected by how school figures into relationships with other people, including parents, teachers, and, as we stress here, friends.

Third, we are interested as well in assessing—monitoring the progress of—the classroom community as a whole, of the kinds of dynamics created by the complex network of children—for the relationships among children matter not only for academic goals but also for grander social goals, for a society where children feel empathy and a sense of their common good (Greene, 1988). This is particularly important in a classroom such as Sarah's, which, like many urban classrooms, is filled with children who bring vastly different life experiences to school. Our challenge, then, is both to assess individuals' strengths and needs and to discover common ground—themes and interests that might foster connections among children from very different places.

Sarah's Classroom: The Riches and Challenges of Diversity

During the 1989–1990 school year, Sarah's first-grade classroom reflected the rich ethnic diversity that has long characterized California. Her 28 children represented African-American, Anglo, Asian-American, and Hispanic ethnicities. Many came from a low-income and working-class African-American neighborhood on the southwest side of the school's attendance area, while others came from the working- and middle-class neighborhood that stretches to its northeast.

In Sarah's classroom, the children selected their own places to sit. Their seating preferences reflected the usual desires of first-grade boys to sit with boys and girls to sit with girls. While there were patches of children of similar ethnicity—a group of white boys, one of black boys—there were also friendships that crossed ethnic

lines. Also, many of Sarah's children were themselves of mixed ethnicity (11 of the 28). "Ain't Xing mixed?" asked Kayla one day,
noticing, perhaps, that Xing, who was Asian-American, was about
the same color as Carla, who was of Mexican and African-American
ethnicity. "I just tan," said Xing.

In a classroom such as Sarah's, it seems important to us that
the children have many open-ended activities in which individuals
can participate in their own ways, using their life experiences and
symbolic resources (their ways of talking, playing, writing, reading,
drawing, singing). And it seems equally important that there be
many group activities, where children can join together and a sense
of class identity can be fostered. The central activities of Sarah's
daily schedule reflected these qualities.

The morning began with journal time. On the first day the children entered Room 205, they were given a composition notebook
and invited to write and draw anything they wanted to. Some simply
drew, others "invented spellings" according to letter sounds. Others
wrote their names. Everyone did something, and the next day, when
they came to school, there were their journals on their desks. So they
wrote again and began to ask their neighbors what they had written.
Sarah encouraged them to read the responses she had written in
each of their journals. Those who wished could share their entries
with the whole class. Thus, over time, this activity came to serve both
the individual and the group, both social and academic ends. Indeed,
even the opening lines of their journal entries reflected these multiple ends: They often wrote "Dear Miss Merritt," "Dear Class," or
"Dear" and the name of a friend.

After journal time, the class read the "morning message," a letter
Sarah wrote on the board to her class. The letter had both personal
news and schedule information—a planned visit from "Miss Merritt's teacher and friend" (Anne), for example, or an upcoming birthday party for Daryll, a compliment for a day of hard work, a wish for a
good day for all. This, then, was another time for individual and
group recognition.

Throughout the morning, there were many opportunities for
reading and for talk, some involving the whole class, some involving
small groups, and others involving "partner" reading by friends or
independent reading. Whole-class sessions often were for enjoying a
story together, for choral reading of favorite poems and rhythmic
stories and songs, and for class study of spelling patterns or handwriting forms. Smaller groups were for talking about how and what
they were reading and, most importantly, for Sarah to hear individu-

als read and support their efforts; in these groups, she used books the school faculty had chosen for beginning readers. Independent and partner reading were for children to select and enjoy a book, together if they wished. For this activity, the children chose literature from the classroom library, which contained multiple copies of many selected children's books. The children chose their own partners and books, planned their own way of sharing the reading, and took responsibility for recording in their reading logs what they had read and their response to the book. In the beginning of the year, Sarah had children who were unconventional readers, fluently reading picture books without really looking at the print, and she had children who already read in conventional ways.

In the middle of the morning, Sarah's children took a break. Out on the playground during recess, groups formed and reformed, as the children took to the bars for climbing, hanging, and swinging, started a soccer game, and walked—or ran—in the large open spaces. When the morning work was done, and lunch was over, the children were off to the playground again. As the children's classroom experiences will reveal, the playground is also a place where significant social work takes place.

The afternoon started with a story time. At first, Sarah led this story time, but, by the spring of the year, the children themselves signed up to read the after-lunch story. Sarah's class studied books by E. J. Keats, L. Lionni, E. Carle, W. Steig, V. Williams, the *Starring First Grade* series by M. Cohen and L. Hoban (1967–1979), and the poetry of Langston Hughes. Many times after Sarah had read a story, a student would make a connection between different characters and authors. For example, Kayla, who struggled with independent reading, noted that Leo Lionni's books have the "same kind of fishes and drawings," and she also commented on the thematic connections between *More Spaghetti I Say* (Gelman, 1987) and *Strega Nona* (de Paola, 1975).

Moreover, the children's talk about these commonly studied books revealed the books that captured the attention of the class as a whole and served as common ground for discussion. For example, Maurice Sendak was a class favorite. Max, the central character in *Where the Wild Things Are* (1963), was often compared to Pierre (1962), the leading character in the book of the same name. Many debates were generated around those two characters. Sendak's book of months, *Chicken Soup with Rice* (1962), was a class favorite throughout the year. The children identified their birthday months, listened time and again to Carole King's musical version ("Really

Rosie"), and made up their own verses based on Sendak's repeating refrains.

After story time came math. The class worked as a whole on new concepts, and then individuals worked side by side on math activities, while those wishing to work together and with Sarah met on the rug. The children made use of the manipulative materials that filled the math corner—the rulers, blocks, geometric sponge shapes, Uniﬁx cubes, flashcards, balance scale, and play money. Math activities were often integrated into science study units; for example, units on nutrition, plants, fruits, and seeds all involved observing, counting, estimating, graphing, measuring, sorting, and classifying.

Many of the science and social studies theme units involved literacy and art activities. The study of countries especially brought in literature, language, story, and song. While time in the afternoon was set aside for the study units, the children's journals, book selections, and free play sometimes reflected the unit themes as well. Moreover, the units were times for children's individual and group identities to be recognized and studied by the class as a whole. Eric and Isabella helped the class learn Spanish during the unit on Chile. Valentina's mother made a map of Chile and sang the children Spanish songs, accompanied by her guitar. Daryll brought in medallions and drums during a study of Africa, while Leaha's mother introduced the children to Chinese calligraphy and helped them make Chinese lanterns during a unit on China.

While child choice of activity or, within activity, of topic and work style (e.g., working alone or with classmates) was a basic part of the classroom day, a block of time was set aside in the afternoon as "free-choice time," a time when students selected activities that were of special interest to them. For example, small groups of children used books or chalkboards to play school, grocery boxes and a cash register (pretend) to play store, or chairs and a large plastic lid to play taxi or "limo." Others chose to classify objects from their study units—model dinosaurs, leaves, stamps or flags from different countries. Some read, some wrote, and some wandered from activity to activity, needing a moment of planning with Sarah about exactly what to do.

It was in the context of these activities that Sarah came to know her children. While there was a standardized test that all first-graders took, Sarah was honest with her children, as they were with her, about the limits of the test. She made sure that the children had practice with the format of the test—the bubbles that must be filled in, the straightforward questions. At the same time, she acknowledged the children's varied reactions to the experience—some children liked the test, some felt it was hard, and some groaned a great deal about it. Sarah told them that she learns about what they really know from observing and listening to them. We consider these informal assessment procedures in the following section.

Tapping Children's Voices, Texts, Pictures, and Play

> Still—in a way—nobody sees a flower—really—it is too small—we haven't time—and to see takes time, like to have a friend takes time. (Georgia O'Keeffe, cited in Callaway, 1989, Red Poppy plate)

Small flowers, like small children, take time to know. In Sarah's classroom, as in many, children's distinctive characteristics became clear over time as Sarah observed her students—and they observed one another—in the course of their daily activities. Their styles—their ways of engaging with other children and with materials—helped shape their academic learning, their network of friends, and the contributions they made to the classroom community.

The value of informally assessing children in the course of daily activities, rather than solely through their products or their performance on particular tasks such as informal reading inventories or spelling dictations, is that it allows us more easily to view the flesh and bones—the voices, if you will—shaping their products and performances. When individual children participate in an activity, they are guided by some purpose, engage in some way with other people, and make use of varied media—that is, they may talk, sing, draw, read, write, and play. Being attuned to the why, with whom, and how, as well as the what, of children's efforts allows us to simultaneously view their social and academic lives.

As an observer, Sarah gave particular attention to children's ways of expressing themselves. She listened to and occasionally taped the children's *conversations* in spontaneous and structured activities; observed and kept anecdotal records of children's *play*; collected samples of children's *drawing* and *writing*; noted what, how, and with whom the children chose to *read*. None of these ways of observing alone allows a complete picture of any one child as a learner and a friend, but they each contribute to an evolving portrait, that is, they each provide artifacts for reflection.

In the next section, we present stories of the classroom lives of some of Sarah's children: Rebekah, Crystal, Daryll, Tahrique, and Justin. These stories will illustrate children learning on several levels—as individuals, as friends, and as a classroom community of learners—and they will include activities across the curriculum— language arts, social studies, science, music, and art. Further, these will be stories in which informal assessment plays a major role in teacher decisions about how best to help students learn.

The Children

We begin with a brief story of Crystal and Rebekah because their story is a relatively easy documentation of steady progress, progress connected in clear-cut ways with their friendship. Then we turn to our major stories, those of the interconnected lives of Daryll, Justin, and their friend Tahrique. Their stories are much less clear cut, more filled with those unsettling classroom times when progress is not so easy to discern, when the energy of relationships is not so straightforwardly positive.

The Best Friends: Crystal and Rebekah

A letter from Rebekah to Crystal:

> Dear Crystal, I am going to
> call you. And I am going to
> play with you. And I am happy about it.
> *love,*
> Rebekah

A note from Crystal to Rebekah:

> Crystal
> 443-5867
> You better
> remembr
> it

Crystal, who was African-American, and Rebekah, who was Anglo, began the school year as strangers. By chance, they ended up sitting back to back at nearby tables. Within days, they were the best of friends. The above exchange, which took place through written notes, was a typical one for them and suggests the interplay between their social and academic growth. "I am going to call you," writes the straightforward Rebekah. "Well then, here's my number," responds Crystal.

Indeed, over the course of the year, the children's journals, which Sarah routinely saved upon completion, reflected the girls' growing friendship as well as their developing encoding skill and the increasing complexity of their messages. They began by writing each other's names; in Crystal's journal, *Rebekah* appeared amidst hieroglyphic-appearing letters, while Rebekah declared "I Loek Crystal a lot." Soon both girls were declaring their affection for each other. Later in the year, they used known words and invented spelling to write letters asking each other questions. "How many grandmothers do you have?" wrote Rebekah to Crystal. "Lots" wrote Crystal back. "Lots?" asked the surprised Rebekah. "I have hundreds of grandmothers," said Crystal, "[of course] some of 'em are dead."

When school began, Rebekah was an independent child who, unlike many of her classmates, did not need constant feedback from Sarah. Rebekah consulted with Sarah on her chosen, free-time activities, but she was serious and confident about her own work and explored the classroom—and its child inhabitants—on her own.

Rebekah was also an eager book lover. Indeed, in the first few weeks of school, she frequently asked Sarah if there would be free-reading time. During free-choice periods, she consistently chose to read books in the classroom library rather than to work puzzles, draw, or work at a study unit activity. This love of reading was confirmed by her father and her kindergarten teacher. By listening to Rebekah read her chosen books, Sarah learned that Rebekah could read some books conventionally, unlike the less conventional readers, who did not necessarily attend to text, match voice and print, or read in a booklike register. When she did not know a word, Rebekah consistently tried to figure it out, using semantic (meaning), syntactic (sentence structure), and graphophonic (sound/symbol) cues as well as her knowledge of the kind of book she was reading.

Rebekah's love of reading was demonstrated in her journal as well. She compiled lists of books in the classroom library and of those which she had read. She was comfortable writing, although it was a relatively new experience for her. Right from the start, she wrote with a clear voice, often about her feelings for her family. And, within the first week of school, she also wrote about her new friend Crystal:

        I loek [like] Crystal
        a lot She loeks
        me to

Unlike Rebekah, who was on the verge of conventional writing
and reading, was the very determined Crystal. Consider her first
journal entry, shown in Figure 4.1, which consists of repeated patterns of letters and letter-like forms. Crystal was not a shy girl in
school, and she wanted to share her journal writing with her classmates. A girl who spoke her mind, requested help, and explained and
defended her positions, Crystal got up and shared her entries by
making up a story on the spot. When the children asked to see her
journal and the picture she had made, Crystal explained that "all I do
is write. I don't draw no pictures." Thus she did not expose the fact
that her writing was very unconventional.

Sarah was concerned about Crystal's writing and reading, but
she also wanted to give her time and space to write in her own ways.
Her classroom aide decided to ask Crystal to write "real letters."
Characteristically, Crystal objected. In a very exasperated tone,
she let Mrs. Puckett know "I am writing! Gosh! What do you want
from me? I am writing. I'm going to start writing on the line when I
am 9."

But, sure enough, by the second week of school Crystal wrote:

        I L U Rebekah
          Rebekah
          Crystal

Accompanying her entry was a picture of two happy little girls
amidst hearts, stars, and a few words, such as *cat*, that Crystal had
copied from the alphabet picture chart. Crystal soon began copying
the "morning message" from the board and, by October, she was
writing full-page stories using invented spellings. Her first attempt
at conventional (alphabetic) writing occurred right after the earth-
quake we experienced in October 1989:

        IYSofrmy   [I was over my
        Grmoshs.   Grandma's house
        Iyntrfc   in the earthquake
        AIySGtWstvy   And I was going to watch TV
        Iwsgtbodttbl   I was going to be under the table (!)]

FIGURE 4.1 Crystal's first journal entry

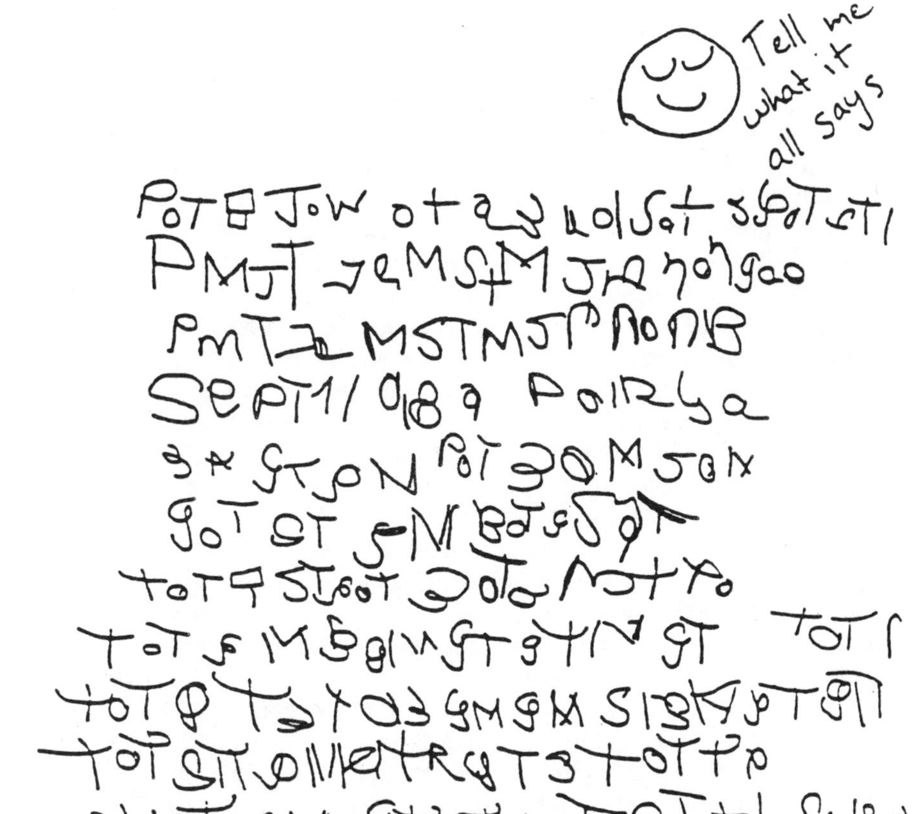

When Crystal shared this entry, Sarah noticed that Crystal carefully read her written words with great pride. Sarah recorded Crystal's reading in small print on her journal to mark this significant change in Crystal's reading and writing behaviors.

Just as Crystal's as well as Rebekah's growth as writers and as friends was reflected in their daily writing journals, so, too, their growth as readers and as friends was reflected in Sarah's observations of their daily book reading. The girls' joint history as literature readers formally began one day when Sarah, noting that they were already writing and reading together during journal time, asked Rebekah to pick a story to read to Crystal. She chose one of the Leo Lionni books, *Swimmy* (1963). This was the beginning of a shared activity that lasted the entire year. During free-choice time, the children could often be found reading side by side. They would read to each other or they would read the same book chorally.

Sarah could not always attend to Crystal's and Rebekah's reading, but she could and did ask them about their reading procedures. When the girls first started reading together, Rebekah explained that Crystal read by guessing from the pictures. Rebekah would gently tell her, "No. Like this," and then Rebekah would read the page. Crystal would nod and then repeat the page after Rebekah. There seemed to be no tension, no feelings of competition, in this activity. Crystal wanted to "really read." And Rebekah helped her in a straightforward, patient manner. Friends. And, while Crystal did not begin to attend to and figure out words herself until the third month of school, she considered herself a reader because of the friend she had. Indeed, by the end of the year, they were *both* among the strongest readers and writers in the classroom.

During free-choice time, Sarah noted that, if Rebekah and Crystal were not reading together, they could be found playing school. Sometimes their classroom consisted of just two people: Rebekah and Crystal, with Rebekah most often in the role of teacher. More often, however, several girls and a few boys would join them. In that case, Crystal and Rebekah became co-teachers. Sharing authority, they would routinely line up chairs in front of the chalkboard, write a morning message, and read it to their students. Then they would flip through the many pages of chart-paper tablets, reciting class poems (using the pointer, of course). They might also give math problems, praising or scolding their students accordingly. To get their beloved reading time in, they would read aloud to their students from a favorite storybook. Rebekah and Crystal seemed to take great pride in having their "classroom" be a realistic, orderly place.

Not only did Crystal and Rebekah take the lead in introducing "school" to the play life of the children in Room 205; in addition, their intertwining of their academic and social lives sparked a favorite classroom writing activity. Crystal and Rebekah were the first students to write to each other in their journals. One day Rebekah stood in front of the class to share her journal and read aloud:

> Dear Crystal,
> > do you like me yes or no
> > I like you
> > > I do   yes
> > > > I do

And then Rebekah gave Crystal the journal so that she could circle "yes" or "no." This peer writing activity became quite the rage for a month or so, surfacing and resurfacing throughout the year. (For a resurfacing, see the Boy Kings' use of it in the next section, "The Boy Kings: Daryll, Justin, Tahrique.")

Crystal and Rebekah's friendship was rooted in an academic partnership. They considered themselves to be "good students," and they enjoyed the challenges of school life. We now turn to a tale of a threesome that was in many ways more challenging than the twosome of Crystal and Rebekah—that of Daryll, Justin, and Tahrique. Theirs was a story in which informal assessment would play a more critical role. These three students were by no means "lacking" or "slow," but, unlike Crystal and Rebekah, they did not consider themselves good students. They tended to avoid academic tasks and sought their most prized success in a kingdom dominated by boy kings.

The Boy Kings: Daryll, Justin, and Tahrique

Justin and Daryll began the year in Room 205, although Justin did not attend school regularly until January. Tahrique entered the classroom in January. In the sections to follow, we concentrate on first Daryll and then Justin, the two children who were members of the class the longest. However, as will become clear, the classroom stories of the three boys, all African-American, are complicated and intertwined, as each child's actions influenced and was influenced by those of the others and, indeed, of the class community as a whole.

Listening to Daryll's classroom talk. Daryll's progress during this first-grade year was linked both to his interactions with key friends and to his active involvement with the classroom community as a whole. We focus on Daryll's classroom talk, his journal drawing and writing, his play, and his reading, aiming to illustrate the importance of teacher sensitivity to individual children's social lives as well as to their academic knowledge and skills.

In the beginning of the year, Daryll was an attentive but quiet student, seemingly quite shy in front of the class as a whole. He was drawn more fully into the community life of Room 205 and, indeed, began to become a significant classroom figure when he brought his out-of-school interests into the "public" arena. Sarah was able to unlock a key moment in Daryll's entry into more active classroom life by attending to and encouraging talk about those interests.

This key moment, which happened in late November, occurred during the class study of Africa. On this day, the children were locating the names of many African countries on a map and talking excitedly:

> "I found Chad. I know a boy named Chad. He goes to another school."
> "I see two countries that begin with Z—Zaire and Zimbabwe."
> "Yeah! I see two that begin with M—Mozambique and the island one—Madagascar."
> "I see the word mad in Madagascar."
> "My brother's name [Kenny] is a lot like that one" (pointing to Kenya).
> "Michael Jackson has a song called Liberian girl—is that Liberia?" (pointing to both Liberia and Libya).
> "Which country treats the black people like slaves?"
> "Where is the desert?"
> "Ghana is the country that Anansi [the Spider] lives in."
> "I know a boy—he's my friend. He comes from Ethiopia."

It was in the midst of this talk, all this blending of personal experiences into the classroom experience, that Daryll raised his hand. He asked if he should bring in something from Africa. Sarah had indeed encouraged the children to bring in anything they had from countries they were studying—coins, books, dolls, clothing, and such. So she said that he certainly should bring in African things.

He then explained that he had a necklace with the shape of Africa on it. Several other children joined in, saying they, too, had these African medallions. Justin explained that he could get a "whole mess" of the medallions—enough for the whole class—at the local flea market. The children began talking about the flea market, which indeed had many African booths, and about the men who danced and played the African drums. "You see them playing those drums—banging all day long." "Yeah and you see 'em dance. Wearing those turbans and all." "Singing and drumming and dancing."

While these conversations were going on, Daryll told the class that his brother had some African drums, which he would bring in—if his brother would let him.

"Do you know how to play them, Daryll?" asked one of the children.

"A little," Daryll replied modestly.

The next day, wearing a painted leather medallion of Africa around his neck, Daryll sat in the teacher's chair and demonstrated his African drums. The children were very excited, most giggling to see Daryll sitting in that chair with drums between his knees. He began to play them—slowly and steadily. The children clapped the same rhythm and began to dance on their knees, and Daryll started beating the drum faster. The drum and medallion stayed in the classroom for the month of Africa study. Daryll was often asked to play his drums, and it was almost always accompanied by wild dancing and chanting.

Observing Daryll write. Another significant change in Daryll's social and academic life in Room 205 occurred in early January; this change was tied to Tahrique's entrance to the class, and it was revealed through Daryll's writing. A friendly student, Tahrique immediately wanted to be friends with Justin and Daryll. Apparently, Tahrique would always ask Daryll about Justin—where he was, what he was doing, if Daryll had seen him yet, and so forth. Daryll was getting desperate—he was tired of having to answer endless questions about Justin. Finally Daryll wrote a letter to Tahrique asking him when he would stop asking about Justin (quoted early in this chapter).

This was a significant change in Daryll's writing. Up until then, Daryll had rarely strayed from writing one or two words to label a Ninja Turtle or superhero he had drawn. To learn of his social world, Sarah had to listen to the talk that went on *around* the journal drawing and writing. For example, Daryll's drawing of a dinosaur and his accompanying label (T-Rex) did not capture his ongoing discussion with Tahrique and Justin of the dinosaur's distinctive features. Nor did it capture how Daryll's talk invited his good friends into the activity or how the boys offered one another encouragement, advice, and laughter.

With his letter, Daryll revealed that he certainly did understand that writing itself could serve a variety of social purposes. He wrote seeking information and, indeed, making a sort of plea. Daryll's note, then, was important to Sarah on two levels: It revealed Daryll's knowledge of the variety of purposes and uses of written language, and it also revealed something of the social networking of her children. Daryll's journal entries began to change from mostly pictures to mostly words, from lists and labels to personal letters.

This change was supported not only by his friendship with Tahrique and Justin, but also by his attraction to Carla, a very popular class member. In early January, when the children chose seats, Justin and Daryll chose to sit by each other—and by Carla as well. Daryll began to use his journal to issue written invitations to Carla, Justin, and Tahrique to write back or talk directly to him, for example:

> Dear Tahrique
> dot [don't] You like
>   Carla
> dot [don't] You like
> Her [her] Four 'a
>   Girl friend?
>   loveD

His strategy had quite an impact on Carla, Tahrique, and Justin, but it also influenced the entire classroom community. Daryll's resurrection of this writing technique (no doubt influenced by Crystal and Rebekah's use of it) was much admired and copied in the classroom. Soon other friends were asking questions aloud during sharing journal time and demanding answers. "Do you like Me—yes or no?" "Can you play with me at lunch?" "Can you play with me after school?" Consequently, these changes revealed growth in individual students and served as a bond of togetherness for all the students. (Other bonds of togetherness were chorally saying "to be continued" if someone's journal entry for the day was not finished and asking through the journal if the class could "see" things, for example, "Do you see that my tooth has fallen out?" "Do you see my new shoes?")

Attending to Daryll's interactions with close friends. As Daryll's journal began to figure more dynamically in his social life, it also began to allow Sarah new perspectives for making sense of how Daryll and his two good friends participated in the life of the classroom. The most revealing entry was made in early March, when Daryll wrote the following entry:

Tahrique is 2 to King Friend
Justin is 1 King Fiend
I   AM 3 three
love Daryll TZX
[three drawn diamonds]
1J   2T   3D

Daryll was using his friends' initials, but to what did the numbers refer? The very feel of the entry was like coded graffiti. With Daryll's permission, Sarah read the entry and showed the picture to the class. The children were puzzled, too. Daryll began explaining—but was quickly drowned out by Tahrique and Justin.

"Well, you see, Miss Merritt," said Tahrique, "it's like this. We are like kings. Justin is the first king, I'm second, and Daryll is third."

"What is a king?" Sarah asked.

The boys explained that it was like being the leader of the school. Sarah asked if this meant that Justin was the best king because his number was 1. The three boys nodded yes. Sarah asked if she could be a king. That got the boys and the rest of the class laughing. Tahrique and Daryll agreed through their laughter that Sarah could be a king—Miss M, King 4. But Justin interrupted and said that she would have to "pass the tests like everybody else" if she was to be a real king.

"Pass tests?" she asked.

Justin explained that during recess, they had to take tests, such as doing back flips, doing splits, performing a new dance, saying the words to a current song on the radio and doing the accompanying dance steps, running a race, and sliding down the playground pole. It sounded like an obstacle course, with Justin running the show and announcing which tests were next.

Through the talk engendered by the journal, Sarah was led to observe the boys' daily recess rituals. Justin (a.k.a. Boy King 1) would run around the yard behind his line of kings, coaching them, yelling the next task, and clapping his hands, as any concerned coach would do. Further, these observations of the boys in their own world allowed Sarah access to the deep roots of this sometimes fragile threesome. This knowledge allowed Sarah to consider ways of structuring learning experiences that would allow her to work with the children's energy rather than to ignore or attempt to undermine it. It was not so easy, however, to know how to translate this knowledge into ways of structuring the children's social networking within the class to support both individual learning and the class community as a whole.

Listening to the boy kings read. The complex nature of the decisions Sarah, like all teachers, made about ways of supporting individuals and groups is best illustrated by considering Daryll's reading. By the time Tahrique entered Sarah's class in January, Daryll was becoming a more confident, more fluent reader. In fact, one day while Daryll was reading to Sarah, he looked up and commented, "I'm reading good, huh?" He and Tahrique, whose reading was similar, were suitable reading partners, provided that Sarah or Mrs. Puckett, her teaching assistant, kept an ear out for them. (Although they were very good at picking books that were the right level for them, they would at times get too silly, seemingly forgetting the purpose of their activity.)

In the following event, Daryll and Tahrique are reading *The Napping House* (Wood, 1984). They are taping it, which means that they have practice-read it at least once. They are reading it quietly. And they are having fun, playing with the tone of voice they are using. However, shortly into their reading, Justin hears them and decides to join:

> DARYLL: (*reading*) There is a house a napping house where everyone is sleeeeeeping. (*giggles from the two boys*)
>
> TAHRIQUE: (*reading*) And in that red house there is a bed a cozy bed in a napping house where everyone is sleeping! (*singing the repeated refrain*)
>
> JUSTIN: (*laughing and moving to join the reading*) My turn. Where are we, right here? Right here? (*general discussion of where they are and whose turn it is*)
>
> JUSTIN: And in (*much laughter*)
>
> TAHRIQUE: And IN!
>
> JUSTIN: And in that bed there is a gr . . . (*again much laughter*)
>
> TAHRIQUE and DARYLL: A granny . . .
>
> TAHRIQUE: Dojy Dottie da da da (*sing-song voice quality*) Where everyone is slee eep ing!!!

JUSTIN: How ya doin girl? How you livin'? Are ya fine? Are ya stinkin'? Are you ugly? Are you honey? Hey babe. Bye Bye. That was Daryll. (*much laughter and confusion over who has the mike*)

DARYLL: (*noble attempt to get back on task*) And on that bed there was a cat . . .

Sarah overheard this last bit of bravado and intervened. It was the end of the taping session for the day. Daryll and Tahrique were a little miffed at not getting to finish. Justin was relieved to be done with his reading. And Sarah considered it a session gone bad, something that seemed to happen whenever Justin entered the reading scene.

In the next section, we turn to the talk, play, writing, and reading of Justin, illustrating how observation from all three perspectives—the individual, the peer group, the class as a whole—allowed Sarah to make sense of and to support Justin's learning.

Attending to Justin's social life. A popular child with both boys and girls, Justin could be found during free-choice time drawing with Daryll and Tahrique, playing store with the girls, or in the dinosaur center with Warren or William. Justin was always in charge. For example, when he played store with the girls, he was the daddy. Sometimes he was a nice daddy, sometimes a demanding one. The girls seemed to like to have him play in either role, as long as he played. Justin would set up chairs as if they were seats in a car. "OK," he would say, "pretend I'm really nice and I'm gonna take all you kids to the store to get whatever you want." (Even children who were not playing in the store game stopped to listen to Justin as he set the scene.) Justin would then make himself a wheel and drive that car to a store some 100 miles away. He would talk to his "kids" about their behavior and ask his wife to get out the sandwiches and sodas for the kids.

During outside play, Justin, as already suggested, had authority over the four or five boys he played with. (Daryll and Tahrique were always with him at recess, as were two or three other boys from different first-grade classrooms.) A strong performance was important for Justin, Boy King 1. The tests or tasks he and his two friends played out were different from most educators' assessments. However, at their core, the children's tests, like the kinds of teacher assessments we are discussing, were concerned with valuing certain goals, trying to achieve them, being able to make others believe in oneself as a competent person, and believing in and feeling good about oneself. At the very least their tests helped make us sympathetic to those who feel defeated from the very start when being assessed in a way that is perceived as unfair—certainly Sarah and, most certainly, Anne could not pass Justin's tests.

Observing Justin read and write.   Understanding the role Justin assumed in his play helped Sarah to understand his behaviors during reading and writing and to understand, too, why taking advantage of the social energy of the three Boy Kings was not so easy. Although Justin was a clear social leader, he was not an academic one. Justin was retained once in first grade for excessive absences. He did not seem to think of himself as "school smart." He would often tell Sarah or one of his peers that he did not feel like doing the work because it took too long to do—or it was too hard or boring. Justin spent a great deal of time avoiding academic tasks or wandering around the room, trying to find something to do that he felt he could succeed at.

Justin sometimes seemed to use his skills as a lively talker to circle around, rather than engage in, activities. For example, he often took a long time settling into the act of writing because he had to check in with everyone. He had to check out his main men—Daryll and, after his arrival, Tahrique. He had to check with the girls at his table—did they have his pencil, his crayons, his dinosaur book? Did Daryll hear M.C. Hammer's latest hit last night? Did he play kickball before coming into school? After a few requests from Sarah to get his work done, Justin would settle in. He usually found a book on his current interest (dinosaurs, racing cars, picture books), drew a picture from it, and then copied two or three words from the book into his journal. Meanwhile, his talk was usually not related to what he was drawing or writing about.

Reading was his most difficult and thus avoided academic task. Yet listening to his talk during study units allowed Sarah to create moments when Justin seemed comfortable with himself as a reader and writer and as a participant in the academic life of the class. Early in the school year, Justin shared with the class the fact that his older brother was a musician. He brought in a tape of his brother singing rap songs. Indeed, Justin was capable of becoming Boy King 1 because of his ability to sing songs so well—to remember the lines and rhymes.

Repetition and rhyme support many young children's comfort with, and willingness to engage, the intricacies of the printed word and their attempts to accurately match voice and print. Children may choose texts with repetitive, predictable patterns that have been read many times to the class to "really read," while they may invent— or, in Justin's case, avoid—stories for more difficult books. Knowing that Justin liked music allowed Sarah to help Justin find reading materials that would support his interaction with the text.

Many class study units (e.g., dinosaurs, sea animals, Spanish, civil rights) involved songs. Justin loved leading the class in these songs. Usually Sarah wrote the words to the songs on large chart paper so the children could read the words as well as sing them. Justin would always volunteer to go up and point with the pointer to the words as they sang. Sometimes, during free-choice time, he would take the pointer, line up several children in chairs in front of the chart paper, and lead them in singing/reading. Daryll, Tahrique, and he also made a rap book, composed of rap lyrics known by most members of the class, which Justin enjoyed reading.

Thus Justin's interest in and knowledge about music not only allowed him reading practice, it also allowed him to assume leadership roles in academic areas. In fact, one day Sarah and the class were trying to remember the four instruments a guest musician had come in and played. They were all stumped after remembering two of the instruments. Justin spoke up and said they should look on the cassette she left behind—that usually the instruments were listed there. Sure enough, the instruments she played were listed on the cassette box. Justin had proved a good researcher!

Justin's interest in songs also translated into his journal writing. For example, Justin drew pictures of Rosa Parks and Dr. Martin Luther King, Jr., both civil rights leaders featured in a song that Justin continually sang to himself during the civil rights study unit. In fact, when the music teacher first sang a song about "Sister Rosa," Justin told her that he had heard it on the radio. The music teacher was obviously pleased with this spontaneous connection. Further, Justin wrote rap songs in his journal, for example:

get up in get get down
911 is joke in your Town
        Justin King 1

Attending to the interplay of Boy King 1's social and academic lives. Through observing Justin's play and listening to his talk, Sarah was able to create situations for Justin to experience both individual success and satisfying participation in the classroom community. Further, the social energy amidst Justin and his main men sometimes could be channeled into academic tasks that were relatively open-ended, such as the journal activity, or that involved familiar materials, such as the chart songs and rap book. However, as already illustrated, the three boys did not do well during partner reading, unlike the very successful partnership of Rebekah and Crystal. There was too much tension to prove oneself, too little cooperation. The boys became very critical of one another and, at the same time, more and more unsure of themselves as readers—and less and less involved in reading. After the initial anger, the boys would laugh and forget about reading.

Sarah tried pairing Justin with a more capable peer reader, but he would sulk and refuse to read; he understood why he was paired with that person—and he resented it. As Daryll illustrated how important a student's evaluation of himself can be, Justin illustrated that the student is often his own worst critic. He was full of assessmentlike comments about himself: "I messed up." "I can't draw." "That book is too hard for me to read." "Can I go to the bathroom?"

As a social leader, Justin did not want it known that he had a hard time reading and writing. He preferred to read with an adult, a well-known adult, who would support his efforts. In fact, with an adult there to support and to help regulate the reading, and with a manageable book, the three Boy Kings could indeed enjoy reading together, which Sarah discovered one day when the boys seemed to be taking a taxicab ride nowhere. Anne was visiting on that day, and she noted both the cab ride and the subsequent reading activity in her notebook.

Sarah had given the children a number of activity choices during a morning work period. They could write in their journals, draw, partner read, play in the store, write Daryll birthday cards, play with the dinosaurs, or work on math. A large group of children, however, chose to go for a taxi ride. Justin was the driver. Crystal, Diandra, Tiffany, and Tahrique were also in the taxi. Sarah was having serious doubts about the learning potential of this day's ride (although Anne wanted "to see where they were going"). Since the taxi seemed headed nowhere and its ride was becoming increasingly bumpy, Sarah intervened.

She asked Justin to come and read to her. He did not want to, but he came reluctantly when she explained that he would be allowed to return to his free choice after a story. His friends were obviously disappointed that the ride had come to an end, but they quickly moved onto other things.

Justin and Sarah settled at his seat and took out his literature reader. She pointed out that he had already read two stories from this book—"The Little Red Hen" and "The Great, Big, Enormous Turnip." This seemed to give him a sense of accomplishment, and so she asked him to read "Dog House for Sale." It was a story that most students enjoy, and one with a familiar story line. Sarah and Justin were not even to the third page of the story when Daryll appeared and asked if he could read along. A minute behind him was Tahrique. After initially struggling to get the newcomers on the right page, the boys settled into their turn-taking pattern. As they read, they supplied one another with needed words, and Sarah, too, directed their attention to varied clues, such as an initial sound or a reference to the sentence sense. Moreover, she established a low-key, supportive atmosphere, one where any insults, playful or otherwise, would be inappropriate. And, since Justin was clearly engaged with the text, Sarah was able to observe his ways of interacting with the text—of making use of orthographic, syntactic, and meaning-based cues, of predicting and commenting on the evolving action—much more easily than she could in the partner-reading episodes.

To both of us, this seemed a significant episode. When we talked about the experience later in the week, we were struck by the contrast between the "Dog House for Sale" experience and *The Napping House* experience, where Justin's social agenda and academic uncertainty had seemed to interfere with what had been a socially and academically successful partnership between Daryll and Tahrique. The contrast between the events highlighted for us children's different academic and social needs.

As much as we value children's social lives and respect the power of peer talk to support children's learning, we realize that, at times, a teacher-structured situation can be more satisfying than a peer-directed one. Many of Sarah's students needed much less support during reading than Justin did. Their talk and writing about their reading suggested real engagement with a book. Moreover, they enjoyed opportunities for sharing a book with a peer. Justin, however, avoided them. For him, reading was a difficult and (as he perceived it) a demeaning act. He felt himself judged by his peers and by Sarah—and he was not proud of his reading performance. Sarah had to provide time and space for Justin to feel successful as a reader, since he needed safety from humiliation when learning or practicing new tasks. During this episode, Sarah was able to do these things—and then she stuck to her word and let him have his free time, taxi and all.

Justin himself demonstrated his own sensitivity to others' need for face-saving, for support, as Sarah noted one morning during journal time. Diandra had just walked in, hiding her face in her hands and crying. She slunk to her table and lay her head in her arms, still crying:

DARYLL: What's the matter, Diandra?

JUSTIN: What's the matter with her?

DARYLL: What's the matter, Diandra? (*Diandra doesn't look up; she just sniffles.*)

SARAH: I think she is wearing her new glasses. She's a little shy about having them. (*Diandra cries louder.*)

DARYLL: You got glasses, Diandra? Don't be shy. You still look cute.

JUSTIN: Yeah! You can still be my girl, anytime. Don't cry, Diandra. I'd be glad to have some new glasses. They could help you see. Then you'd be drawing and reading real good.

WHITNEY: Yeah. I wish I had glasses.

DARYLL: Crystal has glasses and she's OK with them. 'Member she didn't like 'em?

JUSTIN: Yeah. That's right. And now she's wearin' 'em everyday. Look, Diandra. Crystal's got glasses. Don't cry. (*Diandra raises her head and reaches for a pencil.*)

Seeing Justin in varied situations, paying attention to how he expressed himself through play, talk, pictures, and text, allowed a clearer, a truer, picture of him. Yes, he was a student who struggled with reading and writing, but he was also a student who took pleasure in words—who could memorize lines and deliver them dramatically. And he was also one who was curious about the world, who was intrigued by dinosaurs, sharks, whales, and racing cars— and, thus, by the content of books.

Moreover, it was helpful to consider not only his individual progress but his relationships with his friends and, indeed, with the class as a whole. At the end of the year, when Sarah assessed Justin's progress in school, she considered that he no longer had a truancy problem. He came to school every day. That was extremely important. After all, he had been retained an entire year because of poor attendance. Further, she noted that he was considered a leader in the class—not an outcast. His kindergarten teacher, a very dedicated woman, told Sarah that she would consider that a very significant aspect of his school life assessment. Justin *was* considered an outcast in his first years of school. Not only did he seldom attend school, he usually was not clean. The children did not want to be near him. During his year in Room 205, Justin became Boy King 1. His friends supported him and wanted him to be a part of their lives.

Conclusions: The Ways of the Teacher-Archaeologist

Crystal, Rebekah, Tahrique, Daryll, and Justin are unique individuals whose lives, as fellow members of Room 205, were intertwined in complex ways. Through our discussion of those lives, we have aimed to illustrate the potential of informal assessment to help teachers gain a broader and fuller picture of each child. Especially for children such as Justin, whose standardized test scores would suggest only incompetence, informal assessment is a powerful teacher tool for seeing competent children and for understanding the interests, knowledge, and concerns that underlie their sometimes puzzling and frustrating behaviors.

Educators may best tap the power of informal assessment—and thus gain richer, more complex visions of children—by appreciating its multifaceted nature. To these ends, we constructed our stories of children from artifacts and observations that allowed us to view individuals across many contexts involving different kinds of relationships. We emphasized, first, viewing individual children in different kinds of activities. In this way we as educators may discover the texture of individual children's resources and help them "weave" connections among them (Dyson, 1990). For example, knowing about Justin's interest in and knowledge about music and his skill as a singer gave Sarah new possibilities for involving Justin in classroom activities. Indeed, it allowed Sarah to help Justin, Boy King 1, to assume leadership roles in academic activities, including literacy activities.

With the mention of the Boy Kings, we have introduced our second emphasis. Early childhood educators have long been concerned with putting the child at the center of the curriculum and, moreover, with careful observation of the child's interests and activities. But when we put one child at the center of our attention, other children tend to appear as well. Just as our own learning is supported by satisfying, if sometimes challenging, relationships with others, so, too, is children's learning. And, also like adults', children's relationships are complex, filled with needs to be both distinctive from and "just the same as" their friends. We therefore have emphasized that observing children in many different kinds of activities reveals not only their resources as individuals—their interests, knowledge, and skills—but also the network of relationships that energize their lives.

Children's relationships with special others can be an important means for making school itself pleasurable and satisfying. Children can learn from one another, modeling new behaviors, cooperatively completing tasks too hard for any child alone, and raising questions that challenge and stretch one another's thinking (Rogoff, 1990). Moreover, the social talk they engage in can help children make associations between their lives inside and outside of school. Crystal, for example, learned much about reading from her good friend Rebekah, and Rebekah learned, too, as she and Crystal talked together about books and about the personal experiences a book reminded them of. Further, they engaged in many activities together in which neither child had the upper hand. At the same time, however, as Justin illustrated, relationships can also complicate learning. Some children may need private and safe spaces to try out new and challenging tasks, just as they need public times to display their special expertise.

Finally, we have emphasized teachers' sensitivity to the classroom community as a whole. Children need opportunities to build common ground with others, to act as special contributors to classroom life, and to link their lives to others who may, at first, seem quite different from themselves. It is this third area, we believe, that suggests the enormous potential of multicultural classrooms like Sarah's for contributing to the development of adults who may transform social inequities into new social possibilities (Greene, 1988). And it is this third area that also suggests the enormous pain teachers may feel when, in their own classrooms, such social inequities continue to play themselves out.

Children, like adults, may feel most comfortable with others who are similar to themselves in gender, race, and class. Too often, as many have documented, children who are socioculturally different come to feel undervalued and unaccepted in school (Cortes, 1986). And despite the potential for children to learn from one another, situations in which children from more mainstream backgrounds are seen exclusively or formally as "helpers" of children from less mainstream backgrounds hardly seem appropriate.

As teacher-archaeologist, then, Sarah's groundwork in Room 205 involved uncovering and developing a real sense of unique individuals, different friendship networks, and a close classroom community. This three-tiered classroom system was built largely with the tools of informal assessment: observing and listening to individual children, noting and using social relationships and interests, and encouraging open discussions among and with students. It is a circular process—the more the teacher listens and observes the individual child or group of friends, the more she or he is able to use and develop these interests to create powerful community bonds and curriculum themes.

Room 205, then, became a community of friends working hard together and having fun. Sarah was more able to appreciate the individual differences in her class and address them because she was informally noting students' growth throughout the year. Informal assessment allowed her a fuller view of classroom life and, thus, to better understand and support children's efforts to comfortably negotiate their shared lives as individuals, friends, and classroom citizens.

At the same time, talking and writing about informal assessment has helped us both articulate more clearly how the children's social lives mingled with the assessment process and with their academic learning. Teachers at all levels can become unsure of themselves, particularly when they open their curriculum up and allow for the sorts of student action and choice that make informal assessment meaningful. And, just as with their students, sharing experiences and reflecting and laughing about them together can provide social energy, personal confidence, and a deeper understanding of the complexities of learning.

The day Justin filled his taxi with noisy children and took off on a bumpy ride, Sarah and Anne had stood on the side of the road. Sarah wondered aloud, "See any redeeming qualities here?" If she had been alone in her own classroom, Anne would have had the same question. But, not being the teacher in charge, she answered Sarah's wry question with, "Well, don't you want to see where they are going?" Through talking together, Sarah and Anne were able to turn classroom experiences into complex classroom dramas. To appreciate the dramas, they had to be patient in order to see where individual children were going and how and why—the stuff of informal assessment. On the other hand, as Sarah's question made clear, teachers are not just observers but actors in the unfolding plot who must use their observations to influence the outcome of the story for the benefit of the individual and of the community as a whole.

In closing, we recall our opening image of Sarah, gathering artifacts at the end of the day. Some 12 years since she last had a first-grade class of her own, Anne has boxes of such stuff she cannot quite throw out—letters, pictures, cards, even confiscated toy cars that somehow were not returned and freely offered gifts of small dolls and tiny teddy bears. They remind her of children's affections and concerns, and of the social dramas that take place amidst the reading, 'riting, and 'rithmetic. Such is the way of the teacher-archaeologist. To understand our students, we must reach not only across the social and cultural differences that may separate their lives from our own, but back through time. We must reach that childhood place where important social dramas take place right along with the significant learning that will shape the years to come.

Like archaeologists, and the more contemporary-oriented anthropologists, we assume that our children are not wasting time or energy, even when it seems like they are. Through listening, watching, and collecting, we gain clues that allow us to understand all the kinds of problems they are working on and thereby to better support and, indeed, participate with them in the making of the future.

Authors' note. We would like to acknowledge two dedicated teachers, colleagues who teach at Sarah's school, who are themselves skillful "readers" of children and have helped us in our work: Marty Conrad and Louise Rosenkrantz.

References

Callaway, N. (Ed.) (1989). *Georgia O'Keeffe: One hundred flowers*. New York: Callaway and Knopf.

Cazden, C. (1988). *Classroom discourse: The language of teaching and learning*. Portsmouth, NH: Heinemann.

Cohen, M. (1967–1979). *The Starring First Grade* series. New York: Greenwillow Books and Macmillan.

Cortes, C. E. (1986). The education of language minority students: A contextual interaction model. In Bilingual Education Office, California State Department of Education (developer), *Beyond language: Social and cultural factors in schooling language minority students* (pp. 3–34). Los Angeles: Evaluation, Dissemination, and Assessment Center.

de Paola, T. (1975). *Strega Nona*. Englewood-Cliffs, NJ: Prentice-Hall.

Dyson, A. Haas (1989). *Multiple worlds of child writers: Friends learning to write*. New York: Teachers College Press.

Dyson, A. Haas. (1990). Weaving possibilities: Rethinking metaphors for early literacy development. *The Reading Teacher, 44,* 202–214.

Gelman, R. G. (1987). *More spaghetti I say.* New York: Scholastic, Inc.

Greene, M. (1988). *The dialectic of freedom.* New York: Teachers College Press.

Lionni, L. (1963). *Swimmy.* New York: Pantheon.

Piaget, J., & Inhelder, B. (1969). *The psychology of the child.* New York: Basic Books.

Rogoff, B. (1990). *Apprenticeship in thinking: Cognitive development in social context.* New York: Oxford University Press.

Rubin, Z. (1980). *Children's friendships.* Cambridge, MA: Harvard University Press.

Sendak, M. (1962). *Chicken soup with rice.* New York: Harper & Row.

Sendak, M. (1962). *Pierre.* New York: Harper & Row.

Sendak, M. (1963). *Where the wild things are.* New York: Harper & Row.

Vygotsky, L. S. (1962). *Thought and language.* Cambridge, MA: MIT Press.

Vygotsky, L. S. (1978). *Mind in society.* Cambridge, MA: Harvard University Press.

Wood, A. (1984). *The napping house.* San Diego: Harcourt Brace Jovanovich.

Learning with, about, and from Children
Life in a Bilingual Second Grade

JULIA FOURNIER
BETH LANSDOWNE
ZULEMA PASTENES
PAMELA STEEN
SARAH HUDELSON

The theme of "everyone-as-learner" emerges clearly in this chapter. Although theirs is a bilingual program, the teachers have little to say about "limited English" speakers and much to say about children and adults who help one another use oral and written Spanish and English meaningfully throughout the curriculum.

Introduction

It is the beginning of another day at William T. Machan Elementary School. At one corner of the school children are being assisted by the crossing guard. Others are getting off buses parked close to the playground. Some children are dropped off by parents who drive into the parking lot in cars and pick-up trucks. Many children have had breakfast in the school cafeteria before congregating on the playground or outside their classroom doors. Black, white, and brown faces are evident. Children chatter in both English and Spanish.

As the children settle into their classrooms, the principal, Dr. Lynn Davey, greets the school community over the public address system. Each day a different group of children leads the school in the Pledge of Allegiance. Dr. Davey makes the morning announcements, praising those classes with perfect attendance the day before, reminding the teachers of meetings, and noting recipients of such awards as honor table in the cafeteria. Sometimes the student council announces sales, or an individual class reads poetry or announces a special class project. Then classes commence their workday.

William T. Machan is a public elementary school (K–6) in the Creighton Elementary School District in Phoenix, Arizona. The school is located in a residential area of 30- to 40-year-old homes and apartments. The neighborhood originally housed an Anglo middle-class population. But during the last decade, the area has experienced a drastic socioeconomic and ethnic shift. As a result the neighborhood is becoming increasingly Hispanic as more families move north from Mexico, Guatemala, and Honduras seeking economic opportunity and refuge from civil strife. Many of the families are struggling economically, socially, and culturally. About 80% of the children who attend Machan are Hispanic, and Spanish is spoken in many homes. About half of the nonnative English speakers have been designated Limited English Proficient (LEP). Most of the Spanish-speaking families are recent immigrants or first-generation U.S. citizens. Many of the children of immigrant parents did not attend school before their arrival in the United States. The school population is extremely transient. It is not unusual for 25% to 30% of the children in any room to enroll and withdraw from the school within the course of a single academic year.

A current popular term for the children at Machan is "at-risk." Using a specific set of criteria from the state (socioeconomic status, home language, previous academic records, test scores, transiency, previous attendance at school), over two-thirds of the children at the school have been designated as at-risk for school failure. Machan is one of 30 schools that applied for and received a grant from the Arizona State Department of Education to implement a K–3 demonstration project designed to improve academic achievement for the at-risk population. The K–3 project was designed by a team of teachers, parents, school district administrators, and the school principal.

The staff at Machan have been working to improve academic achievement in the following ways: (1) reducing student-teacher ratios by limiting the number of students in the K–3 classes and employing instructional aides; (2) providing workshops for parents to involve them in their children's education; (3) employing a school social worker to assist families with social services; (4) conducting an extended-year summer school program; (5) working on curriculum development based on a sociolinguistic model of learning (meaning a focus on language and literacy development through authentic use); (6) involving teachers in extensive staff development activities that have focused on coming to better understand and implement a sociolinguistic view of learning; and (7) involving instructional aides in workshops and classes to upgrade their performance.

Perhaps the most critical aspects of the K–3 program have been the ones involving staff development and the implementation of curriculum based on holistic views of teaching and learning. These efforts have been led by Lynn Davey, the principal and K–3 project director, and Kelly Draper, the assistant project director. When Davey arrived at Machan five years ago, the instruction was highly traditional and focused on the utilization of basal readers, sequentially based math texts, and content-area textbooks. Since her arrival, Davey has been working to help teachers implement a different approach to instruction. Although traditional approaches are still evident at Machan, there is increased awareness and utilization of other modes of instruction. At all grade levels, many teachers are developing a curriculum that they believe is the most effective for their children. The view of many educators at Machan is that, while there are numbers of children whose family life situations have an adverse effect on their health, school attendance, and attention, the children themselves are not automatically at-risk intellectually because of their language and culture. Rather, schools themselves create or provide a risky learning environment for children when they persist in utilizing traditional, skills-based, teacher-centered, textbook-focused instructional approaches.

The alternative work that many of the teachers are engaged in involves working toward curricula based on a whole language perspective of teaching and learning, with learning occurring in settings where children are asking questions, solving problems, constructing meaning, and taking risks. Children are involved in meaningful content study, utilizing and interacting with a variety of materials, texts, and audiences. Teachers view their roles as facilitators rather than directors. They believe that it is the teacher's job to help children set their own goals for their learning and to work hard to achieve these goals. One indicator of Machan's success in implementing a whole language perspective is its recent designation by the National Council of Teachers of English as a center of excellence for at-risk students.

With regard to bilingualism and whole language, the school believes that children should initially become literate and learn school content in their native language or the language in which they feel more confident (in this case, Spanish), and then use the abilities developed in the native language to construct meaning in another language (in this case, English). The goal is to have children make the transition into English by the end of the third grade. Among the bilingual staff, there is the understanding that essentially individuals learn to read and write only once, since what they have learned in one language they then apply to other languages. As bilingual teacher Beth Lansdowne notes:

> Whenever I have a parent of a Spanish-speaking child wanting to have their child read immediately in English, rather than move gradually through the transition, I use the following statement, which I find valuable: Children only learn to read once. When they have the skills in their native language, those same skills are then applied to English. I really believe that once children reach a certain competence in Spanish reading and writing, they naturally transition themselves. It becomes evident in books that they select, in their journal writing, and in their language.

In many school districts, bilingual education is highly controversial. Even within the Creighton District, not all the schools offer bilingual education. At Machan, there is generally a positive acceptance of the bilingual program by the Spanish-dominant community, especially by families who are newly arrived in the United States. Additionally, the acceptance of the program by the families of English-speaking children is key. The English-speaking models are essential to the program. If there were not sufficient numbers of English-speaking peers, the program would not work.

General community acceptance of the bilingual program does not mean, however, that there are never any problems. Beth's earlier comment suggests that Spanish-speaking parents often worry about why their children are not learning in English. And Julia Fournier, Beth's teaching partner in the bilingual second-grade team, recalls two incidents that also illustrate this reality:

> Last year during the first month of school, I had several confrontational meetings regarding the excessive use of Spanish in my classroom. I had to explain to parents that during the first few weeks, while establishing community, it was essential to everyone that everything be translated in order to ensure that there were no misunderstandings regarding rules, rights, and rituals in the classroom. Most parents were satisfied with this response. I told all of my parents that this was the only

excuse I would make. At my request, some parents asked their children if they would like to switch out of my room. The children objected strongly to this suggestion. So the parents tucked away their fears. With time, some of these parents became some of my strongest advocates.

Another time a Hispanic parent cornered me during open-house night. She wanted a full explanation of why her son had to be exposed to so much Spanish at school. She thought he heard enough at home. None of my responses satisfied her. As a Hispanic woman, she saw the use of Spanish in the classroom as detrimental to her son's educational growth. I went into details of job opportunities for bilingual individuals, using myself as an example. She began to weaken, but she countered that he heard enough Spanish at home to help him. I then talked about the lack of respect the Spanish language has had historically in the United States and how second- and third-generation Hispanics are partly responsible for this situation. I told her that the elevation of Spanish can take place only when Hispanics start seeing their language as power and not as something to be ashamed of. I concluded by saying that perhaps this could begin in elementary school, when children saw their white teachers choosing to learn Spanish because they valued it. She conceded my point and agreed to wait out the month before taking action. The next time I met with her she confessed to me that she had changed her attitude about the bilingual program. She had nothing but praise for the work we did with her son.

The Second Grade Bilingual/Multicultural Team

One of the settings at Machan with a firm commitment to the bilingual and whole language philosophy just outlined is the bilingual/multicultural second-grade team, where two teachers (Julia Fournier and Beth Lansdowne) and two instructional aides (Zulema Pastenes and Pamela Steen) work as a team with a group of about 56 children. Almost all are Hispanic and about half are Spanish-dominant, which means that the children receive a significant amount of their daily instruction in Spanish.

The team formed in 1987 when Julia arrived at Machan. Beth had been at Machan since 1984. Previously she had been employed in a migrant education program on the west side of metropolitan

Phoenix, where she had developed Home Start Program, which involved her working with parents and 4-year-olds in their homes in the labor camps. In addition, she taught English as a second language to non-English-speaking kindergarten children. Beth herself writes: "This job convinced me that my work in education should be geared to the Hispanic community. I worked at this job for a year and moved to Minnesota. I worked with handicapped preschoolers for three years. This job taught me a lot about child development, especially language development, but it was at this point that I really missed the Spanish-speaking children." Beth decided that she needed to be bilingual in order to be most effective as a teacher, so she left her job and moved to Mexico. Living in Mexico and studying Spanish intensively for a school year provided her with the Spanish-language skills she needed to work bilingually. Beth is committed to the students she teaches, and she makes frequent home visits to her children, often assisting families with social services.

Julia moved to Machan from a position in an elementary school in a Mexican–Yaqui Indian community close to Phoenix. Julia also speaks Spanish, although she talks with her students about the fact that she is still learning Spanish and should be considered a model for them only in English. She also does not feel comfortable conducting parent conferences in Spanish, so she uses an interpreter for this activity. A few years before, Julia had been close to leaving teaching for another profession. She felt bored in the classroom and unsatisfied spending her days teaching the prescribed amount of time on each subject using district-adopted texts that left no opportunity for innovation or fun. However, a colleague who was studying at Arizona State introduced her to the idea of whole language, and she began both to examine her own philosophy of teaching and to experiment with such instructional strategies as thematic units, journals, and author studies. According to Julia, she actually changed professions, rediscovering and reinvigorating herself as a "whole language" rather than a "traditional" teacher.

When Beth and Julia started teaming, they had been in one graduate class together. Julia comments:

Construction on our rooms was going on at the school, and we started with nothing, not even lights or air-conditioning. The electricity was not turned on until half an hour before the students arrived for their first day of school. Somehow the experience of readying our classrooms in the dark in the sweltering Phoenix summer heat bound us together from the start. While Beth was not really a whole language teacher, she was open to new ideas, and we began by planning thematic units and community-building activities.

Zulema became a part of the team in late September of that year. Beth and Julia wanted to hire a native Spanish speaker as an instructional aide. Zulema, a native of Chile and a resident of the United States since 1983, bilingual and biliterate, had no classroom experience when she began at Machan, so her first year with the team was really a learning process for her. An energetic and bright individual, she has become an indispensable member of the bilingual team. She reads professional writing on her own time; she has an extra sense about the students' needs; and she works many nights and weekends developing her own checklists and activities or translating concepts into Spanish. She works with Beth in Spanish language arts in the morning and in the afternoon with Julia in math, science, and social studies. This experience has convinced Zulema that she wants to become a bilingual teacher. She notes:

> I think of myself as an example to many children who want to give up on education. Thanks to my proficiency in Spanish, I was able to become as proficient in English. In the 1988–1989 school year I was chosen as educational support personnel staff person of the year. This honor truly reassured me that this is where I belong, where I can really make a change in kids' lives.

Pamela Steen became a part of the second-grade bilingual staff in the fall of 1989. A native of Phoenix, Pam's interest in education began when her own three children entered school. She involved herself in her children's schooling, especially during their preschool and primary years. She became intrigued by the multilingual/multicultural aspects of education when her family lived in a Chinese-dominant neighborhood in San Francisco and her son attended a school where English was the third language down in handouts sent home. She had worked previously in a bilingual first grade at Machan, so that when she moved up to second grade many of the children already knew her. A devoted instructional assistant, she spends hours of her own time doing classroom work and reading professional material, for example, Lucy Calkins' books on writer's workshop (Calkins, 1983, 1986). Pam works in the morning with Julia in English language arts and in the afternoon with Beth in math, science, and social studies. About her work with the children Pam writes:

> I am not a Spanish speaker but I try very hard not to let that fact get in the way of my helping the kids. I will do anything I can to communicate with them. I make a lot of use of bilingual kids as brokers. They help me when I need a translator. The most important thing is that I believe I have the respect and friendship of the kids.

Our Second-Grade Team's Beliefs About Education

While we come from different backgrounds and have different personalities, as team members we share similar views with respect to what teaching and learning should be about. These beliefs have evolved (and are still evolving) as we as team members have planned and worked together, shared professional readings and new ideas, and struggled to teach from a child-centered philosophy that involves constant dialogue with peers, constant thinking and rethinking, and constant working and reworking. In terms of a guiding set of beliefs, we share the views that:

1. There is a special gift that every child possesses. Each child is a unique individual and should be encouraged to develop as such. Each child in the classroom must feel a sense of personal dignity and worth. Classrooms should operate in such a way that children can find and develop their own unique voices.
2. Children want to learn. It is the responsibility of teachers to take advantage of that desire and to use it, as well as to create a place in which each student does his or her best most of the time.
3. Children progress at individual rates. It is crucial to begin by accepting where children are working at a particular point in time and to move from there.
4. Children learn most effectively in classrooms where there is a sense of community, where there is openness and a willingness to share, work together, and help one another. It is essential to build a community of learners. Through shared group experiences, children recognize both their own uniqueness and their contributions to the whole.
5. Bilingual and multiethnic classrooms should facilitate respect and acceptance of other cultures. Multiple cultures and languages should be valued in classrooms.

6. Learners learn best when they are in control of what they are learning, when they feel ownership of their learning. Rather than the teacher assuming all control of the class and curriculum, students must be involved in making important choices concerning the curriculum and classroom management that will affect them throughout the school year.

7. Teaching is a living, breathing profession that changes daily with each child's needs and passions as well as with the teacher's changing ideas. It is not a profession that dictates curriculum on the basis of what is contained in basal readers, geared toward mastery and success on group-administered tests, nor is it a profession that bases itself on what has been done the year before just because the resources have been compiled and are available and easy to get to. Teaching involves constant change.

Our Beliefs About Assessment

Given our beliefs about teaching and learning environments, we believe in and try to use a variety of kinds of assessments that are congruent with our beliefs about appropriate ways of teaching. While the school district requires that we use report cards, and while the district also is concerned with standardized and criterion-referenced tests, we do not believe that these kinds of assessments, which reduce our students to symbols and numbers and which are based on a skills view of learning, give us a true picture of who children are and what they are learning. So for day-to-day work, we rely on a variety of informal, classroom-based kinds of observations of children and documentation of their work. And we are encouraged because our school is moving toward the utilization of more of these kinds of instruments.

At each of the primary grade levels, for example, teachers worked on a regular basis during the 1989–1990 academic year to identify their goals for reading and writing. These goals become the basis of checklists the educators believed reflected their reading and writing objectives and the kinds of literacy behaviors they were working to help their students develop. At the second-grade level, checklists have emerged that are reproduced here as Figures 5.1 and 5.2. We use these checklists at the end of each quarter as one way of reflecting on and documenting student progress. (These checklists were developed with colleagues. See Goodman, Goodman, and Wood, 1988 in Appendix.)

In addition, during the 1989–1990 and 1990–1991 academic years, Pat Carini made several trips to Phoenix to consult with teachers from several schools who wanted to explore innovative ways

FIGURE 5.1   Machan School second grade writing checklist

SECOND GRADE WRITING RECORD
Wm. T. Machan Elementary School

Student _____   Year _____
Teacher _____   Date of Entry into Classroom_____
Primary Language_____   Secondary Language_____

CODES: NE = no evidence, D = developing, C = controls

	DATE	DATE	DATE	COMMENTS
WRITING QUALITY:				
Self selects topic				
Uses expansive vocabulary				
Experiments with style				
Uses revision strategies				
WRITING MECHANICS:				
Handwriting				
Uses periods				
Uses question marks				
Uses quotation marks				
Uses exclamation points				
Uses capitalization				
Uses comma/ apostrophe/accents				
Grammar usage				
% Invented spelling				
% Conventional spelling				

FIGURE 5.2   Machan School second grade reading checklist

SECOND GRADE READING RECORD
WM. T. MACHAN SCHOOL

KEY: D - developing/sometimes
       C - controls/most of the time
       NE - not evident at this time

STUDENT _____ YEAR _____

TEACHER _____ DATE OF ENTRY INTO CLASSROOM _____

A. INTEREST DATES				
1. READS DURING FREE TIME				
2. SELECTS OWN BOOK				
3. READS A VARIETY OF BOOKS				
4. ASKS TO USE LIBRARY				
5. CONTRIBUTES TO BOOK DISCUSSION				
6. READS AT HOME				
7. BRINGS BOOKS AND IDEAS TO SHARE				
8. READS SILENTLY FOR SUSTAINED PERIOD				
B. COMPREHENSION				
1. READS AND REREADS FOR COMPREHENSION				
2. RISKS BY:				
a: making sensible predictions				
b: discussing storyline				
c: identifying elements of literature				
d: explaining cause and effect				
e: drawing conclusions				
f: identifying fiction and nonfiction				
3. BRINGS PRIOR KNOWLEDGE AND PERSONAL EXPERIENCE TO TEXT				
4. RETELLS STORY IN SEQUENCE				
a: after hearing				
b: after reading				
5. MAKES COMPARISONS WITH OTHER TEXTS				
C. STRATEGIES USED - NEW WORDS AND IDEAS				
1. USES ILLUSTRATIONS				
2. USES WORDS THAT MAKE SENSE				
3. USES SENTENCE STRUCTURE				
4. USES WORD STRUCTURE				
5. USES GRAPHOPHONIC CLUES				
6. USES PUNCTUATION				
7. REREADS				
8. SELF-CORRECTS				

of understanding and presenting learners' development. Carini is an educator who has worked for over 20 years with teachers at Prospect School in North Bennington, Vermont. Working together, Carini and her colleagues have developed a process called Descriptive Review. A Descriptive Review is a collaborative description of a child's experiences within the school setting accomplished by bringing together varied perspectives (Carini, 1979, 1986). Two members of the Machan staff attended the 1989–1990 workshops with Carini, who focused on detailed narration as one way of reflecting on an individual's growth. Partly because of Carini's influence and partly because of the K–3 project evaluator, Pat Rigg, teachers have been encouraged to write narrative summaries that provide richer descriptions of children than report cards or checklists.

During 1990–1991 Julia was one of the workshop participants. One of the exercises Carini recommended is identifying a child's strengths and vulnerabilities. Julia decided to begin fall parent conferences by sharing children's strengths. She, Zulema, and Pam generated lists of strengths for each child in Julia's room. After they had a long list of strengths, they listed vulnerabilities and then related the vulnerabilities to strengths. Thus, if a child's strength was verbal ability, an accompanying vulnerability might be not giving others a chance to think for themselves. For example, Antonio's strengths included: dependable, loyal, pays attention most of the time, honest, good insight into literature, watches to see what others do. His vulnerabilities were: friends can easily distract him, will not take risks, and proves loyalty by sometimes goofing around. This exercise taught the team members a lot about the children and reinforced their notions about how to look at learners.

Additionally, multiple samples of children's writing from year to year are kept in their cumulative folders, so that we can examine progress longitudinally and so that teachers can discuss a particular child over time by looking at the child's work. So as a school we are making efforts to assess in ways that reflect our teaching.

Additionally, in our second-grade team, as we consider assessment, we have the following goals and concerns:

1. We want to be able to document individual growth over time. We strive to use assessments that allow us to see learners as individuals and to focus on their individual progress.
2. We work against locking learners into letter or number grades that suggest categories such as low, average, or high. We want to

focus on each child's individual strengths and consider each child's individual potential.

3. We put more emphasis on classroom-based assessments and less on district criterion-referenced or standardized tests. Informal and observational assessments in natural settings give us a more accurate representation of a student's abilities and learning than does a standardized test.

4. We consider where each individual began the school year, the quarter, and even each school day.

5. We consider the prior schooling and background of individual students. This is especially important in bilingual settings. Some children, unfortunately, have not been instructed initially in their native language, even though they should have been. Our assessments should reflect a careful consideration of the learner's educational history.

6. We work together as a team, talking about each child as a whole person before breaking him or her into bits and pieces. In developing a different way of representing on paper what children can do, we have found it valuable to talk first about what the implications are of each item, before plunging into the sometimes tedious task of relating these limiting and limited assignations to an individual.

7. Finally, in assessing children, we must look at what activities have benefited a particular child. If the activities have not been of benefit, they need to be adapted or changed. In evaluating children we must also evaluate ourselves. If we believe that a particular student is not performing to his or her potential, we must look not only at the child but also at the classroom, the curriculum, and ourselves. Have we tried everything? Have we given the student the opportunity to express himself or herself at all times in the manner in which he or she feels most comfortable? What more can we do? We have discovered the values of assessing ourselves as educators on the basis of how we relate to the individual child. We have found that when four people put together all the pieces in a child's school day, we can always think of something new we have not thought of to make an individual schooling experience more successful.

Daily Life in the Second Grade

From this shared philosophy of teaching and assessing, we work together to create a community of learners and to provide opportunities for children's intellectual development, using both their native and second languages to accomplish this. Our second-graders are in two separate homerooms of between 25 and 30 children each. Of the entire population, 85% to 90% are Hispanic, whether they are bilingual or monolingual (in either English or Spanish). Ninety percent of the children receive lunch free or at a reduced fee. In the homerooms, children are grouped heterogeneously according to language, so that approximately half of the children in each room are English readers and half are Spanish readers.

The students' abilities and interest levels are varied. Some come "well prepared" for second grade in terms of previous school experiences, ability to read and write, and mathematics knowledge. Others might be considered "slow learners" by virtue of the fact that they are 8 years old or more and still not reading. Some of the children enter second grade with little or no previous schooling. Many are older than the average second-grader. During the 1989–1990 school year, for example, ten of the children in these two rooms were 9 years old when they entered second grade. Some had been misplaced in English-language kindergartens when they first came to school and had been retained more than once. There is also, as mentioned previously, considerable mobility among the children. During the 1989–1990 school year, for example, Julia lost six students and Beth seven from the beginning-of-the-year class rosters.

Both classrooms have been organized physically to facilitate group work. Desks are arranged in groups of five or six at angles to the chalkboard, which is at the front of each room. There are open floor areas in the front, on the sides, in the center, and at the back of the room. All small-group work with teachers takes place on the floor. In Julia's room there is an elevated platform with pillows in a front corner of the room for reading. Books of various genres are located around the room in tubs. Paper and other work materials are kept on bookshelves located around the edges of the room. The walls are covered with student work. The noise level fluctuates in the rooms, depending on the activity. Usually half of the students are involved in independent work while the remainder are engaged in small-group activities with an instructor. The students are free to work with one another and to help one another at all times. All the materials in the room are available for use at all times.

Children receive reading and writing instruction in their native or stronger language. This means that in the morning, after attendance, lunch count, and opening ceremonies, some of the children change classes. The Spanish-dominant children who work with

Beth and Zulema go to Beth's room, while the English-dominant children or English monolinguals work with Julia and Pam in Julia's room. The same is true for math instruction.

For science and social studies, the children work in their homeroom groups. This is considered instruction in English as a second language, and a great deal of it is carried out through group work, with children using oral and written English in order to investigate a particular topic. In the group activities the children who are fluent in English serve as English-language models for those who are less comfortable with the English language. There is a concerted effort to mix small groups heterogeneously according to language for science and social studies, so that there is at least one fluent bilingual, one English monolingual, and one Spanish-dominant child in each group. The bilingual children thus act as brokers between the English monolinguals and the Spanish monolinguals.

At the beginning of the school year students work on content projects at their assigned tables. As the year progresses, students often choose whom they want to work with based on such factors as respect and admiration or mutual interest in subject matter.

Placement for literacy instruction is usually based on the results of the children's initial language-dominance testing and their literacy instruction the previous year. At school entry, children evaluated as Spanish-dominant by the Idea Proficiency Test (IPT) probably began literacy instruction in Spanish. In the second grade, therefore, Spanish instruction would continue, since in our bilingual program formal transfer to English literacy occurs at the third grade. In contrast, a child initially evaluated as English-dominant would begin literacy instruction in English.

But sometimes we discover children who have been instructed only in their second language for two years, a second language that they use only at school. This may happen because they have transferred from a district without a bilingual program; it may be that there was not room in the bilingual program; or they may have been misplaced initially. Some of these children have very little confidence in their abilities to perform in school. In these cases we may have to make a decision about whether to move a child from one literacy program into the other.

Before we do this, we attend very closely to these students' use of oral and written language. We watch for progress over several weeks. We note whether we have to clarify directions by giving them in Spanish. We also ask the child what language he or she feels comfortable in. If we decide to move a child back into the first language for instruction, we continue to watch carefully for the same things, especially for comfort level and progress.

For example, this fall, one of our children, Leonel, came into our bilingual rooms from a monolingual English first grade. Originally he had tested as more proficient in English than Spanish on the IPT. Yet he came from a home where only Spanish was spoken, and he was having a lot of difficulty with English literacy. After extensive observation and a reevaluation using the IPT (his Spanish had improved and his English had not), we decided to move him into Spanish literacy in December. He has made rapid progress in Spanish. Between December and February his writing has become easily readable because his inventions are based in Spanish orthography. He has broken code and become a reader in Spanish. And his mother is pleased about his move to Spanish because now she can help him at home.

At the beginning of the year, we take time in our homerooms to establish an environment in which all class members feel free to express themselves without embarrassment in either language. In working as a team, some aspects can be more time-consuming and involve more thought. One of these is forming multiple learning communities. One community is the homeroom, one the English-dominant class, one the Spanish-dominant class, and one all of us combined. We accomplish this by exposing ourselves—our own levels of language proficiency and our own educational vulnerabilities. From the first day, the children are mindful of our language diversities, and they accept them. They therefore accept the language differences in one another. We all agree that practice by speaking and listening is the way to become proficient in our second languages, and we also agree to help one another. The English-dominant students from English-only families are the members of the community who have to make special efforts to use Spanish in order to become bilingual, or just familiar with a second language.

Our Instructional Program and Our Ways of Assessing

While there is variation between the two rooms, both teams make use of the following instructional strategies and ways of assessing.

Book sharing/reading aloud.   In both classrooms, children are read aloud to several times a day. Reading aloud is a central feature of each classroom, because we believe that a love for literature will develop if the children are immersed in an environment that is full of good books. The adults share a variety of kinds of literatures, including picture books, chapter books, nonfiction works related to content study, poetry, wordless picture books, and books created by the children themselves in writer's workshop. The adults choose some of the books, and the children also make requests. Favorite books may be reread several times. All the adults read to the children, and frequently guests are invited in to read to the children. Children are encouraged to make personal responses to the books. In addition, adults may use a particular story to generate a discussion about a particular literary element—such as character, conflict, or climax—as exemplified in the book. This kind of discussion serves as a prelude to literature study, described below. After books have been read aloud, they are available in the classroom for children to peruse.

We do not carry out any evaluations of the children during read-aloud time. However, we do find this a good time to make observations of children's behavior. One day, for example, Julia observed Charlotte and wrote:

> Charlotte sits at her desk. Pam reads to the class from *The Witches* (Dahl, 1972). Charlotte takes her sweatshirt from her desk and runs the seams through her mouth. She takes out a pencil, checks the graphite point, sniffs the eraser. She finds another pencil and repeats her inspection. Outwardly, Charlotte appears restless and bored. Since I have known her for over a year now, I am certain she is listening and interested. My previous experience with Charlotte reminds me of how Charlotte lives through chapter books and tells me to ignore outward signs. She is paying attention. I can trust with Charlotte because I have had a previous relationship with her (her mother is our aide, Pam). So, why can't I trust those other students who outwardly seem to be goofing off?

GRAB or DEAR time.   These acronyms stand for Go Read a Book or Drop Everything and Read. During this time children read a book of their choice. The activity is introduced to the children and demonstrated after the first week of school, when various kinds of books have been read to the classes. Adults explain DEAR or GRAB time, noting that everyone will read for the entire time. The adults also model good reading behavior for the class. A timer is set, and everyone reads until the timer rings. Generally the groups begin reading to themselves for a short period of time, perhaps 4 or 5 minutes. As the children become more comfortable with this activity, the time is lengthened gradually to 10 or 15 minutes. To familiarize them with the literature in the room, children may initially be directed to read a certain kind of book on a certain day, for example, fiction on Monday and Wednesday, nonfiction on Tuesday and Thursday, and poetry on Friday. Eventually, however, learners choose any book they want to read.

We evaluate GRAB by writing down the titles of the books the children choose to read. Periodically we discuss interesting patterns in an individual child's choices or in a general classroom trend. We also make note of whether or not the child is paying attention mostly to text. We also make notations regarding choices in fiction, nonfiction, or poetry.

One of the children describes GRAB in this way:

> Do you know want G.R.A.B. stande for. its stande for Go read a book and the teacher sace timeer and the kids get book and thay read for 10 minutes

Literature study. For both English and Spanish reading we use children's literature rather than basal readers. Our classrooms have multiple copies of a variety of titles, and extra money received is often spent on more books. Generally we begin to work in literature study groups about the fourth or fifth week of school, after the children have become accustomed to DEAR and GRAB time, and after they have had experiences responding to literature shared out loud in the class. A literature study usually lasts four or five days. On the day prior to the first day of literature study, the students have examined three or four books and prioritized them according to their interest. We then meet and assign children to literature study groups. Generally children are grouped into literature study groups based on what they would like to read rather than on their reading ability.

The first day of the literature study consists of meeting as a group. Each child receives a numbered copy of the book, and this number is written on the form where we keep track of literature study response. Frequently an adult then reads the book aloud and the children follow along. The session ends with a group commitment to read the book at home with an adult or older sibling and make notes. It is the children's responsibility to reread the book before coming to the literature study group so that they can participate in group response, discussion, and interpretation of the book. The adult

will also be a member of the literature study group and will participate by offering her own impressions of and ideas about the book.

At the end of the first session, students receive a half sheet of
paper with lines on it. There is a place for them to write their name,
the title of the book, and notes for the group, as well as a line for their
parent's signature. (See Figure 5.3.) On the back of each sheet is a
place where they can web the story if they want. Figure 5.3 illustrates a
kind of skeleton web for *The Funny Little Woman* (Mosel, 1972), with
some of the elements of literature (characters, place, plot) outlined.

The second day, students come to literature study with their
books and papers. On our record-keeping sheets, we note whether
students remembered their book and whether they came prepared.
When we have recorded this information, the children read aloud,
volunteering to read the pages they feel comfortable reading. We may
jot down some of the miscues. While we know that the miscues a
child makes while he or she is reading aloud do not give us a
completely clear idea of a child's reading strategies, they do give us
some idea. We also note what the child does when he or she comes to
a trouble word (looks at illustrations, goes back and reads over, skips
the word, substitutes, sounds out, etc.), as well as how many times
the child volunteers to read.

On the third day we are ready to discuss the book. In the first
group session, the children discuss their impressions of the book. In
a subsequent session, the children focus on a certain element of
literature in the book or on a certain kind of response or theme that
came out of the initial discussion. These may include character
study, plot, main idea, the climax, problems or conflicts in the book,
change, lessons learned, the theme of the book, how the book connected to the children's own experiences, the use of illustrations,
and so on. Initially adults may demonstrate the kind of language to
use in discussing literature. As the year progresses the children are
generally able to exchange ideas and analyze elements of literature.
During these response/study sessions, we continue to note on our
forms whether children have come prepared to the study group. We
also note the responses children make to the books (e.g., relating the
books to their own experiences, commenting on what they liked,
discussing the characters, commenting on the resolution of conflict
in the story).

On the day of the final meeting, we go on to self-evaluation. For
this, we use a form consisting of a sheet with statements the students must respond to in terms of their own performance during the
literature study. These include statements about whether students

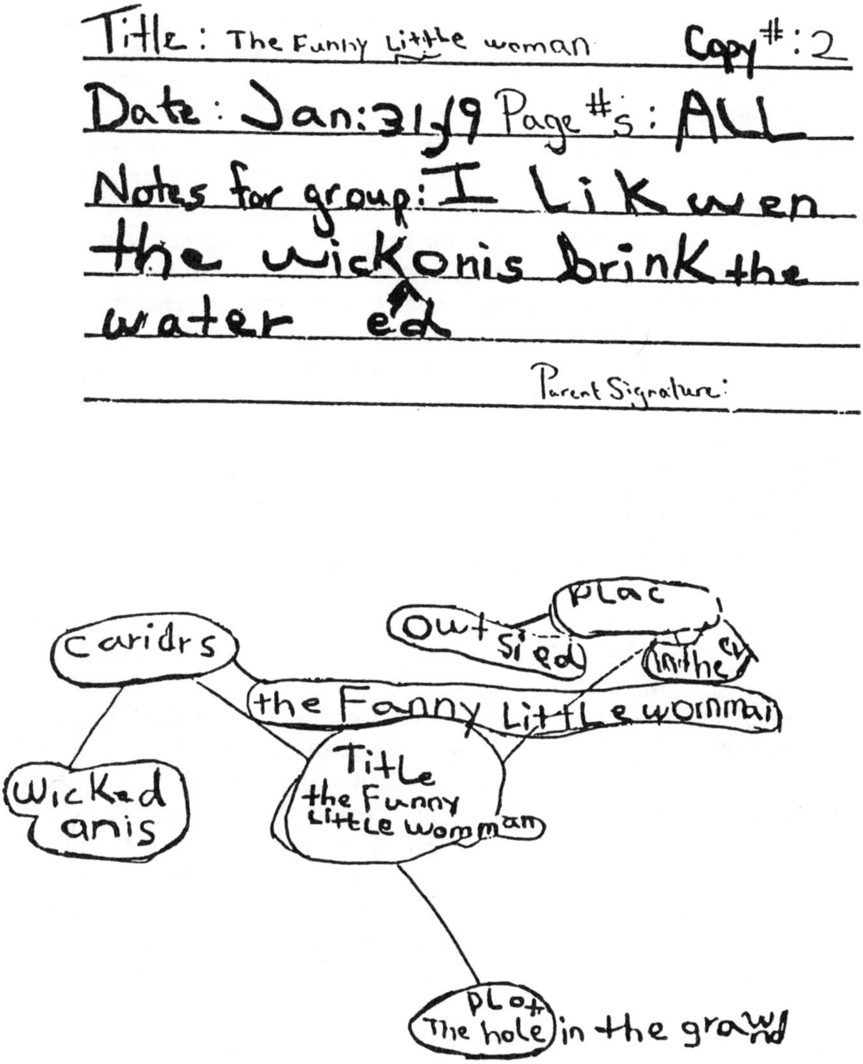

FIGURE 5.3   Individual child's literature study notes and webbing

have done their reading, brought their books to literature circle, shared their opinions and ideas, and listened to the ideas of others. Each student evaluates him- or herself, and then the group has a chance to disagree with the peer's self-evaluation. We operate in a circle format during this time. Someone will read the statement, "I bring my book to literature circle."/"Traigo my libro al círculo de literatura." The learners will have a moment to write down their grades. Then each child in turn shares the mark he or she has assigned him- or herself. We then ask for disagreements. If others in the group disagree, they state their reasons for disagreeing, and the group's grade also is noted by the child. At the bottom of the self-evaluation sheet, there is a chance for the children to respond to the just-completed book, indicating what they liked or did not like.

The practice of self-evaluation takes time to initiate, both because of the children's inexperience with attributing an abstract mark to their own work and because of the notion of disagreeing with a peer's evaluation of his or her own work. When we start this procedure, we have to demonstrate how to talk about our disagreements, and we have to refer to our own notes to make our points. But we have persevered, and this is now an essential part of literature study. It makes all the group members accountable not only for their own performance but also, to a certain extent, for their peers' performance. These records, which we keep on file for the school year, give a picture of a child's development over time. For example, an examination of the literature study group forms accumulated last year reveals much about Hector, a Spanish-speaking child who entered second grade as a nonreader and was involved initially in literature study groups with repetitive, highly predictable books. Early on, Zulema's and Beth's notes document that, even though he could not read himself, he enjoyed having others read to him and he loved to talk about books. By mid-November, when reading orally, Hector was sounding out words on his own in the context of stories. He began to work with children who were reading less predictable material, and he seemed comfortable in these more challenging settings. By January Hector was blending sounds together more easily, and his oral reading was becoming more fluent. He was able to talk about books in terms of his likes and dislikes. He also would read a book so many times that he would memorize parts of it. By February Hector had begun to concentrate on the details and the sequences of books he was reading. He continued to discriminate fiction from nonfiction. In April and May he chose to read longer and more difficult books to challenge himself. He had really developed confidence as a reader.

The forms also serve as a basis for a weekly discussion of the work we have been doing in groups. We share what has happened in the sessions, focusing on improvements noted or changes that need to be made to keep a child or group of children challenged. For example when we (Beth and Zulema) talked about Hector in November, we decided that he needed to be challenged by less predictable/patterned books, and we arranged to have him participate in literature study groups that were reading more difficult stories. We also talk about potential subsequent books and about different techniques to use with children with special needs. These weekly meetings give us up-to-date knowledge of what the children are learning and what they need to learn.

In addition to the forms, sometimes we take notes on or tape-record literature study sessions. This allows for a more in-depth consideration of both the children's responses and our own work as teachers. For example, Julia was working one day with a group that had read *The Tenth Good Thing About Barney* (Viorst, 1971). She had asked them the day before to think about what conflicts they could identify in the book. The discussion went something like this:

JULIA: So, I asked you all to think about the conflicts in this book.
BLANCA: The cat died and the boy is sad.
ALEX: He's supposed to think of ten things but he can't think of ten.
JUAN: Only nine.
JULIA: And how is that conflict resolved?
(*Flipping through pages*)
OLIVIA: Here. Here. When the father is in the yard.
JUAN: (*reading*) "He'll change until he's part of the ground . . ."
NANCY: (*reading*) "And that's a pretty nice job for a cat." That's the tenth good thing.
JULIA: So they resolved the conflict by . . .
YOLANDA: They talked and they thought of it together. The dad said it.
ALEX: Then there's the conflict about Annie and heaven or the ground.
JUAN: Huh?
(*Flipping through the books*)
ALEX: Here (*points to illustration of cat heaven*)
NANCY: (*laughing*) Yea, they were arguing.
BLANCA: The dad comes in and he tells them about how no one know for sure about heaven.

JULIA: So the conflict is resolved by . . .

NANCY: Well it's kind of not because Annie still says, "Heaven."

ALEX: And the boy says, "Ground."

YOLANDA: He was really sad.

ALEX: He was sad, he wouldn't watch TV.

JUAN: He gave his seconds on cookies to Annie.

ALEX: He wouldn't eat chicken or pudding.

MARICELA: When my grandpa died, my mom didn't want to eat very much, she was sad.

JULIA: Yeah, it's sad when someone dies.

NANCY: Barney died. That was a conflict. They resolved it by having a funeral and saying good things.

JULIA: Has everyone here been to a funeral?

(*Nods*)

OLIVIA: A guy gets up and says nice things.

ALEX: People are sad.

MARICELA: They cry.

BLANCA: But they feel better afterwards because they get to hear all the good things and then they can't be so sad because then they can remember other things that aren't sad.

NANCY: People get mad and sad at the same time.

JULIA: I wonder why people get mad?

EVERYONE: Because they died.

JULIA: Does that make sense?

ALEX: Noooo . . .

BLANCA: No, because the person didn't do it on purpose.

NANCY: But sometimes people don't get a chance to say things or goodbye or do something

YOLANDA: Like say some things you wanted to say.

NANCY: Or the last thing you said was bad and you wanted to say something good.

ALEX: You never see the person again—like my kitty . . .

JUAN: But you can remember.

NANCY: That's why the funeral's good.

YOLANDA: Everything dies.

BLANCA: It's part of life.

As Julia reflected on this discussion, she noted:

The kids came prepared to discuss the conflicts—more prepared than I, who had not anticipated the maturity and intensity with which these 7- and 8-year-old proceeded. I had thought of the same conflicts, save one. In my own mind I had determined that there is no resolution for the conflict of death, but these children came to their own conclusions and left me standing still as they raced ahead. This experience caused me to change my view of literature study, to expect more of the children participating in the groups and to have more faith in the children's ability.

Children also keep a literature log to record books they have taken home and read with their parents. Children bring these logs to group during the evaluation portion of the literature circle to ensure that no one falls behind in record-keeping.

Sometime after school resumes after the winter break, we introduce literature journals. We wait until this time because we find that the children are more confident in their writing abilities and have, for the most part, developed a code that we are able to interpret. We also are sure that the students have the basic sense of story and are familiar with the common language we use to talk about story. We use the literature logs as another way for students to express thoughts they have about the story they have read. Some students give only the most basic responses to a particular story orally but write elaborate or revealing responses in their literature journals. We use the journals to ask students to explore one of the themes or questions that kept arising in the discussion.

For example, on one occasion a group of English readers had studied Steig's *Brave Irene* (1986). The following exchange took place between Julia and a student:

QUESTION: Why is Irene a hero or heroine?
RESPONSE: Because she got the dress to the diances. She got the dress back
JULIA'S COMMENT: You're right! She accomplished her mission! Did she have to sacrifice anything? Did she change?
RESPONSE: Dear Ms. Fournier
Yay she sacrifice something. At the starting of the story she was a sweet littil garle. And at the end she was a brave Irene. Becus she sacrifiset a brocun ankle. And geting lost.

Similarly, the following response to *Guillermo Jorge Manuel José* (Fox, 1984) was made:

QUESTION: ¿Por qué la memoria es importante? (Why is a memory important?)
RESPONSE: eso es lo que está en el corazón y es muy valioso
(it's what is in the heart and it is very valuable)

We read the journal entries and record them as we would the group's discussion. We give our reactions by responding in the journals.

We must also mention that not every second-grader comes equally able in the area of language arts. During the first literature studies, we talk frequently, wondering about the learners who struggle aloud, worrying about the meaning they are constructing. For these children, we may (with parental permission) modify the curriculum somewhat. We need to build their confidence by giving them books that always offer a successful experience, such as the highly predictable books from the Wright Books program. So we give these less confident and able readers (as was Hector at the beginning of the school year) choices of books for literature study with less text than those of the other literature study groups. One child describes literature study in this way:

Literature Stude
in literature stude we gave to go back and we had to read the book to the teacher we are reading Mirandy and Brother Wins I think that book is a rele good book for us to read it has same intesed part B—like this book and the people in my gerup to

Journals.   From the first day of school, the children keep personal dialogue journals in which they record events of importance to them. We collect the journals on a daily basis and respond to them. Children may write in either language in their journals, and no overt correction is made of the entries. Standard language use is demonstrated in the adults' responses to the children. Journal writing is the first kind of writing the children do. After that has been established, we add on writer's workshop.

Our earliest assessments of our children's writing come through reading their dialogue journals. After the first week of school, we look carefully at the journals to give us a baseline on the children. We make notes about content, length of entries, invented spelling, conventional spelling, letter formation, punctuation, and capitalization. If we know that a child writing in English comes from a Spanish-language background, we also look to see if there are influences of Spanish orthography on the English. Since we also read the journals daily, we use them to take note of breakthroughs or new features in a child's written language. For example, one day when she was reading Carla's journal, Zulema noticed that for the first time the child was using selected consonants as well as vowels in her writing. This breakthrough signaled to her teachers that she was ready for more direct instruction focusing on sound-symbol relationships in her own writing.

We keep the children's journals on file until the end of the year, so that we can also use them over time to see how the children's writing has developed. Returning to Hector, for example, his journal entries from the beginning of the year make clear that he was struggling both with letter formation and with a consistent utilization of sound-letter correspondences. This made his writing difficult to read, both for himself and for adults. As the year progressed, his use of the alphabetic code became more consistent and he included more of the sounds of the words he was writing. He and the adults began to be able to read his writing. Hector began to carry on conversations about selected topics that lasted several days. He became more communicative in his journal writing.

We have also used some of the children's journal writing to help us figure out appropriate instructional strategies for individual children. Susana, for example, was a child in Julia's and Pam's English language arts group. From the beginning of the year Susana was an enthusiastic participant in journal writing, but the adults could not understand her written code. As a team we discussed what we might do to steer Susana toward a more universal code without turning her off to writing. Initially we would sit together with Susana's (and other children's) journals to figure out their meanings. Then one of us would write back to Susana using standard English. We gradually became more skilled at reading Susana's code, and our demonstrations of standard English assisted her in figuring out the more universal code. However, as she became more invested in journal writing her entries became longer and more complicated, and once again hard for us to interpret. If we asked Susana the next day what she had written, she often had a hard time remembering everything she had meant to say, which was embarrassing for her. This led us to begin having Susana read to us what she had written immediately after writing. This she could do.

Journal writing means this to one of the children:

Journals is fun to rith in. And when we do journals we rith
tell the bell ring. And the teacher rith back.

Writer's workshop. We generally begin writer's workshop
around the middle of October by introducing the idea of telling
stories. Beth, for example, has asked children to bring in stories
from home, stories that someone else has told them or written down,
and to recount them for the class, providing time for the listeners to
ask questions and make responses. After this, children begin to
identify topics for their own stories, talk with a partner about their
ideas, and write these topics down in their writing folders.

Julia has started by telling her own stories and then encouraging the children to ask questions, tell what they liked and did not
like, and so on. She then asks the children's advice about which
story to write down, which she does to demonstrate this part of
writer's workshop. By the time the children have seen her story in
written form, most are eager to write their own. These activities lead
logically into partner talk, where children tell stories to each other
and ask questions. After a few days of that, they begin writing stories
down. Drafting of stories leads to sharing, revising and editing,
conferencing with the teacher, and rewriting and publishing selected pieces. Published works are celebrated as children read them
aloud to their classmates during La Silla del Autor/Author's Chair.
Published books are displayed prominently in the rooms and made
available for reading. Usually the children's topics come from their
own personal experiences, but often, as the year progresses, the
students venture into fiction. As they begin to feel more comfortable
with writing, some even move into chapter books. Once writer's
workshop has been established, it becomes a major part of each day
in both English and Spanish.

On a daily basis, we adults work with children on their writing.
We conference with children, both about the contents and about the
form of what they are producing. We also attend closely to what the
children are producing, so that we are able to present minilessons
on specific aspects of writing as needed. If, for example, many of the
children are not using periods in their writing, we may present a
minilesson on periods at the start of the daily writing time. The
reverse may also be true. If several of the children are using periods,
we may comment on this in order to demonstrate for the group at
large what some children are doing. As the year progresses, certain
children are identified as expert in some particular area (for example, spelling or punctuation), and others often consult them. During

individual and group conferencing, the children assist one another in using what they have been taught.

While we do spend some time with whole-group lessons on a specific aspect of writing, most of our direct teaching takes place in small-group or individual conferences, in peer discussions, or when a student reads a draft of a story to the class and the class members offer suggestions or ask questions about the piece. Children keep their work-in-progress in writing folders, and we save their drafts in permanent files. We keep track of the suggestions and ideas that are generated in individual and group conferences by recording them on conference/editing forms. These provide information about each child's accomplishments and challenges. For example, in reviewing Lorena's form we can see that (1) she has been asked to add some information about who the story characters visited and why they ran to the bathroom; (2) she has checked to see if she has capital letters and periods in the edited draft of her story; (3) her story was strong in that she used a lot of details; (4) her story had a clear sequence and ending; (5) her spelling was accurate; and (6) she had given her story a title. When they conclude work on a piece, children also use a self-evaluation checklist, which includes a final examination of their work and a requirement that another child read and comment on the piece.

Working with children individually and in small groups allows us to assess children's growth. It also provides us with information that influences instructional modifications to meet individual children's needs.

For example, as with her journal writing, Susana's writing was difficult to read early on in writer's workshop. Our assessment resulted in a decision to work with Susana in a special way during writer's workshop. When Susana finished a draft, she would bring it to one of us for a conference. She would read her piece, and we would transcribe as she read on a separate piece of paper. In this way, Susana retained artistic control and ownership, yet we understood what ideas and elements she was working with. By writing Susana's stories in standard English, we provided her with the opportunity to read and reread familiar text while at the same time validating her writing and her experiences. By December and January we were able to read most of Susana's written work without interpretation from her; therefore we moved away from transcribing and toward the more standard writer's workshop strategies we employ with the majority of the second-graders.

As mentioned earlier, we save all the drafts of the children's stories for our own records. These pages and our written comments and observations allow us to document each child's progress over the course of the year. They give us an appreciation for what learners can accomplish. A careful look at Hector's work, for example, reveals a child who made tremendous strides. Early in the year, Hector's code was difficult to read because so many of the letters were missing. He was also a reluctant writer, one who seemed to lack self-confidence. As he became more accustomed to the class, however, he began to take risks in his writing and to write about his own life experiences. He published his first book at the end of November, which gave him a sense of authorship. Since he was one of the first children published, the other children viewed him as an accomplished writer. When other children were working on their books, they would often seek out Hector for advice about the authoring process. Hector benefited from the attention to his expert abilities and from others' interest in his stories. Over time, he developed a sense of audience. He did not want to publish all of his work, as many children do. He published some books just for himself and some books solely for the class. By the end of the year, he had assumed the role of co-author and illustrator for other students' books. Reflecting on Hector, Beth commented:

> Hector taught me a lot about the virtues of trust and patience. I learned to trust the process of learning, rather than always looking ahead to the product. Although Hector is an individual case, he reminds me to have the patience to allow children to unfold when they feel safe enough to begin to take risks. Hector has reinforced my belief in the individual gifts that each child has to offer.

One child explains writer's workshop this way:

> We do Writer's Workshop after journals. What we do is this . . . we talk to somebody about something that happened to us or a story we made up in our mide. Then we get some paper and write our story down. Next we get what we call a coversheet. We put it on top of our papers and staple it. Now you put it in the blue box. The next day Ms. Fournier will call you to the back and conferins with you, She will tell you that you can read it to the class. After you read it people will ask you questions or coments that will help you make the story better. The next day you write your story again. After your finished writ-

ing your story again you put a cover on it. Then read it to the class again. Now we're all done with your story. The End.

Independent jobs and spelling time. Because adults are frequently working with small groups of children in literature study or writing conferencing, the others must work on their own. They accomplish this through such independent activities as jobs and spelling time. Jobs are usually listed on the board in order or importance or urgency, meaning jobs with deadlines will be listed first and optional jobs will be listed last. Some jobs are daily jobs whose importance is understood by all. Examples of jobs may be pen-pal letters (last year correspondence was going on with people from Wales, Australia, and Japan), a page to be a part of a class book, or a pull-up (opposite of a put-down) to be written for a classmate. An optional job may be exploring a map of Paris and counting the number of hospitals there.

Since spelling receives a grade on the report card, we spend some time on it every day. Generally four to eight words (depending on the specific children) for spelling come from frequently misspelled words in the learners' journals, words they are using in writer's workshop, or words in the books the children have been reading for literature study. Children are grouped heterogeneously (not by ability) for spelling, so that not everyone is working on the same spelling words. Each group is on a five-day schedule of activities focused on the spelling words, with a test on the fifth day. Each day the children do one spelling activity, such as putting the spelling words in alphabetical order, making sentences with their words, making flash cards, writing their words using stencils, and so on. On the day of the test the children's work is to study their words with someone in their group.

In terms of assessment, we record both daily performance of their work and their test results. We try to deemphasize the importance of the tests, and we try to emphasize children's approximations to standard spelling. Thus, if a word is misspelled we may point out that only one letter was left out. We continually evaluate whether the number of words is appropriate. If we determine that we are setting certain children up to fail by assigning the normal number of words, we reduce the number or discuss with parents at conference the possibility of doing so. Similarly, if children are not being challenged, we may increase the number of words. Through writer's workshop we try to give the students spelling strategies that they can use for life. We talk about what they might do if they do not know how to spell a word, for example, skip the word, use another word, use something in the room to find the spelling, ask a good speller, or write the word three times and circle the spelling that looks the best.

Problems.   Problems is the time of the day when the children have the opportunity to discuss any problem they have been experiencing. During this time they talk to the person they have had the problem with, and they try to agree on a consequence or a solution. For example, if Irma calls Dora a bad name, Irma must say five nice things about Dora in front of the class. In the beginning of the year this takes a lot of demonstrating, but by the end of the year the children are working privately to solve their problems. Children work out problems in whatever language they want, and if they need an interpreter, they ask for one.

Mathematics instruction.   Math sessions are taught in the children's dominant language, using a variety of different materials and strategies. We begin each afternoon math session with Mad Minute, a one-minute timed paper with 30 math problems on each sheet. When a student can answer all 30 problems correctly in one minute, he or she moves on to the next level. Immediately after the Mad Minute, we check each student's paper and record the number of problems each student completed correctly. The children really do not compete against one another, only against themselves. They love this activity, and they share their progress with one another.

Another ritual in math involves the use of the calendar. We do the calendar in a manner we learned in a *Mathematics Their Way* (Barrata-Lorton, 1976) workshop. In carrying out this activity, we use odd and even numbers, counting by 2s and 5s, rote counting, patterning, days of the week, ordinal numbers, birthdays, and numbers of lost teeth. The amount of language that this activity requires is also extensive. At the beginnng of the year we demonstrate the routine. Gradually the children take over the activity, taking turns assuming the teacher role. We evaluate informally by observing that everyone participates, both in the teacher and student roles.

The remainder of the math time is spent on the math skills that the school district and the state of Arizona deem appropriate for second grade (for example, estimating, measuring, finding patterns, sequencing, place value, time, money, word problems, and number sequence). Given an option, we have elected to purchase only the practice books from the district-adopted math program. We use the practice book as a guide for what we could be studying. A major component of our math programs is *Mathematics Their Way*, which is a hands-on approach to allowing children to experience and experiment with basic mathematics concepts. *Mathematics Their Way* involves children, in pairs or small groups, working on problems that call for thinking mathematically rather than simply memorizing isolated facts.

During these worktimes we ask students to assess themselves, evaluating both their own participation in activities and how they work together. We also move among the children as they work on *Mathematics Their Way* activities, observing and noting how children are doing, making inquiries about how they are going about the activities, and assisting those who need help. We may also use some chapter tests when we feel that the students have received instruction in the concepts the district-adopted text has targeted.

A child views *Mathematics Their Way* like this:

> When we do Math their Way it means we do math that doesn't look like math But it really is math It just looks like a bunsch of games They call it Math their way because smaller kidns think its hard for them to learn regular math the teachers can trick them to do math and the kids won't know they are really doing math they think its just a regular fun game.

Science and social studies thematic units. For science and social studies, the children regroup into homerooms. This is a time when English-language acquisition is facilitated through content-area study (although the children's native language may also be used to assure comprehension of content and child participation). Science and social studies are carried on, from 40 minutes to an hour a day, through the use of thematic units and expert projects. Children choose some of the units of study by selecting topics and issues of interest and concern to them. The units involve hands-on experiences with specific content. Through the use of such strategies as brainstorming, children reflect on what they already know about a topic and generate questions that they would like to explore. Then, working in small groups, children seek answers to their questions, recording the results of their research and organizing information to be shared with others. At the end of each unit of study, each small group shares information and experiences with the large group. Language learning occurs throughout the process of working in small groups.

In the spring of 1990, for example, one of the units of study was the desert. After the children had determined what they already knew and what they wanted to know, each small group researched a specific desert plant and animal. In some groups, the English reader in each group would read the material, the bilingual child would translate for the Spanish-dominant child, and another bilingual child would transcribe the information. Then each group decided how it would contribute to a class mural on the desert. Each group made its own decision and created something for the mural. One particular pair, Ricardo and Eric, consisted of a Spanish-dominant and an English-monolingual child. Although these two never socialized, they respected each other as learners, and they chose to work together to study the jackrabbit and to describe its environment both above and below ground. They made a diagram of its environment by laying a box on its side and illustrating the jackrabbit's tunnel with tubing and play dough. Then Ricardo wrote a description of the environment in both Spanish and English.

Because so much of the work on thematic units is done in small groups, we believe that it is important to assess how children are working together. To do this, we ask the members of each group to evaluate themselves on whether they contributed to the group, whether they stayed on-task while in the group, whether they listened to others in the group, and whether they assisted in the group project. Group members may evaluate their performance in these categories as unsatisfactory, satisfactory, good, or excellent, and we write down how they have evaluated themselves. After each group member has evaluated him- or herself, we ask the other members of the group if they agree with each member's self-evaluation. If the teachers agree or disagree with the individual's or group's evaluations, we indicate that, also. In addition to this process evaluation, we have the product evaluation of the expert project or report, and that work receives a grade.

Because our science/social studies work is also officially our English as a second language (ESL) time, we do make concerted efforts to pay attention to the children's efforts to understand and use English, so that we can share this information among ourselves, with parents at conference time, and with other personnel at the school. We think that this is particularly important, because the Idea Proficiency Test, used to evaluate ESL ability, does not accurately represent what children can do in English. In our informal observations, we become aware of individual children's growth in English. Susana, for example, was a Spanish-dominant child who had not been instructed in Spanish when she entered school, because there was no bilingual program in the school where she had gone to kindergarten and no space in the bilingual program when she had come into the Creighton district for first grade. At the beginning of the year she was reluctant to use English; she chose to work with children who were bilingual so that she would have Spanish translations handy. Early on in the year she would observe closely whatever was happening in content study, but she would never make a contribution in small-group or whole-class discussion. She would not make eye contact with adults. After about a month Susana began to make eye contact, but she still refused to talk. Her first verbalizations in English took the form of repeating responses or comments that had been made by another student.

As a team we talked about this and considered the possibility that Susana might be thinking so hard about her response that she might not even realize that she was repeating another child's response. Another possibility we explored was that Susana was waiting until someone had said what she was thinking to verbalize her response. So perhaps she used others to determine whether or not the words she wanted to use were correct English. We were convinced that Susana was making strides in developing confidence as an English speaker. By mid-October Susana's hand was always the first one up. Sometimes she would shake her head, but more frequently than not she would articulate her idea. She no longer relied on hearing other English responses first. She was sure of her place in the classroom community and not afraid to take the risk of speaking her second language in front of the group. Susana's desire to be heard overshadowed her fears of not being completely accurate in English. Overcoming her concern for correctness, Susana took on more of a leadership role in content studies.

Conclusions

In this chapter we have shared some of the ways we work with our children and how we observe and document their learning. While we have focused on what we do, a major area of concern for us is the children's self-evaluations. We want children to be involved in thinking both about what they have learned and their participation in the learning of others. A major goal for us is that children begin to take responsibility for their own learning and contribute to the learning of others. This is central to our community of learners.

In this chapter, too, we have reflected in some depth on our own work. But we do not work in isolation. Rather we teach and learn within a community of individuals who support us in our efforts. It seems appropriate to conclude our chapter by acknowledging that community. While we can trace philosophies of teaching partly to reading and listening to influential leaders in our field (see Appendix for a partial list of titles referred to and shared by Machan teachers), we must attribute much of our development as teachers of children to the environment at Machan created by Lynn Davey and Kelly Draper. These two individuals have worked together to assemble a staff of energetic and innovative people dedicated to the children and families of the community of Machan School.

Our teaching staff is made up of many teachers who are products of Arizona State University's post-baccalaureate program, and they have brought their energy and creativity—and the energies of ASU faculty such as Ralph Peterson, Maryann Eeds, Carole Edelsky, Irene Serna, and Sarah Hudelson, to name a few—into our community. Many of the "postbac" teachers did their student teaching with some of the metropolitan Phoenix whole-language community's finest teachers, Chris Boyd, Diana Doyle, Mary Glover, and Karen Smith.

There are teachers at Machan who are artists and musicians. They have enriched the school with their ideas. Most of us at Machan are involved in some kind of cross-grade buddy program. We have special-interest groups both in and out of school. Across grade levels we share insights into children. We enjoy talking about our students and what they are doing in other rooms. What children accomplish over time is really interesting to us. We share one anothers' frustrations and celebrate one anothers' successes.

Many experts have pointed out that learning is social. As educators we are involved in the learning process. We often attend seminars, conferences, and workshops together. Sometimes our exchanges of information come across a podium at a formal meeting, but more often they occur over a cup of coffee. More important than the information itself, however, is the freedom to practice our philosophy and the encouragement we receive from those around us. There is an energy at Machan that supports the program we are struggling with, and colleagues such as Cecilia Espinosa, Karen Moore, Mary Blask, Nancy Keahon, Cherry Dellios, Sandy Hilligass,

Susan Timmer, Lori Elander, Mark Routhier, and Tom Tracy contribute in a major way to that energy.

Finally, there are the children and parents at Machan, who inspire us in our work. In spite of the transiency at the school, there is a core group of families who have stayed in the neighborhood, and brothers, sisters, and cousins have come through the bilingual program. By the time younger family members come to our second-grade rooms, they have heard a lot about us from their older relations. There is already a personal connection among the children. They know that we care about them and their families as people, and that we will listen and respond to them in a human-to-human way. So we are kind of like a family, with a special kind of intimacy and caring. Naturally it is not a family without problems. Our children have tremendous needs. In general they are not worried about acquiring a certain kind of Barbie doll. Many of them do not have food on the table. So there is a sense of urgency and importance to our teaching. But in addition to their needs there are also a richness of culture and an intellectual potential and eagerness to learn that motivate us. We want to be at school. We need the children as much as they need us. We do not want to miss out on the learning. All of us are richer for the experiences we share, for the teaching and learning all of us participate in in our community.

References

Barrata–Lorton, M. (1976). *Mathematics their way: An activity–centered program for early childhood education.* Menlo Park, CA: Addison-Wesley.

Calkins, L. (1983). *Lessons from a child.* Portsmouth, NH: Heinemann.

Calkins, L. (1986). *The art of teaching writing.* Portsmouth, NH: Heinemann.

Carini, P. (1979). *The art of seeing and the visibility of the person.* Grand Forks: University of North Dakota.

Carini, P. (1986). *Another way of looking at education and evaluation.* North Bennington, VT: Prospect Archive and Center for Education and Research.

Dahl, R. (1972). *The witches.* New York: Puffin Penguin.

Fox, M. (1984). *Guillermo Jorge Manuel José.* Caracas: Ediciones Ekare-Banco del Libro.

Mosel, A. (1972). *The funny little woman.* New York: Dutton.

Steig, W. (1986). *Brave Irene.* New York: Farrar, Straus & Giroux.

Viorst, J. (1971). *The tenth good thing about Barney.* New York: MacMillan.

Appendix

Atwell, N. (1987). *In the middle.* Portsmouth, NH: Heinemann.

Calkins, L. (1983). *Lessons from a child.* Portsmouth, NH: Heinemann.

Calkins, L. (1986). *The art of teaching writing.* Portsmouth, NH: Heinemann.

Clay, M. M. (1975). *What did I write?* Portsmouth, NH: Heinemann.

Edelsky, C. (1986). *Writing in a bilingual program: Habia una vez.* Norwood, NJ: Ablex.

Goodman, K. (1986). *What's whole in whole language.* Portsmouth, NH: Heinemann.

Goodman, K. S., Goodman, Y. M., & Wood, W. M. (Eds.). (1989). *The whole language evaluation book.* Portsmouth, NH: Heinemann.

Graves, D. H. (1983). *Writing: Teachers and children at work.* Portsmouth, NH: Heinemann.

Rigg, P., & Allen, V. (Eds.). (1989). *When they don't all speak English.* Urbana, IL: National Council of Teachers of English.

Short, K. G., & Mitchell, K. P. (Eds.). (1990). *Talking about books.* Portsmouth, NH: Heinemann.

Smith, F. (1986). *Insult to intelligence.* New York: Arbor House.

6

Informal Assessment in Second Grade

A Foxfire Story

JANET MOBLEY
SHARON T. TEETS

The core principles in this chapter are those of Foxfire, a program that originated in rural Georgia and is now nationally known. For both authors, working in Tennessee, it has represented a new direction in their careers. They recount the process of shifting directions, Janet toward more student-centered practice and Sharon toward "older" children in public schools.

A Developmentalist Meets Foxfire: *Sharon's Voice*

Erik Erikson theorizes that the task of midlife is to choose between generativity versus stagnation, to contribute to something larger than one's own personal development (Erikson, 1963). While most psychologists use Erikson's theory to explain personal rather than professional development, I suspect that the stage applies to career development as well. At midcareer some of us struggle for new meaning in our work, perhaps taking a new direction or reflecting on our past experiences and formulating a statement about what one's professional life means, either in general or in regard to a particular issue. I suspect that this happens with many people, and we might see the results of each person's struggle in the form of books or articles. However, we see little of the struggle itself—the in-process grappling with the issues that the person faced.

This chapter is different. This *is* the in-process thoughts of a classroom teacher and a college faculty member who have chosen paths toward generativity. As we struggled with what to write, we found ourselves continually assured with what goes on in the class-room—it "felt" right. But as we tried to put in writing what we had done together, it all seemed so ordinary. It seemed like common sense. On the other hand, when we hear the questions teachers ask about assessment and evaluation and the fears they express about their own evaluations as teachers, we think that we do have something to share.

When confronted with the task of describing how assessment, documentation, and evaluation occur in the classroom, we found ourselves providing isolated examples of various strategies, but the examples always led to a discussion of a rationale for the strategy, which in turn led to sharing our own past training and emerging philosophies. So we need to share a little bit about our backgrounds so that the rest of this chapter will make more sense.

An Integrated Approach to Assessment and How It Came to Be

I sometimes consider myself a "womb-to-tomb" teacher. By that I mean that I have worked in both public and private settings as a teacher of infants and toddlers; preschool children; elementary, junior high, and high school students; undergraduate and graduate students, and other retooling adults in their thirties through their sixties. I also teach human development courses—stages of development from prenatal through death. However, I consider my primary area of expertise to be working with young children between birth and 8 years of age. I was trained from a child development perspective. Over the years, I have come to regard that perspective as unique, as one that differs from the traditional educational perspective and that happens to be compatible with the views of children, learning, and teaching expressed in the previous chapters. Therefore the focus of planning educational experiences for groups of young children, including assessment and evaluation, is to meet the individual developmental needs of each child, in an integrated way, within the context of his or her environments in school or at home.

The theories of Jean Piaget (1955) and Erik Erikson (1963) guide the teacher in making decisions about what is important about each child's development. Piaget theorizes that educational experiences for young children in the sensorimotor and preoperational, and to a certain extent the concrete operational, stages should be based in concrete, action-oriented activities. Piaget also states that individuals move from stage to stage through active involvement with concrete materials, through social interactions with peers and adults, through maturity, and through the internal balancing of assimilation and accommodation. Stated simply, Piaget would believe that young children "learn by doing" with their peers and real materials, with observant adults who add language to help children extract the maximum meaning from each experience. Educators who use Piaget as a guide see the child as an intellectually active individual who is motivated to seek out challenging activities in order to move to more abstract levels of thinking.

Erikson (1963), on the other hand, provides the social-emotional balance. Erikson sees the young child as moving through stages as well, with a crisis to be resolved at each stage. From infancy through early childhood, the child needs to resolve the crises of trust versus mistrust, autonomy versus shame and doubt, and initiative versus guilt, as well as begin to tackle industry versus inferiority. Teachers who use this stage theory as a guide will manage the environment, including the assessment and evaluation process, in a way as to make sure that children do become confident, autonomous, and industrious individuals.

Developmentalists recognize that many factors contribute to variations in children's current behavior and overall development. Maslow's hierarchy of needs (1970)—in which he proposes that individual physiological, safety, love, self-esteem, and self-actualization needs must be met, in that order, at any given point in time—is integrated into an understanding of a child's present behavior and overall development. For example, a teacher of young children would not evaluate a child at a time when he or she knew the child was tired, hungry, or suffering from some emotional distress.

In addition to the hierarchy of needs, developmentalists also recognize that there are many other influences upon children's development. Bronfenbrenner (1979) emphasizes reciprocity in relationships as a contributor to overall human development, as well as the influence of the "ecological" settings of the individual—whether it be the home, the school, the relationships within each immediate environment, the community, or the culture at large.

The basis, then, for planning experiences is rooted not only in a general knowledge of developmental principles but also in the knowledge of how children of a given age or developmental level progress normally, within the context of each child's setting. Within a given classroom of individual children, experiences are planned to meet the general needs of children of a given age, but beyond that, observations of individual children's needs are made before selecting activities that can meet the varied needs of the children in the group. For example, a teacher might observe that some children need considerable work with fine-motor skills, that a number of children seem to have some tension about them that needs ventilating, and that a few children seem to be exceptionally creative and need additional open activities that will provide a vehicle for the creativity; the teacher might then select modeling dough and/or clay as the activity that accommodates the varying needs of the children. That is a condensed version of how a child development person, in early childhood education, goes about the planning process. The schema for such a planning process, adapted from one used by the staff at the University of Texas at Austin Child Development Laboratory, is shown in Figure 6.1.

Beginning to Link the Assessment Approach to Practitioners in Public Schools

For a number of years, I implemented the planning process for children as the director of the child development laboratory school within the Department of Home Economics at Carson-Newman College. It is a small program, so I frequently taught in the group with the children in addition to handling administrative and parent-involvement issues. I also taught a variety of courses in child development, family relationships, and early childhood education for undergraduate students. Occasionally I taught graduate courses in the Education Division. And I have spent several years working on various state curriculum projects, conducting workshops for teachers in the public schools.

Late one December, in the midst of a sabbatical year, the chair of the Division of Education asked me if I would be interested in moving to that division, for the purpose of heading up a new program at the college—the Foxfire Teacher Network. This was the first time I realized Foxfire had teacher networks. Having grown up in the heart of Appalachia, I had religiously bought those books for my father as perfect Christmas gifts. My parents not only could remember many of the Appalachian traditions that the books documented; they were still practicing some of those "traditions." The books validated a lifetime of hard work. But back to the networks: What was it that they were supposed to do? The division chair said that perhaps I should read *Sometimes a Shining Moment* by Eliot Wigginton (1986), the high school English teacher who had, with his students, published the Foxfire books with which I was so familiar.

I read. The book is divided into three parts, with the first being a personal history of how the Foxfire approach to teaching came into being. At one point in the book, I thought, "This is ridiculous—I am

FIGURE 6.1 Planning process

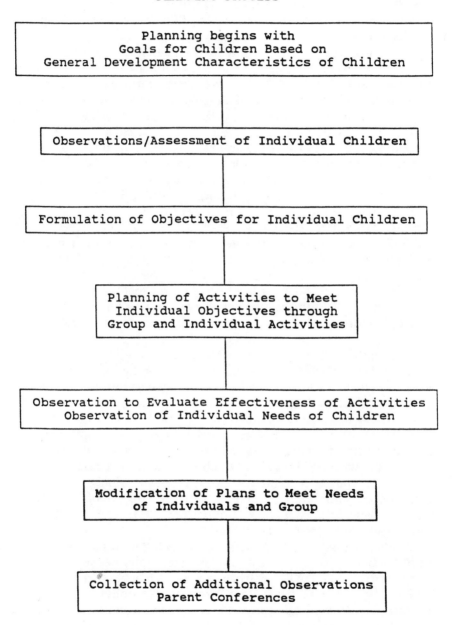

PLANNING PROCESS

Planning begins with
Goals for Children Based on
General Development Characteristics of Children

Observations/Assessment of Individual Children

Formulation of Objectives for Individual Children

Planning of Activities to Meet
Individual Objectives through
Group and Individual Activities

Observation to Evaluate Effectiveness of Activities
Observation of Individual Needs of Children

Modification of Plans to Meet Needs
of Individuals and Group

Collection of Additional Observations
Parent Conferences

not a high school English teacher, and I have not been a teacher employed by the public schools for some time now, and I don't see why the division chair could possibly think that I could do this job." Then I read on, and I read about how Eliot Wigginton, during his first year of teaching, failed on many counts.

But I also read about what he learned when he spent individual time with some of the "worst" students in his classes, and I realized that the Foxfire approach, as it has evolved, works with adolescents because it is an approach that is developmentally appropriate. If one draws implications from Piaget's (1955) stage for adolescence, formal operations, one sees that the child is now capable of abstract reasoning and hypothetical thinking. The child should be given opportunities to engage in problem solving. Erikson (1963) suggests that it is during the adolescent period that children develop a sense of identity—as students engage in meaningful work, linked to others in their communities, they begin to formulate a sense of who they are. At the heart of the Foxfire approach is a genuine respect for young people's ability to engage in responsible decision making, within the context of a safe environment, guided by a skillful teacher. Students have the opportunity to form hypotheses, test them out, and formulate new ones for the ones that did not work.

I had finally found an approach, used in a public school, that I could support. One of the frustrating things about working with preschool children has been to talk with their parents *after* the children have experienced public schools. While many do quite well, I am haunted by the stories from parents about children who left the child development lab as competent youngsters but are now experiencing failure in the public school setting. I have always wondered what would have been the outcome if these children had been allowed to continue to encounter developmentally appropriate experiences, rather than being required to fit into a rigid curriculum in classrooms with large numbers of children and inadequate staff. In the Foxfire approach, I could see that developmentally appropriate experiences *could be* provided, within the context of any public school classroom, given the willingness of the teacher and the administration.

So, yes, I made the leap back into working with teachers in the public school setting once again. We, like ten other networks around the country, offer Foxfire courses for K–12 teachers in all subject areas. The teachers from East Tennessee enroll in an intense summer seminar on campus at Carson-Newman, and then they are provided with support throughout the year as they try to implement the approach in their classrooms. Teachers meet together regularly and visit one anothers' classrooms, as time and budgets permit. Ongoing professional development activities are provided to teachers as they identify their needs and interests regarding additional training. Finally, teachers provide the leadership for the networks—the goal of the entire Foxfire process is to enable teachers and children to develop skills for living democratically in their classrooms and society. If teachers are not empowered to take leadership for their own growth, the approach would be hollow.

Although teachers are offered support, guidance, and leadership opportunities, some simply take the course, try out a few ideas, and then go back to business as usual. Some teachers change their teaching, indeed their whole lives entirely, frequently reporting, "This has changed me forever—I'll never teach the same way again!" For other teachers, the approach so naturally complements what they have already been doing that they become resources for new or struggling teachers.

Janet Mobley was one of those for whom this approach just clicked! She was fortunate to have a principal whose philosophy on staff innovation is, "I'd rather have them try anything than do nothing—at least I know they're thinking!" He was thrilled with Janet's initiative in writing grant proposals with her children to support their activities in their classroom, and he offered to help in any way possible. Each time I entered her classroom, located in a small rural community in East Tennessee, she and the children beamed with enthusiasm as they discussed their work. It was such a delight to see second-graders rush to grab my hand to guide me to see their latest brainstorming list of writing topics or tell me how they were budgeting their money for a current project. What a contrast to the quiet classrooms where every head is bowed penitentially, laboring over endless worksheets that look the same every day of the year.

Foxfire as a Reflective Model
for Assessment: *Janet's Voice*

I have been teaching in elementary school for 15 years. Although I have always been interested in each child in my classroom, I would say that I have been more teacher-directed and subject-centered than child-centered throughout the years.

I teach 24 second-graders, mostly from low income Caucasian families, in a small rural school. Even though we have been emphasizing the basic skills during the last five years, we have not been afraid to try out new programs. I am like most teachers: I have always been eager to try new ideas. I try out many things to see how they work, and I keep the things that seem to be consistent with my basic philosophy of teaching. I want children to show growth from the beginning of the year to the end, and I want them to enjoy the process. I want them to see school and learning as pleasant experiences, because I think the development of positive attitudes during the early childhood years is what is most important for children in our school.

The Foxfire approach was consistent with my own ideas, but I had never thought about involving students in evaluation. As I started to share the learning objectives with students, I gradually began to be more child-centered in general. In my most recent graduate work, I have also begun to try to analyze how the Foxfire approach contributes to the developmental stages of Erikson (1963) and Piaget (1955). I now see that the core practices of the Foxfire approach (Wigginton, 1990) do contribute to children's overall development. Perhaps a brief history and description of the core practices would provide a better understanding of how assessment, documentation, and evaluation fit into the Foxfire approach.

History of the Development of the Core Practices

When Eliot Wigginton decided in October of his first year of teaching that the standard approach to teaching English was not working, the students and he decided to create a magazine that they called *Foxfire*. Foxfire is the name of a lichen that grows on rotting wood in the southern Appalachians and glows in the dark; it seems an appropriate word for describing the difference in the way students had performed in the standard English approach, as opposed to their involvement in the magazine format for the course.

The first magazine was to be filled with student work, much like any student literary magazine, and also featured pieces that the students had been able to get authors to contribute. When the students began discussing who would buy the magazine, some of the local students suggested that if it were to sell locally, then there should be something of local interest in the magazine. Wigginton's students collected superstitions from community folks to publish in the magazine. When the first issue sold, general reaction was that the superstitions and local stories were great, but "whose idea was it to put in that haiku poetry stuff?" The format had been set for the successful magazine.

When teachers began to ask Wigginton to help them generate the same kind of interest in English as his magazine students apparently had, Wigginton began to conduct workshops and courses on cultural journalism. Magazine projects sprang up around the country. But in a few years, it was apparent that some students had no more interest in the magazine projects than they had in the traditional English assignments. Why was that happening? Was it just something magic that Wig had that no one else could reproduce? Wigginton began to look at the way other English teachers developed their magazine projects, and he began to look at his own work, trying to figure out essential differences. From this process, the core practices evolved.

The core practices, eloquently stated by Eliot Wigginton (1990), appear in a number of Foxfire publications; these core practices are examined regularly and reconstructed as teachers around the country try the approach in their diverse settings. A shortened summary of the existing practices follows:

1. Activities are selected based on student interest.
2. Learning experiences are characterized by active student involvement in the planning, implementation, and evaluation process.
3. Teachers serve as collaborators or leaders in the learning process, rather than as bosses.
4. The community is viewed as an important resource for learning and as a way to connect what is learned in the school setting with the world outside of school.
5. Each person in the classroom is viewed as a person who contributes; there is an emphasis on teamwork and peer teaching.
6. An audience for student work beyond the classroom is taken into consideration in the construction of learning activities.
7. Aesthetic experiences are viewed as being the most powerful experiences a student can have.
8. Students are encouraged to reflect upon their learning experiences, extracting from them the meaning of each experience, in order to plan more effectively for future experiences.
9. The academic integrity of student work is a constant concern; both meeting state-mandated objectives and engaging in intellectually challenging work are considered to be important parts of the process.

10. Ongoing evaluation of experiences is an essential part of the process; student involvement in the selection and implementation of evaluation strategies is significant.
11. Finally, each set of experiences should lead to another set of experiences that will challenge the learner further. Asking "What next?" is an important part of the process of becoming lifelong learners (Wigginton, 1990).

Although each teacher and class use the approach in their own ways, a typical pattern is to do some preliminary reflecting upon past or favorite learning experiences in order to determine what makes a good learning experience. Then children are shown the state-mandated curricular skills and objectives for their particular grade level and subject-matter areas. Each teacher makes the decision about how many or which objectives are examined first, depending upon his or her preferred way of tackling the first learning experiences. Children and teachers brainstorm about why they need to develop those skills, concentrating on where these skills are used in the real world. They then generate ideas about how to meet the objectives through a real-world experience, incorporating the children's ideas about what makes learning experiences meaningful. At every step of the way, when the approach works well, students and teachers are involved in designing ways to meet objectives, including ways to evaluate individual and group progress.

Probably the greatest difficulty teachers have with the Foxfire approach is evaluation. Teachers and administrators alike will tell you that they intuitively feel that the approach is the most valid way to teach. But the nagging questions continue to emerge: "How can I demonstrate that each child is making progress? How will the children do on state-mandated achievement tests?" One of the major areas addressed in the Foxfire courses is that of evaluation; a variety of evaluation strategies are discussed, and the importance of selecting strategies that are in line with the Foxfire approach is stressed.

As Wigginton has honed the Foxfire approach, he has recognized that the philosophy underlying the approach is most compatible with that of John Dewey. As teachers trying to figure out ways to implement the approach, we find ourselves turning to Dewey increasingly for guidance. Regarding evaluation, Dewey wrote (1919), "The criterion of the value of school education is the extent in which it creates a desire for continued growth and supplies means for making the desire effective in fact" (p. 62). He also asked:

What avail is it to win prescribed amounts of information about geography and history, to win the ability to read and write, if in the process the individual loses his own soul: loses his appreciation of things worth while, of the values to which these things are relative; if he loses desire to apply what he has learned and, above all, loses the ability to extract meaning from his future experiences as they occur? (1938, p. 49)

As we struggle with the choice of specific evaluation strategies that will document progress on state-mandated learning objectives, we feel that it is also necessary to evaluate the effectiveness of the educational process in general. If the choices we make do not foster the overall development of children, and if the choices do not stimulate an interest in continued learning, we may as well quit—it is as simple as that.

The Core Practices in the Classroom

After I took the Foxfire course at Carson-Newman College in the summer of 1989, my philosophy of education began to evolve slowly toward that of student-centered, rather than teacher-directed, activities. In *Sometimes a Shining Moment* (1986), Wigginton suggests that teachers often devise and construct projects and impose them on the students. He suggests that the process of learning is more essential than the final product, and he emphasizes that subject matter should involve human and physical resources from the real world. He stresses an integration of academic approaches, class decision making, and problem solving. Assessment should be a continuous and ongoing collaboration between the teacher and students, including student-student assessment and evaluation.

The core practice that emphasizes centering learning activities around student interest takes different forms at various grade levels. Those teachers who work with younger children infer interest from observations of children's actions and language. It was no secret that, from Halloween onward, the children in Maynardville Elementary were interested in anything to do with Christmas. I always have been challenged to keep children on-task during the pre-Christmas excitement, and I have been concerned that the children focus only on the receiving of presents, many of them too expensive for their parents to buy. I decided that this might be the perfect time to try to integrate all the core practices into a project in which children had real interest. With my newly acquired philosophy entrenched in my mind, I proposed a project to my second-grade students that I hoped would combine the teaching of skills with a community service project. I was right. They were excited about being able to focus on the holidays as a legitimate way to get school work done! I had envisioned what I thought was the perfect project: My class would visit the local nursing home, bring gifts, and sing carols. I had planned for the students to write a skit, perform it, and sing the Christmas carols before an audience. Instead of exchanging names or bringing gifts for one another in class, as we had traditionally done, the students would write letters to the nursing home personnel to see what gifts would be appropriate for the elderly patients, such as tissues and lotion.

With great enthusiasm, I proposed my "student-centered" project to the students to elicit their input—approval actually. In reality, I had ascribed my values and ideas to the project, allowing the students little opportunity for decision making. During the silence that ensued, Joey raised his hand tentatively and suggested, "Why can't we do something for kids instead of the people at the home?" Jamie chimed in, "We could all bring in our old toys and give them to kids that don't have any!" As we brainstormed possibilities, the children became animated, thoughtful, and totally involved. For the first time in my twelve years of teaching experience, the children were dwelling not on what they would receive but on what they could do for others less fortunate than themselves.

After the suggestion to bring in toys for Toys for Tots, a project to distribute used toys sponsored by a civic organization in Knoxville, I suggested doing something for children in our own community. The possibility of adopting a needy child was brought into the dialogue. True to Foxfire methods, we voted on the Christmas project the children had suggested, which was in part based on their experiences with other children. We then worked to raise money to "sponsor" two economically disadvantaged children for Christmas. The children wrote to the Department of Human Services to find children whose families were in difficult circumstances.

In my journal entry of November 8, I wrote that my grandiose idea of the nursing home project had been soundly defeated. The students had moved beyond self-concern and self-indulgence to address a real need in the community. From their own perspective, based on their experience, they were able to empathize with other children. Developmentally, this was sound. The importance of the choice related to their newfound realization that parents play the role of Santa. Intuitively, they realized that children whose parents could not afford gifts would have no Christmas.

As I watched the children's enthusiasm grow, I sometimes thought about what was being accomplished—beyond the state-mandated objectives. One of the chief functions of education is to guide young people toward an appreciation of and participation in their communities. It is the duty of teachers to acquaint their pupils with all the factors that comprise their social, economic, and political heritage—and to help them integrate the basic skills and knowledge that are taught in separate units with their real-world experience outside the classroom.

Dewey expressed the concern that:

> There is the standing danger that the material of formal instruction will be merely the subject matter of the schools, isolated from the subject matter of life-experience. The permanent social interests are likely to be lost from view. (1919, p. 10)

Dewey and his followers felt that the separation of the schools from the community could be eliminated if the curriculum were built jointly by pupils and teachers; having the students engage in socially useful work in the community would result in their acquiring the culture of varied settings. Home, church, and social agencies share the responsibility of molding the life and character of American youth. By involving community members in the functioning of the classroom, and providing the students with an awareness of the community, a lifelong reciprocal commitment can be established.

The goal of the Foxfire approach to teaching is to create a more "effective and humane democratic society" (Wigginton, 1990). As a teacher working in a traditional school setting, I was in a situation that required me to use the school's traditional methods of assessment but afforded me the opportunity to use informal methods to monitor the student's mastery of state-mandated skills. To monitor and assess this mastery of skills, I used a variety of methods, which I will now describe.

Awareness of Mastery of Objectives

One of the first techniques I employed was to allow the students to know up front what was expected of them. Applying the Foxfire approach, I posted state objectives in the room or provided them on handouts so that students knew what was expected of them. The Tennessee State Department of Education has mandated a list of basic skills and provided a test booklet for the second-grade classrooms across the state. In my school system, it was a given that the tests be administered. Teachers were required to teach/test/re-teach/retest each student.

Instead of teaching the basic skills in isolation, I began to integrate them into a project that the students had not only helped develop but that made them responsible for gauging their own mastery of the skills. The Christmas project allowed us to assess and master our knowledge of these essential skills while still meeting the objectives of the school system. For example, as children planned the budget for the purchase of toys, they had opportunities to practice at least 15 mathematics skills. Because they *needed* to be accurate with their computations, they were willing to spend the time it took to get their skills down pat—they wanted to be sure they got their money's worth when they bought toys!

The students began with an awareness of the objectives I wished to teach, then worked independently and in small groups to achieve those objectives. Through being aware of what they needed to know, students became actively involved in their own learning. One example of this was the combination of peer tutoring and mastery evaluation. As part of providing an audience for daily journal writings, my class and I planned to publish a book of stories. As we approached the publishing deadline and students selected the stories they wished to publish, two slower students, Troy and Cara, had few stories from which to choose. Although they had stories in their portfolios, some were not legible. Several of the more able students were more than willing to write the stories as Troy and Cara dictated. The students who took the dictation were mastering a language arts skill: "to write simple sentences from dictation." Troy and Cara were eager to copy the story in their own handwriting, thus mastering the required skills: "to print legibly and neatly and to copy simple sentences using proper spacing between words, within words, and between sentences." Thus mastery of state-mandated basic skills was achieved by all students involved in the cooperative endeavor.

Knowing the Student:
Observing Individual and Group Response

Working in small groups with children on a project allows the teacher to observe the students as they work. By getting to know individual students through observation, I was allowed to meet their needs more fully because I could identify those needs. It was satisfying to observe the ongoing development of students as the year progressed.

I was able to monitor their acquisition of knowledge and, perhaps more importantly, to observe a change in their attitudes. Often I did this by noting their facial expressions—something that is much easier to do in a small group. For example, I had been concerned about Jamie's self-concept and social skills. When he first entered second grade, he rarely interacted with other children and he rarely changed facial expressions. He did his work quietly and reasonably effectively, but he simply seemed to lack affect. After having begun to concentrate on social and emotional development as well as academic objectives, I developed an objective for Jamie. I wanted to encourage more spontaneous expression and greater interaction with other children in the group. As I worked in small groups, taking care to note small changes in his attentiveness or expression, he gradually became more of a participant. Although these changes were gradual, I tried to note carefully the situations in which he became more interactive, then placing these notes in his folder to document the progress he had made. At parent conference time, it would be important to share not only his academic progress but also his social progress.

We had agreed it would be necessary to request permission of the principal for our Christmas project. The small group's purpose was to write him a letter, which the students dictated as I wrote on a large chart. The students were to copy the letter as neatly and legibly as possible, so that Dr. Shoffner, the principal, could read it. The students were writing for an intended audience, but also with a purpose in mind. They were eager and attentive as our task evolved.

One student in particular showed greater enthusiasm and more on-task behavior than previously. Beth, a 10-year-old handicapped student with cerebral palsy, had been assigned to my classroom both because it best matched her assessed grade-level ability and because it was close to the bathroom and playground. As I tried to work with her on handwriting skills, her regular response was, "That's not how I did it in my other school," which had been a special school for handicapped students. As a classroom teacher with no special education training, I did not feel qualified to disagree. But as Beth copied the letter to the principal, I was amazed. Her letter spacing and sizing, although not perfect, were neat and legible, and the entire task was completed on time. I realize not only Beth's capabilities but also the benefit of applying a learning situation to a real-world, student-centered situation.

Monitoring Student Attitudes

The opportunity to monitor student attitudes is probably the most important aspect of this type of evaluation. Some of the ways to monitor attitudes include:

Performance
Willingness to participate in class activities
Willingness to learn by asking questions about problems on topics that are not required
Willingness to do extra, independent projects

Characteristic behaviors of second-graders include a growing capacity for self-evaluation and responsiveness to group activities, both spontaneous and adult-supervised. By observing individual student progress, I was able to assess growth in school performance as well as development of a positive attitude toward schoolwork. In one instance, working with a small group in charge of counting money derived from the sale of baked goods for the Christmas project, Jamie, a student who is shy and tentative about expressing himself in a large group, came to me and said that he did not have enough quarters to make a complete roll of $10. He then went on to say that he needed three more quarters to finish the roll. He had not only demonstrated the ability to solve a number sentence for subtraction with money, he had also identified the problem and offered a solution. He then suggested that he and a friend go to another class to sell more baked goods, which they did.

By working with the group counting the money, Jamie was able to demonstrate a knowledge of basic skills by performance and a willingness to learn by asking questions about problems or topics not required. He was also able to assert himself in a subject in which he felt confident, which raised his self-esteem to the point where he was able to contribute more to large group discussions.

Another method I used to assess student attitudes was their willingness to do extra, independent projects. After writing in class daily for several months, Bonnie brought in a story from home that she had done on her own. She and her grandmother discussed school life when the grandmother was a student. Bonnie then wrote a one-page story about life in her grandmother's era. The grandmother had helped with spelling and punctuation, which further made Bonnie proud of her efforts. She even confided that her mother made her copy the story in her best handwriting. I was pleased to note the interaction between the adults and the child, as well as Bonnie's willingness to do additional work on her own. A friend, May, spent the night at Bonnie's house months later. May brought in a three-page chronicle of their adventures. May's and Bonnie's attitudes about writing were certainly that writing could be a positive, creative, and expressive endeavor.

Monitoring Individual Students During Class

Another method of observation I used more effectively this year was to monitor individual students during class. As I walked around the pods, as we called the clusters of four desks, I was able not only to assess their written performance but also to provide immediate feedback.

Mason, a victim of sexual abuse, displayed an eagerness to learn but an inability to stay on-task for an extended period of time. Although he had excellent math skills and was able to master each state math objective, he was not able to stay on-task long enough to complete a lengthy test. By praising him often and keeping his attention on his task, I was able both to assess his ability and to prevent a possible behavior problem. Unfortunately, the teacher is usually not able to do this during standardized testing conditions, which are rigid and structured. Such conditions do not meet the special needs of 7-year-olds, two of which are the need for praise and encouragement from adults and reminders of responsibilities. It became important for Mason and for me to document, with anecdotal records, the times when he was able to work math problems on an individual basis, as opposed to his performance on the required standardized test at the end of the year.

In order to provide children with some experience with standardized testing procedures, mastery tests were given periodically throughout the year. As I observed Mason's pattern of errors during the short mastery tests, I was able to counsel him on how to check for his errors. The combination of praise and training to look for errors helped Mason lengthen the amount of time he was able to stay on-task during more structured situations.

Using Results to Determine if There May Be Other Problems

Working in a small group and monitoring individual students also allows the teacher to determine if there might be other problems, as with hearing, sight, emotional stressors, and home-life difficulties. One student published a story in our class book in which he said he hoped his dad would marry his girlfriend who was living with him because his mom was big, fat, and lazy. I used my teacher prerogative to quietly edit that story. But I did gain a greater understanding of Joey's home life and was able to understand why he did not bring money or permission slips to class trips. Using the Foxfire approach on projects, especially the use of small groups, allows the teacher time with individuals to *know* students. This good relationship with students aids in assessment as well as helps to improve student performance.

Knowledge of Students' Abilities

Getting to know individuals helps a teacher build a curriculum around student interests and to evaluate students by their own progress rather than a norm-referenced measurement instrument. The students in my rural second-grade classroom on the border of Appalachia are not able to compete with students in suburban Knoxville in terms of experience, home involvement, and motivation. The child who has been sexually abused or who is emotionally disturbed will not progress at the same rate as other children. But the teacher, the child, and the parents need an instrument to measure that progress.

In the area of mathematics, students kept a checklist in the front of their state-mandated test booklets. (See Figure 6.2.) The children were allowed to check each skill as it was mastered. However, the skills were not necessarily taught in isolation. Although drill and repetition are essential to the mastery of calculating skills, a stimulating classroom goes beyond that. Children should be encouraged to think and apply those skills to real-life situations, just as Jamie did with the coins. After reading about the U.S. Census in *Weekly Reader*, we did an informal class census and graphed the results. One student suggested that our class conduct a schoolwide census. As we brainstormed the possibility, one student even suggested that we might be counting households twice if students had a sibling in another grade level. Were the students applying mathematical concepts to the real world and learning to think? I think so.

FIGURE 6.2 Second grade mathematics skills checklist

Name _____ Second Grade Mathematics Skills

Dates of Mastery/Notes:

Match word names to numbers _____
Count/write by twos through 98 _____
Read/write numbers through 999 _____
Count/write by threes through 99 _____
Place/total value through 999 _____
Greater/lesser of two numbers _____
Number before/after given number _____
Order numbers through 999 _____
Addition facts (sums 0-18) _____
Add two 1-digit numbers _____
Add 2-digit and 1-digit/regrouping _____
Add 2 digit and 3-digit numbers _____
Add 2-digit numbers/regrouping _____
Add three 1 digit-numbers _____
Basic subtraction facts _____
Subtract 2-digit numbers _____
Subtract 1-digit from 1-digit _____
Subtract 2-digit from 3-digit _____
Multiply numbers (1-5) _____
Match fractions/shaded regions _____
Match word names/fractions _____
Write fraction for shaded region _____
Interpret picture graph _____
Units of capacity/customary _____
Units of weight/customary _____
Tell time to quarter hour _____
Compare indoor/outdoor temps _____
Use calendar date to name day _____
Units of capacity/metric _____
Units of mass/metric _____
Value of coins _____
Measure objects _____
Name solid shapes (cone, etc.) _____
Continue pattern of shapes _____
Solve 1-step word problem _____
Complete a number sentence _____
Write number sentences _____
Solve problems/picture graphs _____
Solve number sentences (money) _____
Determine value of coins _____

Oral Examination by Questioning During Discussions

Another method of assessment used was oral examination by questioning during class discussions. As the year progressed, more students became involved in class discussions. I tried to create a risk-free, positive environment to facilitate this. I tried to affirm the incorrect answer in order to praise the child for his or her attempt, then provide the correct response in discussions of such straightforward content as math problems. In any discussion, I often turned to the class for help in providing responses. An example of a more open-ended discussion was the one in which I suggested visiting the nursing home for the Christmas project. Rex responded for the class when he said the class would like to do something for other children. Max, a shy child who rarely volunteered, chimed in by saying that he agreed. I was elated to hear Max speak out and voice his opinion. These kinds of views are responses to be "examined" as well.

Use of Portfolios

Foxfire, along with a variety of other approaches to language arts instruction, recognizes the importance of children's learning to read from material they have written themselves. Language arts objectives were accomplished more through writing than through working with the basal reader. Children brainstormed topics about which they would like to write, then voted on the kinds of stories to work on each day. Some teachers report that children do not like to write, but when given the choice of topics, the children were eager to begin. The favorite topic this past year was, of course, Ninja Turtles. Some teachers do not like children to write about television characters, but the enthusiasm for learning how to spell *Michelangelo* and *Raphael* convinced me that the subject matter was just fine!

The writing samples, or stories, as we called them, were not graded or marked in any fashion. Each story was read daily by the student-author to the class only if he or she chose to read it aloud. The class was invited to critique the story or offer suggestions for improvement. The students filed their own stories daily in their portfolios. On each portfolio was stapled a checklist of basic skills that the student could check as he or she mastered them.

The reading skills checklist, shown in Figure 6.3, contains a listing of the basic reading skills that children in second grade are required to master in Tennessee. The writing and reading of stories was an efficient way to meet those objectives. Providing the checklist for the children and their parents simply allowed them to recognize the skills that they were developing. The children could measure their achievement relative to their own progress as well of that of their peers. By doing this, I was able to enlist peer support to help notify the students periodically and verbally of their performance as

FIGURE 6.3   Second grade reading skills checklist

Name _____   Second-Grade Reading Skills

                                  Date of Mastery/Notes:

Identify new words _____

Identify synonyms _____

Identify antonyms _____

Sequence events _____

Select a title _____

Identify story elements _____

Describe characters _____

Verify conclusions _____

Identify the main idea _____

Identify cause/effect _____

Reality and fantasy _____

Initial consonant blends _____

Final consonant blends _____

Vowel digraphs _____

Long vowels _____

Identify base words _____

Form contractions _____

Form compound words _____

Count syllables _____

the stories were filed and the checklists were completed. For example, as Bonnie and May shared their stories about the night they spent together, they not only compared the sequence of events in the story but also checked each other's sentence structure and mechanical details.

Writing skills were then retaught to the class as a whole after the stories were read aloud. I used charts for spelling words the children identified as those words they wished to spell correctly for their stories. Since students were not criticized for incorrect spelling, the vocabulary the children used in writing was extensive and colorful. Again, their attempts at using large, new words (we called them "50-cent" words) were encouraged. They became intrigued with correctly spelling "big" words, such as *gorgeous* and the Ninja Turtles' names. These words made up their own dictionaries, which they alphabet-ized and kept in their own desks. The use of correct grammar, sentence structure, and capitalization were retaught to the entire class. Often I used examples of student sentences to emphasize or reinforce a skill the students were having difficulty mastering.

The portfolios also became an important tool for parent confer-encing. Some parents are concerned that their children are doing too little work and making no progress in reading and writing; others are concerned that their children are doing very well yet are not being recognized as the best students. When writing samples from several weeks of work are shown, documenting student pro-gress over time, parents can easily see how their children are doing. With the attached skills list, the parents can also see how they can help their children to move on to the next skills as well. For example, in less than eight weeks' time, Brad had moved from drawing pic-tures with a few words scrawled unevenly on a crumpled page to a story with five paragraphs—complete with correct grammar and spelling. The parents were naturally delighted with his progress!

Homework Assigned Only to Those Who Need Extra Practice

By using a continuous ongoing assessment of student perfor-mance, I was able to report progress to parents if a student began to have difficulty. Homework was then assigned to those who needed extra practice. Often this was done with an accompanying note or phone call to parents; they were willing to help their child if only they knew what they could do to help. The portfolios were invaluable in demonstrating to parents the need for additional work. For example, Barry seemed to have difficulty with story construction, which was obvious from the disjointed nature of his writing samples. A conver-sation with the parents about talking about events and then writing them down proved a helpful strategy in improving his in-class work as well.

Concluding Thoughts

Language arts skills were easier to assess by observation techniques than mathematics skills. In an elementary classroom, more time is devoted daily to language arts, and language skills can be assessed more by observation than specific performance and mastery. The use of checklists and portfolios was advantageous in a number of ways. In one respect, it gave importance and credibility to the child's work. Rather than being sent home, the papers were placed in the child's portfolio. By reviewing these, the children were therefore able to evaluate their own progress on a daily basis and receive instant knowledge of its results. The emphasis on process, not product, allowed the goal setting and attainment of those goals to be ongoing through the school year.

Another outgrowth of using this type of assessment relates to Dewey's (1938) concept of learning, in which new activities grow out of previous learning and past experiences. The acquisition of new skills through experience leads to the desire for further knowledge, which is fostered by a child's naturally inquisitive mind.

Is this type of project difficult for the teacher? Absolutely! But the challenge, enthusiasm, and creativity generated by the students makes each day a learning adventure for teacher and students alike.

In order to provide a rich background of experience that allows the child to use and assess the basic skills and knowledge that are taught in separate units, the teacher must connect these skills to real-world experiences beyond the classroom. By using a variety of methods and assessment techniques, the curriculum can be built jointly by the students and teacher to allow for a total-language approach to the teaching of essential skills in order to further the total growth of the individual child.

Reflections on Our Collaboration: *Sharon's Voice*

As I think about how Janet goes about assessing, documenting, and evaluating her children, it seems like a very natural process. Janet exudes confidence, and the relationships she has established with the parents of her children facilitate an easy exchange of information. If skills are being mastered satisfactorily, they are checked off. If there is any concern about a child not mastering a skill or concept, parents are notified quickly so that they can be enlisted to help in remediation. Janet is alert to identifying potentially gifted or talented children in her classroom. She provides enrichment activities or involves them in peer-tutoring activities that will enable them to grow rather than stagnate. Providing grades, then, on report cards is as painless as it can be—parents and children alike are prepared for what they may receive at each reporting period because both have been involved throughout the process.

For some teachers, this whole process looks and *is* much more difficult. The key, I think, is to begin to really look at the dimensions of the evaluation process in terms of the three parts which we have mentioned earlier—assessment, documentation, and evaluation. As Hilton Smith, the Foxfire Teacher Outreach director, said in a conference on November 17, 1990:

> Assessment strategies tell you "what is." Documentation provides proof of "what is." And evaluation tells you "what is in light of what should be." Too often we use all of the terms interchangeably and then we get into trouble.

As the Foxfire teachers work together in East Tennessee, the assessment of student understanding and progress seems to come fairly easily. In the training course for teachers, we emphasize the importance of observation. For a teacher of young children, observation is the primary means for assessing children's developmental progress. My first training in observation came from the classic *The Nursery School: A Human Relationships Laboratory*:

> Perhaps the first step in understanding the meaning of behavior is to be able to look at the way a child behaves without feeling a necessity to change his behavior. We must learn to look at behavior as it is rather than in terms of what we want it to be. (Read, 1966, p. 176)

In agreement with good references on observation (Almy & Genishi, 1979; Cohen & Stern, 1975), I highlight the need for objective observations, with behaviors and settings recorded accurately. Interpretations or impressions of the teacher need to be recorded apart from the observation itself.

The reliance on observation as a means for assessment implies that classrooms are structured in a way that allows for learning through observation. There is not much to be learned about individuals' behavior when children are engaged solely in seatwork or teacher-directed activities. What teachers observe becomes varied in self-chosen activities, in small-group work, and in open-ended activities. The use of open discussions and brainstorming sessions with small groups and the entire class provides insight into children's perceptions of content and process.

The documentation process is more difficult. Observation is one thing—keeping records of those observations is yet another. Teachers committed to the use of anecdotal records, as well as the use of checklists, devise clever ways to manage the task. Sometimes I arbitrarily decide to observe a certain number of children each day, just to make sure I have records each week. Sometimes, especially at the beginning of the year, I try to sit down and recall every child, from memory, in the classroom and write down something about that child's day—this quickly points out who is being ignored, which is one of my greatest fears. Teachers are beginning to use checklists for student as well as teacher use in evaluating skills, attitudes, and behaviors. Journal entries and portfolios provide documentation of progress throughout the year. In one school, children and teachers are compiling a group journal—at the end of each day, they reflect on the day and record progress and things to consider for the next day. The growth in their ability to reflect as a group can be seen in the quantity and quality of ideas generated by students. Photographs, slides, and videotapes of activities in process provide insight into what children are learning throughout the year.

Evaluation, "what is in light of what should be," is the biggest challenge. Janet has little trouble with this, and the key to her success is experience, knowledge of the state curriculum requirements, and her relationships with her administrators and parents. She assesses and documents continuously; therefore, evaluation appears to be less subjective to both parents and children.

A discussion of an individual's approach to assessment, documentation, and evaluation would not be complete without setting it in the context of the larger educational community (Puckett, 1989). The last decade has produced more recommendations for educational reform than perhaps any other in the history of public schools in the United States (Gross & Gross, 1985). Although the recommendations take many forms, almost all states have implemented some sort of mandated "back-to-basics" curriculum, with a standardized testing package to assess whether or not children and teachers are "making the grade." Teachers frequently express frustration about the pressure to "teach to the test," and many report that they feel they have been stripped of their creativity. They are concerned that children are spending their lives in meaningless and repetitive activities in order to do well on tests (Bennett, 1990). Teachers in all of the Foxfire networks have expressed similar concerns; they like the "feel" of the Foxfire approach, but they are afraid of what will happen to the end-of-the-year scores.

The professional literature is now filled with calls for alternative forms of assessment (Bredekamp, 1987; Democracy and Education Editorial Board, 1990; National Commission on Testing and Public Policy, 1990; Neill & Medina, 1989; O'Neill, 1990), including teacher/ student constructed pre- and posttest measures (Goswami, 1989; Valencia, 1990). The sentiment is clear, at least among some educators, that standardized testing is not the best way to measure student achievement.

However, before changes are made in existing testing practices, convincing evidence will have to be presented that the alternative forms of assessment are as valid than standardized tests. In a recent study conducted with the Foxfire teachers in East Tennessee (Teets & Mobley, 1991), we found that children in Foxfire classrooms did at least as well as, if not better than, children in classrooms where the Foxfire approach was not being used. In addition, in comparing the performances of children on alternative forms of assessment with their performances on standardized tests, there were no great discrepancies. Teachers reported that they felt much more confident about their evaluations of children with the documentation provided by alternative forms of assessment and documentation.

Students reported a preference for involvement in the evaluation process. Perhaps one child's quote says it all: "This is the best I've ever been in school—I usually spend most of my time in the principal's office!" When one child in a third-grade classroom told a group of administrators that he liked the Foxfire approach because "we didn't use boring textbooks so much," I shuddered! I quickly asked, "So, you mean you didn't work very hard?" The child was quick to reply, "No, it was harder than working out of the textbook, because we had to think for ourselves and we had to . . ."—and he listed all the ways in which they had learned throughout the year.

As we noted at the beginning, this chapter is a document in progress. As such, we have shared our thoughts about the philosophy underlying our approach to assessment, documentation, and evaluation in the elementary school classroom. We have tried to provide examples of how the process works, but we realize that our discussion was sometimes abstract and theoretical. Janet and I were purposeful in this choice. We believe that the underlying philosophy is critical in the selection of instructional and assessment strategies, and we have delighted in our opportunity to discuss the blending of theory and practice. We both think that there is not enough of this kind of discussion among teachers in public schools, teacher educators, and students preparing to be teachers. We hope that our chapter will contribute to a thoughtful dialogue among these people. If we do not engage in these dialogues, the real price is paid by the children whose futures lie in the hands of those who take assessment and evaluation lightly.

References

Almy, M., & Genishi, C. (1979). *Ways of studying children* (rev. ed.). New York: Teachers College Press.

Bennett, K. (1990). Qualitative research. Paper presented at Carson-Newman College, Jefferson City, TN.

Bredekamp, S. (Ed.). (1987). Position statement on standardized testing of young children of 3 through 8 years of age. Washington, DC: National Association for the Education of Young Children.

Bronfenbrenner, U. (1979). *The ecology of human development.* Cambridge, MA: Harvard University Press.

Cohen, D. H., & Stern, V. (1975). *Observing and recording the behavior of young children.* New York: Teachers College Press.

Democracy and Education Editorial Board. (1990). Toward authentic assessment: Testing and evaluation for democratic education. *Democracy and Education, 5*(1), 5–10.

Dewey, J. *Democracy and education.* (1919). New York: Macmillan.

Dewey, J. *Experience and education.* (1938). New York: Macmillan.

Erikson, E. H. (1963). *Childhood and society.* New York: Norton.

Goswami, D. (1989). Assessing assessment. *Bread Loaf News, 3*(3). Middlebury, VT: College of Middlebury, Bread Loaf School of English.

Gross, B., & Gross, R. (Eds.). (1985). *The great school debate.* New York: Simon & Schuster.

Maslow, A. H. (1970). *Motivation and personality* (2nd ed.). New York: Harper & Row.

National Commission on Testing and Public Policy. (1990). *From gatekeeper to gateway: Transforming testing in America.* Chestnut Hill, MA: National Commission on Testing and Public Policy, Boston College.

Neill, D. M., & Medina, N. J. (1989). Standardized testing: Harmful to educational health. *Phi Delta Kappan, 70*(9), 688–697.

O'Neill, J. (Ed.). (1990). *The Update, 32*(7), 1–7. Alexandria, VA: Association for Supervision and Curriculum Development.

Piaget, J. (1955). *The language and thought of the child.* New York: Meridian.

Puckett, J. (1989). *Foxfire reconsidered: A 20-year experiment in progressive education.* Urbana: University of Illinois Press.

Read, K. (1966). *The nursery school: A human relationships laboratory* (4th ed.). Philadelphia: Saunders.

Smith, H. (1990, November 17). Personal Interview. Rabun Gap, GA.

Teets, S. T., & Mobley, J. (1991, April). *The Foxfire approach and the teacher researcher: Student performance on alternative forms of assessment and standardized tests.* Paper presented at the annual meeting of the American Educational Research Association, Chicago.

Valencia, S. (1990). A portfolio approach to classroom reading assessment: The whys, whats, and hows. *The Reading Teacher, 43*(4), 338–340.

Wigginton, E. (1986). *Sometimes a shining moment.* New York: Doubleday.

Wigginton, E. (1990). Core practices of the Foxfire approach. Rabun Gap, GA: Foxfire Teacher Outreach.

—————— **7** ——————

Looking Forward
Toward Stories of Theory and Practice

CELIA GENISHI

This concluding chapter begins with a presentation of contrasts and similarities in Chapters 2 through 6. It ends with a call to action to those interested in linking theory with practice through the use of stories and other accessible forms of public discourse.

> Finally, stories are powerful research tools. They provide us with a picture of real people in real situations, struggling with real problems. They banish the indifference often generated by samples, treatments, and faceless subjects. They invite us to speculate on what might be changed and with what effect.
> (Witherell & Noddings, 1991, p. 280)

The stories from our classrooms have now been told, about the individuals and groups, personal and programmatic motives, plots enacted by children and teachers living in communal spaces and framed by the temporal boundaries of the school year. We described the "whys" and "hows" of our child- and teacher-developed curricula in detail, as well as our ways of assessing them. As pictures of "real people in real situations," each story, like each collaboration, was unique. Some teachers worked in teams, others on their own; some teacher educators were involved in the assessing, others were not. Voices, too, varied—some reflected many years of teaching experience; others, a few. Some voices were conversational, others polished and "like a writer's." Some voices were heard in unison, others in sequenced solos. This final chapter is my attempt to sort out, then harmonize the voices by identifying both differences and recurrent themes and common goals for learning and teaching. Sections on contrasts and commonalities in curriculum and assessment are

191

followed by a discussion of the relationship between theories of development and practice and, finally, by a call to action to those trying to create bridges between practitioners and theorists.

Looking for Contrast and Recurrence

Our stories featured children within an age range of six years, and the many examples of classroom life differed considerably across that span. Preschool children, in keeping with tradition and state regulations, enjoyed a low adult-to-child ratio in the settings we described. (The state of Ohio, for instance, requires 1 adult caregiver for no more than 14 4- and 5-year-olds, though our collaborators had lower ratios.) The preschoolers' curriculum revolved around play, which was inseparable from learning about complex social relationships, solutions to problems, aspects of oral and written language, or science. What children did and said while playing was a valuable source of information, something to be observed and assessed by the teachers, from preschool through first grade. In the second grade children did not stop playing, but the focus in the classroom shifted, so that children spent more time with printed materials and sustained topics of study.

On the topic of assessment through standardized testing, there were again some variations. A number of teachers felt pressured by them but judged them to be irrelevant to their interests in individual development; others were straightforward with their children about tests, since school districts required them. In one second-grade classroom, for instance, Janet helped children practice standardized testing skills occasionally throughout the year. All authors, however, focused primarily on assessing *individual* children's progress, the kind group tests cannot—and are not intended to—measure.

In contrast, curricula showed shifts in focus from individual children to groups, as well as from individual to group goals. Children who were 2 or 3 years old, such as Morgan in Chapter 2, were sometimes caught up in the difficulties of separation from their parents, so teachers often made plans specifically for Morgan. The 6- or 7-year-olds, however, were more often enacting scenes with peers, trying to balance an interest in friends or making friends with becoming literate or "numerate"; for example, second-grader Jamie in Chapter 6 figured out how much money he lacked to fill a roll of quarters for a class project and suggested that he and a friend sell some baked goods to another class to make up the difference. His solution worked toward a group goal to earn money, at the same time that he and his classmates accomplished academic goals by applying state-mandated math skills. Thus curricular shifts, sometimes reinforced by those outside the classroom, seemed matched by developmental shifts that children demonstrated across the chapters.

More striking than the contrasts across the age span were clear commonalities revealed within the framework of child-oriented curricula. The curricula, as defined in Chapter 1, included some pre-planned activities as well as the countless spontaneous interactions and experiences among children, materials, and people that made up school life. Several characteristics recurred in every chapter, like themes uniting the teachers who worked in different locations across the country but shared a vision of learning. First, teachers saw the establishment of a *safe environment* as a primary task. Mary, Stephanie, Joanne, and Jan called this "emotional safety" in Chapter 2; Sarah and Anne referred to "safety from humiliation" in Chapter 4; and the other collaborators all described in their own ways an environment safe enough for exploring freely, taking risks, and making mistakes—in other words, safe enough for learning.

Second, children had *choices* to make. The play and work choices varied depending on the classroom. Sometimes children recorded their own "worktime choices," as Evan and his kindergarten classmates did in Chapter 3; sometimes the teachers, as in Chapters 2 and 3, kept records in daily notes. As children grew older, some choices were closely tied to academic goals. Children in every classroom had opportunities to select books to hear or read, but the second-graders in Chapters 5 and 6 also chose what they wanted to study about topics, such as the desert, or what project they wanted to engage in, such as buying toys to give as gifts. And there were countless other choices—who will be a friend or partner, is this block construction finished now, what shapes should be on this collage? Preschooler Ellis in Chapter 3 clearly made such artistic choices with care.

Third, teachers recognized the importance of *children's own "cultures,"* in terms of both child lore and their family backgrounds, which differed from chapter to chapter in terms of social, ethnic, and economic characteristics. The ubiquitous Ninja Turtles entered classroom curricula, as did rap music and children's stories as expressed through play and print. As the Boy Kings—Daryll, Justin, and Tahrique—in Chapter 4 showed, children set physical and artistic tasks for themselves; and their self-assessments remind us of the ways *they* view life in school. Family members, of course, are often important aspects of children's cultures; and every chapter included references to parental roles. These ranged from being consultants who problem-solved with teachers about their child to occasional visitors—guest speakers for the class—to parent skeptics who questioned school policies.

Fourth, all teachers arranged for experiences that were *integrated* across subject areas. Determining when a group was engaging in "social studies" would be difficult because children might be taking a walk, reading a book, having a debate, or interviewing someone in the community. Also, different aspects of learning were integrated: the social, cognitive or academic, emotional, aesthetic, and so on all blended. When Adrienne in Chapter 2 learned about climbing, the task was not just motoric—it was cognitive, emotional, and often social as well. Many children, especially in the first- and second-grade classrooms, became readers and writers in the company of friends. How could Crystal and Rebekah's social purposes in the first grade, for example, be separated from the emotional or academic?

The specifics of what teachers did, such as documenting the learning of skills or attending to state requirements, varied within and across grades. In that sense each teacher or team integrated in their own way curricular purposes with "outside" goals. But there was also a sense of "vertical integration" across the years, a developmental continuity reflected in the curricula. If all the collaborators were in the same school, they might see a few practices with which they would disagree, but they could also see satisfying "extensions" of their activities in one anothers' classrooms. For example, primary grade math was "hands-on," and *Mathematics Their Way* was used in both kindergarten and second grade. And in every classroom, literature—real books—served to integrate both subject matter and personal experience. Jan's story about 4-year-old Morgan and Danny's kitten and Julia's group dialogue about *The Tenth Good Thing About Barney* (Viorst, 1971) involved the same book. In the preschool setting, Jan chose to read it aloud as an appropriate follow-up to a conversation about Danny's kitten, who was killed by a car. The boys expressed their sadness and suggested Ninja Turtle music for an imagined funeral. Julia's second-graders, in contrast, talked about aspects of the book's plot and discussed what they knew about the funerals they had experienced. One child commented on death in general, "It's part of life." The same book elicited discussions that could only be described as "developmentally appropriate" as teachers allowed for children's own responses. Thus integration across the curriculum incorporated flexibility in choice and use of materials.

Finally, the kind of curriculum just summarized implies orchestration by a certain kind of teacher, one who believes that *children and teachers are learners*. Few would claim that the classroom teachers contributing to this book are "typical"; in fact, they are probably exceptionally good teachers and committed educators who are blessed with high energy and optimism. Like many other teachers whose voices may not be public, though, these teachers assume that human beings are learners. So in their classrooms there was the expectation that everyone could learn, or there was "the absence of the expectation that learning will not occur" (Smith, 1981, p. 635). There was therefore an absence of fixed ability groups, which categorize children as high, medium, or low achievers. Instead children—people with preferences and choices to make—formed their own groups, or teachers grouped them heterogeneously or according to interest.

Equally important were the concepts of teacher-as-learner and teacher-as-researcher. When teachers had conversations or discussions with children or adults, they asked genuine questions. As a character in a novel put it, they were "questions that show she's been listening. Real questions, I mean. Not those who-cares questions most other grownups ask" (Tyler, 1991, p. 26). Careful listening was as evident as informed telling while teachers learned what was on a child's mind and where her or his thinking was headed. Moreover, the teachers took their learning beyond the boundaries of the classroom. They learned from parents and other family members, from other teachers, who in turn learned from them. Some belonged to national organizations or networks, for example, of Foxfire teachers or those interested in early childhood education or "whole language." Some were also part of college or university courses or groups, so that their learning was both formal and informal. Every one of them was "resisting professional arrest" (Edelsky, 1988), reflecting on the daily events and dramas of their classrooms and raising questions about their own practice and about policies that affect children and teachers. Thus they resisted classifications they felt were misleading, stereotyping, or constraining, such as "at-risk," just as they resisted overly academic or narrow curricula and a reliance on standardized test scores.

Summing Up the Ways

Resisting narrowness in both curriculum and assessment was another theme the teachers shared. Of course, their ways of assessing were hard to separate from the features of their curricula and their views of children and learning. In fact, a number of teachers presented their activities and instructional strategies *with* their ways of assessing, since they were so closely linked. The major "way" that all teachers shared was *careful observation.* They were people who knew how to look—at individuals and the networks that formed around them, at groups as their purposes varied across situations, and at the classroom as a community. Thus Stephanie knew of the subtle things that relatively quiet children like Jimmy of Chapter 2 did as he accomplished tasks and slowly formed friendships. In a similar way Martha and Patsy knew of the progress of Ellis and Evan of Chapter 3. Julia, Beth, Zulema, and Pam watched and listened to Susana of Chapter 5 as she began to learn English as a second language. During social studies and science, an initial period of silence was followed by efforts to express herself in English, which she used more and more freely even as she made mistakes. Systematic observation keeps every child in the foreground for some period of time, so that all children become part of remembered scenes. These can be revisited through notes and other written records, conversations, the children's own work, or occasional audiotapes. Naturally there were changes in assessment as children got older. Although all teachers integrated different aspects of the curriculum, things such as focused lessons in science or social studies became more distinct and prolonged in the primary grades. In Chapter 6 Janet provided examples of how terminology changes when learning goals become more differentiated. She named evaluation of "state-mandated skills," "monitoring student attitudes," and "oral examination by questioning" as aspects of assessment that she and other Foxfire teachers were committed to. What was significant about her ways of assessing was that they were clearly student-centered; like teachers of younger children, Janet based her assessments on careful listening, record-keeping by the children and herself, and open-ended discussion. Further, she "taught" and assessed writing by having the children write and read. The children saved what they wrote in portfolios and assessed their own progress in writing skills. Thus developmentally appropriate curriculum and assessment can be maintained even as outside agencies impose their own standards, a common occurrence in public schools.

In short, there was a notable consistency throughout the chapters regarding ways of assessing. Whether children engaged in block play, Ninja Turtle sewer construction, shared writing and reading, or a focused discussion of a class project, teachers assessed children in the curricular context in similar ways: a quick conversation begun by children's questions, careful reading of a child's letter, discussion of a book, including teacher questions, review of a child-done checklist, sometimes longer planned observations or audiorecordings. Just as everything a child experienced contributed to the curriculum, every interaction teachers participated in offered a chance for assessment. Not every interaction was preserved, of course, but those that were shaped the children's and teachers' stories of classroom life.

Keeping the Faith: Toward Theories of Practice

Even as the stories in each chapter presented the contrasts and similarities just discussed, each group of authors also had an overriding concern, a uniquely expressed force that shaped their work and kept their faith in learning and teaching alive. In Chapter 2 this was an initial focus on "emotional safety" for individual children and adults, then a concern with free-flowing communication—about what was felt, questioned, known—among children and adults. A curriculum rooted in knowledge of how children develop was in the foreground in Chapter 3. The teachers here demonstrated how tight the link is between assessment and curriculum when children are given the opportunities and *time* to be at the center of both. Chapter 4 revealed a dominant theme of social cohesion. It is a story of how children of different social and ethnic backgrounds create bonds among themselves at the same time that they respond to the demands of the curriculum and the classroom community. Two themes, children as users of "whole language" and teachers as learners, emerged in Chapter 5. Meaningful uses of oral and written language, whether Spanish, English, or both, drove the curriculum. Teachers together with children were learners-through-language. In Chapter 6 the principles and practices of Foxfire teachers were featured. At the core was a concept of schooling as a democratic process, one that allowed for children to make choices as well as to become participants in a society with rights and constraints.

The contrasts, similarities, and especially the overriding forces—what Maxine Greene (1988a) has called "governing obsessions"—

summarized here tell a lot about what we collaborators believe is "good practice." In fact, the practices described may be the features of our *theories of practice*, or those theories about children, development, learning, and assessment that underlie teachers' curricular decisions and interactions. They contrast in important ways with *theories of development* (Fein & Schwartz, 1982), which give systematic accounts of human growth and change from birth to adulthood. According to Fein and Schwartz, a theory of development is descriptive. The theorist makes no judgment about how development *should* occur, but instead describes and explains how it *does* occur in human beings in general. A developmental theory is also passivist with respect to children's learning environments. It does not address questions of how adults can actively enhance development through specific teaching strategies or activities. Piaget's theory of intellectual development (Piaget & Inhelder, 1969) is a prime example of a developmental theory.

In contrast *theories of practice* apply to particular children and teachers in educational settings. These theories are prescriptive and lead to recommendations about how adults should view development and, moreover, how they should arrange environments for children. The theories, like those you have encountered here, are focused on individual children in real classrooms—not the "universal child" or all children—and they are activist. Adults take an active role in their own settings to provide experiences that benefit the greatest number of children. The guidelines of the National Association for the Education of Young Children for developmentally appropriate practice (Bredekamp, 1987) represent a broad-ranging theory of practice, as does the "whole language" philosophy (Edelsky, Altwerger, & Flores, 1991). Also, published curricula and textbooks imply their own practical theories, which may be broad or narrow in focus.

How are theories of development related to those of practice? And how are they related to the thinking displayed in our earlier chapters? Fein and Schwartz (1982) recommend the creation of a relationship of "reciprocity and mutual dependence" (p. 99) between theorists of development and those of practice. They suggest working toward rules about practice that clearly stem from developmental principles. The recommendation is a logically powerful one: practitioners and researchers might verify aspects of a theory to demonstrate that practices are theoretically sound. For example, teachers might choose to study aspects of attachment theory (Bowlby, 1972), an account of how children establish and maintain their first social relationships. The theory is relevant to caregivers of infants and prekindergartners who wonder how long hours in early educational settings, away from parents or primary caregivers, affect those early critical relationships (Caruso, 1989). Through systematic observation teachers might document events that verify or challenge aspects of Bowlby's theory. Eventually they might try out specific practices that build on their observations. Fein and Schwartz (1982) present an example of such a practice, which is similar to one the preschool teachers in Chapter 2 described: the use of a "decompression" area that allows children to enter a new setting with few children, appealing activities, and a responsive teacher. The practice helps "detach" children from familiar adults and ease the separation process.

Did the authors of Chapter 2 arrive at their procedures by a careful reading and verification of theory? Teachers' own references to theory, which appear throughout our chapters, are only a rough reflection of the theorists who have influenced them. A look back at Chapter 2, though, shows a link to a theory of *practice* (Balaban, 1985) that incorporates aspects of developmental theory about attachment and separation. Other collaborators mention multiple theories, some developmental and some theories of practice.

Yet the chapter authors in general did not dwell on the theorists they mentioned as sources of their philosophies of teaching. Instead the teachers provided many of the concrete examples of classroom activities and events so necessary for filling in their own theories of practice. They did this *without* first verifying aspects of developmental theory, such as stages of attachment or intellectual development. The collaborators tended to be eclectic, mentioning contemporary theorists of practice, such as Calkins (1986), Carini (1975), and Wigginton (1986), and classic theorists of development, such as Erikson (1963), Maslow (1970), and Piaget (Piaget & Inhelder, 1969). Their work touched responsive chords in the teachers even though some of the theorists are not currently "popular." So questions arise: Is the recommendation that practitioners *verify* or elaborate on developmental theory a practical one? As they attempt to link theory with practice, should practitioners bear the responsibility for verification of theory? The logic of the recommendation is powerful, but the teachers have shown here that their own preoccupation is with the elaboration of theories of practice, a struggle shaped more by the complexities of classroom life than by the scientific process of verifying theory and deducing procedures.

Thus we are left with questions waiting for answers about the relationship between theory and practice. How does an intimate understanding of theory help practitioners work on behalf of their governing obsessions, those overriding concerns that keep them in the classroom? Is knowledge of theories of *practice* enough? How do we develop an ideal, mutually dependent relationship between theorists and practitioners that honors both—that does not diminish the value of the knowledge of teachers or oversimplify theory? And that does not romanticize teachers or glorify theory? In view of these challenges, the nature of this mutually dependent relationship still needs to be articulated. A possible approach to this articulation, for forming bridges between theories of development and practice, is considered next.

Taking Control: The Power of Teachers' Stories

You get what you settle for. (Louise, in the movie *Thelma and Louise*)

Power is the ability to take one's place in whatever discourse is essential to action and the right to have one's part matter. This is true in the Pentagon, in marriage, in friendship, and in politics. (Heilbrun, 1988, p. 18)

It is also true in the field of education, of which politics is a part. Figuring out what action to take on behalf of children and their learning does depend on having a mode of discourse—a way of articulating and using language in interaction—that brings about change. Those responsible for broad-scale change, often policy makers and administrators, quote theorists, researchers, and testmakers to support their arguments. They borrow the words and work of others, sometimes of developmental theorists, to make their discourse more powerful. They have seldom borrowed the stories of teachers, especially those that are richly detailed like the chapters presented here. "Persuasive discourse" often has the sound of an essay, a sense of objectivity, and a sprinkling of numbers that many find the most persuasive (numbers of students who are or are not able to do something, scores on achievement tests, and so on). It is what Donaldson (1978) would call a "disembedded" style, which stands outside individual—storylike—experience and what many call a "male" style.

A "female" style, on the other hand, is storylike; the content of what is said is embedded in everyday life. There may be commitments to particular theories or movements, but data in the statistical sense are seldom used to argue points. Thus stories strike many as too ordinary to hold persuasive power. Yet we have just presented our stories in an effort to persuade, to demonstrate that *classroom life is indeed complex and that there is no short route to assessing when the object of our assessments is children's development it- self.* For development is a story, and along with other features of story, it possesses the dimension of *time*. Teachers and peers can act to promote learning and enhance development in children, but children need time to experience, re-experience, think, and under- stand. And for those who make judgments about practice and set policy, it takes *time* to hear or read, and especially understand, developmental stories.

It may be no surprise that all of us co-authors are women, although this was not consciously planned. Most people who work with and write about young children in classrooms are women, and the topic of children is seen as womanly. There are, of course, men who are exceptions, who both work with children (and women) and write about them (Ayers, 1989, and Corsaro, 1985, are just two examples). *We propose that stories by women and men about life in classrooms be made more prominent—and powerful—in the pub- lic discourse about education and its improvement*, and we hope our stories are now part of that discourse.

Story, or narrative as it is also called, is not only a mode of discourse or articulation; it is a way of thinking as well (Bruner, 1986; Egan, 1988). It incorporates lived experience in ways that are sequenced in "real time" and thus recognizable and accessible to most readers. Further, stories allow us to generalize to our own experiences, to see ourselves in new scenes or scenes similar to those we know, such as others' classrooms. We can make comparisons between their theories, decisions, and behaviors and our own; and we can imagine changes, new directions in plots, different scenes or endings in our classroom stories, as Witherell and Noddings (1991) suggested at the beginning of this chapter.

People often view theories in general, and in our context espe- cially developmental theories, as *unchanging*. They are a form of language or discourse that literary theorist Mikhail Bakhtin (1981) terms *authoritative*, like the language of religious litanies, legal texts, or a favorite theory if it is recited like scripture. The eternal authoritativeness of theories is something practitioners, along with researchers and theorists, challenge when they try to see how stories of everyday life fit the theory, or when they see if the scripts played out in classrooms challenge it.

Any theory, like any text, is interpreted—responded to by a thinking, meaning-seeking reader or listener (Rosenblatt, 1978). It does not need to remain frozen and will not as long as individuals respond to its content in their own ways, for their own situations. As soon as that responding begins, as soon as readers or listeners begin to comment on or question aspects of the theory, it becomes less authoritative. As Bakhtin (1981) says, resisting authoritative discourse makes it less distant and transforms it into *internally persuasive* discourse; that is, language that belongs to both the theorist and ourselves. It becomes a *dialogue* to which we contribute our own words and thoughts. So understanding theory can be an interactive—*sociolinguistic*—event: It involves writers and readers or speakers and hearers who make their own interpretations and use language in their own ways, depending on the situation. In other words, understanding theory can be a variable process. It might be a scientific investigation, based on hypothesis testing and deduction; but it can also involve the actions and reactions of story, which links us in imaginative ways back to the logic of theory.

If *understanding* theory is a goal, it makes sense to allow and encourage the forms of discourse that make it interpretable, that transform it into dialogue that is internally persuasive rather than authoritative and distant. Participation in a dialogue that leads to modifications in theory, research, or practice also becomes a goal (see Florio-Ruane, 1991, and Lather, 1991, for other perspectives on interpretation and dialogue, theory and research). So in considering our own theories, those we collaborators have built up ourselves and those of theorists we find persuasive, we want to leave open the dialogue so that neither the theory itself nor our view of it becomes authoritative—frozen. Seeking appropriate forms of discourse for that dialogue is as challenging as the verification of theory and generation of principles of practice, discussed by Fein and Schwartz (1982).

Clearly dialogue, collaboration, and story are all appropriate aspects of discourse in our search for principles embodied in this book. We tell stories to link theory with practice, as some collaborators have done here, and to challenge theories some have accepted for years: for instance, the theory of practice that second-language learners must be proficient in spoken language before they can become literate, or a piece of developmental theory that 2-year-olds are egocentric—unable to take others' perspectives—and thus not sociable. The testing of theory was not one of our goals, so it remains for us to see whether and how our stories of learning, teaching, and assessing are taken up by others who write in essayist style or think mainly in the disembodied, highly objective mode of the scientist.

It is not in the nature of people or language to create a "unistyle" of speaking or writing. We think, though, it is possible to provide bridges or forums that bring contrasting styles of expression and thinking into contact. A recent example is Scales, Almy, Nicolopoulou, and Ervin-Tripp's collection on play (1991), spanning practice, research, and theory in several disciplines related to early education and development. There is no effort here to create a "unistyle," but there is a unique ensemble of different styles, a setting down together of voices with contrasting but related missions. This is one kind of bridge that links two previously divided, often antagonistic or indifferent, communities (researchers and theorists versus practitioners).

Another example is conferences that highlight dialogues among practitioners and theorists or researchers. A recent workshop held at Teachers College, Columbia, entitled "Building Learner-Centered Schools" (1991), drew people from across the country who were engaged in or wanted to be engaged in changing schools. Like the characters in the movie *Thelma and Louise*, who decided not to settle for constrained lives that they did not control, the conference participants were unwilling to settle for constrained learners and schools. Workshop leaders were primarily practitioners, and speakers included theorists of practice and policy makers. Any observer could see it was an event full of dialogue, not just during sessions but between them as well. This was one instance among many of the communities trying to form or maintain themselves, to make space for creating internally persuasive dialogues about practice and theory.

So there are positive signs for creating bridges, for integrating "the felt and the known, the subjective and the objective, the private and the public spheres" (Greene, 1988b, p. 79), for making dialogues externally persuasive in arenas of power in writing and through talk. But there are also the contrary signs presented in Chapter 1, most notably a presidential agenda for *nationally* coordinated programs for school improvement. This means that proponents of grass-roots alternatives—alternative child- and teacher-developed curricula and assessment—have much to do. And one thing we can do is tell our own stories in a way that asks for responses from others, as we have tried to do here. With Harold Rosen we think that

[N]arrative must become a more acceptable way of saying, writing, thinking and presenting. I am not proposing that anecdote should

> drive out analysis but that narrative should be allowed its honour-
> able place in the analysis of everything, that stories-in-the-head
> should be given their chance to be heard. (Rosen, 1985, p. 20)

Narrative can humanize and give us routes into clearer visions,
analyses that come more easily because of striking examples or
parables that draw us into both story and discussion.

We suggest that those who do not favor stories in the literature
of education and social science consider the purposes of that literature. If social and educational change is one of its goals, then it
should be everyone's responsibility to create ways of communicating
that touch others—that are open and not obscure. *There should be
an attempt on the part of theorists, researchers, and practitioners to
speak and write plainly, to make ideas and findings accessible to
an interested public.* This is not easy, just as writing publishable
stories from the classroom is not easy. Some have already made their
voices accessible, through story (Paley, 1981, 1986, 1990) or "plain-
speaking," and through a growing body of teacher research. We
invite others to join in developing a more inclusive range of styles of
speaking and writing, by imagining conversations with new audiences—by exercising a greater *sociolinguistic imagination.*

In particular, we invite them to consider the potential of story, a
form that can bridge two divided rivers, one full of centuries of
cherished thinking and research, the other a communal river of
memory, full of the ordinary events of daily life, in classrooms and
out, sometimes written and often not. For what is memory but, as
Robert Coles says, "a story, an aspect of experience that lives in a
particular mind" (Coles, 1989, p. 183)? As happens in some conversations and meetings, bridges can begin to form as people discover
memories in common, through talk, as Carolyn Heilbrun notes:

> I do not believe that new stories will find their way into texts if they
> do not begin in oral exchanges among women in groups hearing
> and talking to one another. (1988, p. 46)

Underlying this belief is another, that people do not see themselves
as *actors,* people who accomplish things, unless someone demon-
strates that they are actors, unless someone places them in a story.
As Heilbrun also notes, the main characters in novels are often part
of a *quest,* the heroic seeking of a grand goal. Oral exchanges among
women or, preferably, among all teachers and their collaborators,

may be the first steps that give substance to their quests for enhanced development and learning in children and themselves and to a new quest for more varied forms of public discourse, spoken and written. Those new forms, which may imaginatively blend a conventional objective style with classroom stories, could further empower and broaden the movement toward alternative assessments.

We have come full circle; many of us collaborators began work on our chapters through talk, and we end by emphasizing its importance. Conversations helped us place ourselves in a story about experiencing life in classrooms and sharing the story with others. Over time and through talk, then print, our stories have demonstrated developmentally appropriate, grass-roots ways of enacting curriculum and assessing it. We have now all become characters in a continuing quest for improved practices and meaningful links between curriculum and assessment, theory and practice.

References

Ayers, W. (1989). *The good preschool teacher: Six teachers reflect on their lives.* New York: Teachers College Press.

Bakhtin, M. M. (1981). *The dialogic imagination: Four essays.* Austin, TX: University of Texas Press.

Balaban, N. (1985). *Starting school: From separation to independence.* New York: Teachers College Press.

Bowlby, J. (1972). *Attachment and loss: Vol. 2. Separation.* London: Hogarth.

Bredekamp, S. (Ed.). (1987). *Developmentally appropriate practice in early childhood programs serving children from birth through age 8* (expanded ed.). Washington, DC: National Association for the Education of Young Children.

Bruner, J. (1986). *Actual minds, possible worlds.* Cambridge, MA: Harvard University Press.

Building Learner-Centered Schools. (1991, May). Conference coordinated by Ann Lieberman, Linda Darling-Hammond, & Ann Spindel. New York: Teachers College, Columbia.

Calkins, L. (1986). *The art of teaching writing.* Portsmouth, NH: Heinemann.

Carini, P. F. (1975). *Observation and description: An alternative methodology for the investigation of human phenomena.* Grand Forks: North Dakota Study Group on Evaluation, University of North Dakota.

Caruso, D. (1989). Attachment and exploration in infancy: Research and applied issues. *Early Childhood Research Quarterly, 4,* 117–132.

Coles, R. (1989). *The call of stories: Teaching and the moral imagination.* Boston: Houghton Mifflin.

Corsaro, W. A. (1985). *Friendship and peer culture in the early years.* Norwood, NJ: Ablex.

Donaldson, M. (1978). *Children's minds.* New York: Norton.

Edelsky, C. (1988). Research currents: Resisting (professional) arrest. *Language Arts, 65,* 396–402.

Edelsky, C., Altwerger, B., & Flores, B. (1991). *Whole language: What's the difference?* Portsmouth, NH: Heinemann.

Egan, K. (1988). *Primary understanding: Education in early childhood.* New York: Routledge.

Erikson, E. H. (1963). *Childhood and society.* New York: Norton.

Fein, G., & Schwartz, P. M. (1982). Developmental theories in early education. In B. Spodek (Ed.), *Handbook of research in early childhood education* (pp. 82–104). New York: Free Press.

Florio-Ruane, S. (1991). Conversation and narrative in collaborative research: An ethnography of the Written Literacy Forum. In C. Witherell & N. Noddings (Eds.), *Stories lives tell: Narrative and dialogue in education* (pp. 234–256). New York: Teachers College Press.

Greene, M. (1988a, June). *Beyond the predictable: Possibilities and purposes.* Paper presented at symposium on Defining the field of early childhood. Lincolnwood, IL.

Greene, M. (1988b). *The dialectic of freedom.* New York: Teachers College Press.

Heilbrun, C. G. (1988). *Writing a woman's life.* New York: Ballantine.

Lather, P. (1991). *Getting smart: Feminist research and pedagogy with/in the postmodern.* New York: Routledge.

Maslow, A. H. (1970). *Motivation and personality* (2nd ed.). New York: Harper & Row.

Paley, V. G. (1981). *Wally's stories.* Cambridge, MA: Harvard University Press.

Paley, V. G. (1986). *Mollie is three: Growing up in school.* Chicago: University of Chicago Press.

Paley, V. G. (1990). *The boy who would be a helicopter: The uses of storytelling in the classroom.* Cambridge, MA: Harvard University Press.

Piaget, J., & Inhelder, B. (1969). *The psychology of the child.* New York: Basic Books.

Rosen, H. (1985). *Stories and meanings.* Sheffield, England: National Association for the Teaching of English.

Rosenblatt, L. (1978). *The reader, the text, the poem: The transactional theory of the literary work.* Carbondale: Southern Illinois University Press.

Scales, B., Almy, M. Nicolopoulou, A., & Ervin-Tripp, S. (Eds.). (1991). *Play and the social context of development in early care and education.* New York: Teachers College Press.

Smith, F. (1981). Demonstrations, engagement, and sensitivity: The choice between people and programs. *Language Arts, 58,* 634–642.

Tyler, A. (1991). *Saint Maybe.* New York: Knopf.

Viorst, J. (1971). *The tenth good thing about Barney.* New York: Harper & Row.

Wigginton, E. (1986). *Sometimes a shining moment.* New York: Doubleday.

Witherell, C., & Noddings, N. (Eds.). (1991). *Stories lives tell: Narrative and dialogue in education.* New York: Teachers College Press.

About the Contributors

Harriet K. Cuffaro is a member of the graduate faculty at the Bank Street College of Education, where she teaches courses in the foundations area and curriculum and supervises teachers. As a curriculum specialist, she has contributed to the development of nonsexist and multicultural programs and materials. Her publications and research reflect her interests in issues of equity, the history of early childhood curriculum, and young children's dramatic play and block building.

Anne Haas Dyson, a former classroom teacher, is a professor in the Graduate School of Education, University of California, Berkeley. She is also a co-director of the Center for the Study of Writing and the author of *Multiple Worlds of Child Writers: Friends Learning to Write* and, with Celia Genishi, of *Language Assessment in the Early Years.*

Martha Foote received a B.A. in art history from Swarthmore College and her master's in Early Childhood Education from Bank Street College. She has taught the 4- and 5-year-olds at Manhattan Country School since 1987.

Julia Fournier is a second-grade teacher at William T. Machan Elementary School in Phoenix, Arizona. She also has taught in Tempe, Arizona, and in Grand Junction, Colorado. She received her bachelor's degree in special education and elementary education from Arizona State University.

Joanne Flynn Frantz has been a head teacher at the School for Young Children (SYC), Columbus, Ohio, since 1983, and was a teacher there for 11 years before that. She has offered workshops on play and is currently community relations liaison of the Columbus Association for the Education of Young Children. She holds a B.A. from Connecticut College in history and an M.S. from Ohio State University in family relations and human development. She is married with two teenaged children.

Celia Genishi, a former secondary Spanish and preschool teacher, is on the faculty in early childhood education in the Department of Curriculum and Teaching, Teachers College, Columbia. With Millie Almy, she is co-author of *Ways of Studying Children*, and with Anne Haas Dyson, co-author of *Language Assessment in the Early Years.*

Sarah Hudelson is associate professor and program coordinator, Multicultural Education Program, College of Education, Arizona State University. A former elementary school teacher, she received her Ph.D. from the University of Texas at Austin. Her research has focused on bilingual children's first- and second-language and literacy development, and she has published a monograph on the topic: *Write On: Children's Writing in ESL.*

Beth Lansdowne is a second-grade bilingual teacher at William T. Machan Elementary School in Phoenix, Arizona. She has also taught in Litchfield Park, Arizona, and in Minnesota. She received her bachelor's degree from the University of Illinois at Champaign-Urbana, and she has her bilingual education endorsement from Arizona State University.

Sarah Merritt has taught primary grades in the Bahamas; Prince George's County, Maryland; and Berkeley, California. She received her M.A. in education from the University of California, Berkeley. She currently teaches in Dedham, Massachusetts, where she lives with her husband John and two cats.

Janet Mobley holds a B.S. in elementary education from the University of Tennessee, Knoxville. She has a master's degree in counseling and guidance from Lincoln Memorial University in Harrogate, Tennessee, and has taught elementary school for 15 years. A second-grade teacher at Maynardville Elementary School in Maynardville, Tennessee, she was state evaluator for the Tennessee State Department of Education in 1991–1992.

Zulema Pastenes is a bilingual instructional aide at William T. Machan Elementary School in Phoenix, Arizona. A native of Chile, she is bilingual and biliterate. She is presently working toward her bachelor's degree in bilingual education.

Stephanie Rottmayer became interested in teaching at SYC when she was a volunteer aide while her sons attended the school. A teacher there for 14 years, she enjoys music and teaches beginning piano. She is currently working toward a B.S. in the College of Human Ecology at Ohio State. She is married and has two sons.

Patsy Stafford received her master's degree in early childhood education from the Bank Street College of Education. She has taught kindergarten at Public School 11 in Manhattan since 1988.

Pamela Steen is an instructional aide at William T. Machan Elementary School in Phoenix, Arizona. She became interested in education when her oldest child enrolled in Head Start in 1974. She has been working in classrooms since that time.

Sharon T. Teets holds a B.S. in home economics education from West Virginia University. She completed her master's degree at the University of Tennessee, Knoxville, and she holds a Ph.D. in curriculum and instruction, with a specialization in early childhood education and child development, from the University of Texas at Austin. She is associate professor of education at Carson-Newman College and coordinator of the Foxfire Teacher Network in East Tennessee.

Mary Trickett has taught at SYC since 1985 and taught in day care and preschool for five years before that. A 1975 graduate of Ohio State University with a B.S. in family and child development, she has taught parenting courses. She is married and has three sons.

Jan Waters was a psychiatric and school nurse before teaching at SYC for 16 years and directing it since 1986. In 1990 she received an M.S. in family relations and human development from Ohio State University. She gives workshops on play and issues related to separation and conflict. She is married with three children.

Index